AF178801

Māndhātr̥durga

A Preliminary Catalogue of the Historic Monuments at Oṃkāreśvar-Māndhātā

Jürgen Neuß

xasia eBooks

About the author

Jürgen Neuß, PhD (2007), studied Indology at Berlin and Allahabad. He worked at Free University Berlin from 2000–2010 until the closure of the Indological Department. He works on the cultural history of the Narmadā valley since almost two decades and has already published a number of related contributions. He presently lives in Berlin as an independent scholar and author.

Bibliographic information published by the Deutsche Nationalbibliothek
The Deutsche Nationalbibliothek lists this publication in the Deutsche Nationalbibliografie. Detailed bibliographic data are available on the Internet at http://dnb.ddb.de.

xasia eBooks

This book is published under the Creative Commons Attribution 4.0 License (CC-BY-SA 4.0).

The electronic Open Access Version of this work is permanently available on the website of CrossAsia-eBooks: http://crossasia-books.ub.uni-heidelberg.de/xasia

doi: https://doi.org/10.11588/xabooks.269.355
urn: urn:nbn:de:bsz:16-xabooks-269-8

The cover illustrations are based on photographs by Jürgen Neuß.
Front cover: The Gayāśilāmaṭh
Back cover: Bhairava sculpture near the North gate on Māndhātā hill

© Jürgen Neuß 2017
All graphics and plates are by the author, unless otherwise indicated.

ISBN 978-3-946742-29-6 (Hardcover)
ISBN 978-3-946742-28-9 (PDF)

—

In memoriam

Paṇḍit Kailāś Dattātrey Jośī and Paṇḍit Nārāyaṇ Prasād Bhāṭe

—

Contents

PREFACE

In an earlier mainly text-based contribution I have argued that Māndhātā island and its surroundings have been of considerable religious and historical importance which may probably be traced back to about the sixth century CE.[1] On the basis of historical records found at Māndhātā which refer explicitly or implicitly to the Paramāra dynasty we may safely infer that Māndhātā flourished between the tenth and the thirteenth century. In view of the fact that information about the place's history beyond these limits is extremely scarce, it is all the more striking that Māndhātā has till date retained its importance as a religious centre.

The period when Māndhātā flourished falls into the so–called 'early medieval' phase (ca. 600–1300) of South Asian historiography, which, as Jason HAWKES has recently conclusively argued, remains "ill-defined and poorly understood" and is "arguably the most poorly represented period archaeologically in the entire subcontinent".[2]

The Central Indian site of Oṃkāreśvar–Māndhātā is located in the East Nimar district of the state of Madhya Pradesh and represents an island in the river Narmadā.

In his Progress Report of the Archaeological Survey of Western India for the months May 1893 to April 1894, Henry Cousens, then Superintendent of the Archaeological Survey in Bombay, wrote:

> Compared with the antiquarian remains in the Bombay Presidency, and Western India generally, those of the Central Provinces are few and poor. Even those of the Mândhâtâ and Mârkanda, which are generally looked upon as among the most interesting in the Central Provinces, are neither extensive nor of any extra merit architecturally. The valley of the Narbadâ, from Burhânpur to Jabalpur, is perhaps the most scanty in this respect; but this is chiefly due to the fact that railway contractors, when constructing the G.I.P. line, found, in the many remains that then existed, material ready to hand for their bridges and culverts. (COUSENS 1894: 1).

1 NEUSS 2013: 144–145.

2 HAWKES 2014: 95 and 96.

This statement is one of the early professional documents that laments the loss of archaeological remains in the wake of large infrastructure projects in the Narmadā valley, a phenomenon which has acquired new significance with the construction of large dams on the Narmadā river.[3] In the nineteenth century it has, for instance, caused the destruction by "the cruel hands of the vandals and the uninterested" of the famous historic city of Tripurī,[4] one of very few early cultural centres that existed in the Narmadā valley at all. Apart from a few sculptural fragments, the remains of Tripurī were almost entirely lost to historical and archaeological research.

With all due respect and admiration that the eminent archaeologist Henry COUSENS deserves, it must be stated that his judgement about the remains at Māndhātā was misconceived. Given COUSENS' merit, this error would of course be tolerable if only would it not have had such a lasting impact on the assessment of Māndhātā's historical importance. In fact, COUSENS' unfortunate judgement appears to have influenced the scale of research at Māndhātā till date. A note written by the then Vice-Roy of India, Lord George Nathaniel Curzon,[5] in which he stated: "I visited this renowned and sacred island in the Nerbudda on October, 31st, 1902, and was equally disappointed with its beauties and its monuments [...]" turned out even more devastating, and ultimately limited the extent of expenditure on the remains at Māndhātā to a minimum.[6]

What has never been realized since COUSENS' times is the fact that the historic remains at Māndhātā are much more extensive and coherent than the few brief archaeological notes suggest, that all exclusively focus on a few isolated monuments, which COUSENS had, in retrospect, selected rather arbitrarily. Such notes appeared between COUSENS' first report of 1894 and SPOONER's note about the end of the Archaeological Survey's conservation work on those monuments in 1924.[7] What has been lost till date is a broad view of the whole area which fundamentally represents a conglomeration of three extensive settlements with a thoroughly

3 NEUSS 2012b.

4 CHOUBEY 2006: 1.

5 Cited in MARSHALL 1909: 6–7.

6 This is corroborated by MARSHALL: "[...] it is on the note which he left behind him [...] that all subsequent measures have been based." (*ibid.*: 6) In his note, Curzon had further stated: "The only building of any real character or distinction on the island is the Hindu Temple of Siddheśvara Mahādeva. [...] But it can never at anything except a wholly disproportionate cost be made into anything but a ruin."

7 SPOONER 1924: 192.

structured fortified city in the centre that were built in the latter half of HAWKES' 'poorly-understood early medieval phase' in the art-historically scanty Narmadā valley.

The remains on Māndhātā island in fact represent the only preserved fortified city of the Paramāras of Dhāra presently known to us. Of course it was not an isolated outpost, but stood in correspondence with settlements on the north as well as the south bank of the Narmadā river which connected the place to the two principal cultural areas of North and South India of which the course of the Narmadā river represents the natural boundary.[8] Although Māndhātā has yielded the second most number of inscriptions of the Paramāras found at a single place, its historical significance has never been adequately investigated.[9] Frederick Eden PARGITER's repeated claim that Māndhātā held an important position in the cultural history of (Central) India,[10] was apparently overshadowed by his identification of Māndhātā with the famous ancient city of Māhiṣmatī that was later supported by John Faithfull FLEET.[11] Already disputed in their times, this identification was later, conclusively as it seems, refuted on account of the excavations at Maheśvar.[12] This appears to have shifted Māndhātā completely out of the focus of historical research.

While remains of the mainland settlement on the south bank are partly preserved in the present village of Godarpurā, the remains of the corresponding settlement on the north bank around erstwhile Panthiā village, already severely disturbed in the early twentieth century, have irretrievably been destroyed almost in their entirety in the course of the construction of the Oṃkāreśvar Hydroelectric Project. It is here, that COUSENS' lament and CHOUBEY's bitter remark, cited above, have acquired new significance. Additionally, the remains which are still extant on Māndhātā island are under threat from local building activities despite the fact that many areas are under a nominal protection of either the

8 Thus the Narmadā is called "*centre of the earth – mahī-madhyam*" in the Devīpurāṇa (HAZRA 1963: 51).

9 NEUSS 2013: 140ff.

10 PARGITER 1904: viii–xiii, and 333–334, note ‡.

11 FLEET 1910 and PARGITER 1910.

12 The case, it seems, has been settled once and for all in favour of Maheśvar by Hasmukh Dhirajlal SANKALIA (SANKALIA & *al.* 1958: 1–15). In the course of his line of argument, he refers to all previous writers on the subject and the four different opinions which identified ancient Mahiṣmatī either with Maheśvar, Māndhātā, Maṇḍlā or Maisūr. One of the strongest arguments in favour of Maheśvar is the fact that of all the places proposed, only Maheśvar really seems to lie on the ancient route from Paithān to Ujjain.

Archaeological Survey of India (subsequently: ASI) or the Directorate of Archaeology, Archives and Museums (subsequently: DAAM), Bhopal.[13] For instance, large areas near the Gaurīsomanātha temple have already been profoundly disturbed by the erection of large building complexes of private, pseudo-religious institutions. These activities represented, in fact, illegal encroachments on government land, and some of these structures have already been demolished again on government order.

In the following report I shall briefly, yet in some detail, describe the remains and monuments at Māndhātā. I hope to show that the number, extent and complexity of the remains, of which considerable and significant portions are still lying underground, urgently demand archaeological investigation. In my view, Māndhātā's significance for the history of Central India and especially the history of Central Indian art and architecture is comparable to that of the recently much celebrated site of Āśāpurī,[14] now so aptly investigated by a high-profile team of experts at P.R.Ā.S.Ā.D.A, located at the Welsh School of Architecture[15] and headed by Adam Hardy in collaboration with the World Monuments Fund.

I hope that this work may be received with interest. Admittedly, the descriptions could in many cases be more detailed and the treatment of the individual monuments and artefacts may in some cases appear somewhat arbitrary. The responsibility for all such shortcomings, as well as for errors and and mistakes that one may find in this contribution lies, of course, entirely with me.

J.N.
Berlin, May 2017

13 The DAAM has placed information boards at many places on Māndhātā island and at Godarpurā which declare the surrounding areas as protected ancient monuments and archaeological sites ("*yaḥ kṣetra prācīn smārak tathā purātattvīya sthal* [...] *hai*") under the Ancient Monuments and Archaeological Sites and Remains Act, 1958.

14 See HARDY 2015b.

15 See http://www.prasada.org.uk.

ACKNOWLEDGEMENTS

I wish to express my gratitude to all my friends in Oṃkāreśvar. Special mention deserve Kālūrām Bhoī, Manu Tīṛke, Bhavānīrām, Brāhmacārī Narmadāśaṅkar, Paṇḍit Nārāyaṇ Prāsād Bhāṭe (†) and Paṇḍit Kailaś Dattātrey Jośī (†) who have accompanied me on many occasions and supplied me with much valuable information. To the memory of the latter two fine individuals I dedicate this work.

I further thank Patrick Held for discussions which have incited many insights and supplied a host of information that had escaped me. As he is the only other person who presently works on Māndhātā, our interesting e-mail exchanges have very often reassured me to carry on.

Thanks are also due to the British Library, London and the Victoria and Albert Museum, London for the permission to publish some of the historic photographs taken at Māndhātā in their holdings.

I am greatly obliged to Dr. Adam Hardy who kindly spared his valuable time to go through an earlier draft of this book resulting in a number of valuable suggestions and corrections.

My deepest gratitude is, however, due to my wife, Birgit Stein. Without her forbearance, patience and support, I would not have been able to complete this work.

INTRODUCTION

In this study I shall present a description of the vast and still mostly undocumented archaeological and art historical remains at Oṃkāreśvar-Māndhātā (subsequently: OM).[16] Besides generally adding to the scanty knowledge of the 'early medieval' period in India,[17] it specifically focuses on one of the rare extant historic cities in the Narmadā valley which simultaneously represents the only known full-fledged (and still largely preserved and excavatable) fortified city of the Paramāras of Dhāra. The study summarizes and illustrates the results of several surveys undertaken to trace, document and map as many historic artefacts as possible in order to draw a rather comprehensive, yet preliminary picture of the Paramāra city at Māndhātā.[18]

The idea for this survey arose from a map of OM which I prepared on the basis of satellite imagery obtained from Google Earth.[19] The latter's history function enabled me to stitch together a detailed map of the island and its surroundings from about 80 satellite images taken on March, 17, 2001. This map depicts OM on a scale of approximately 1:3000 a) prior to the construction of the Oṃkāreśvar dam, b) prior to the numerous encroachments and building activities that occurred during the last decade, and c) almost at the peak of the dry season. These particularities and the map's comparatively high resolution, which is unfortunately impossible to reproduce here (its print size is 55x94 cm), facilitated to trace not only the course of the remaining fort walls, but showed also many interesting details, lines, spots and structures, that elicited my curiosity resulting in the idea to conduct a systematic survey of the remains at OM. In the field I was able to trace almost all of these objects, which turned out to be various structural remains, most of which indeed seem to go back to Paramāra

16 A very brief description of sculptures found along the pilgrim's path on the island has more recently been published by Tamara SEARS (2014b).

17 See HAWKES 2015: 95–96.

18 It is very likely that archaeological excavations at the site would yield evidence of pre-Paramāra occupation.

19 The utility of data from Google Earth for archaeological research in India has been demonstrated with regard to the early historic site of Śiśupālgaṛh in Orissa by Tilok THAKURIA & *al.* (2013).

times. Viewed together and set in context all these remains render a relatively clear picture of the structure of the fortified city, Māndhātṛdurga,[20] which existed at Māndhātā about a millennium ago. Moreover, the multitude of artefacts are of considerable importance especially with regard to the development of Paramāra art and architecture.

The scope of the present catalogue is necessarily limited by the fact that it is confined to surface finds. But it is not merely the lack of substantial archaeological investigations which allows only for a 'preliminary catalogue', but also the vastness and variety of remains, which give opportunity for a number of specific studies, especially with regard to Paramāra art – architecture and sculpture alike – of which OM bears vast treasures. For an assessment of the state of research concerning the antiquarian remains at OM see the respective section in my earlier paper.[21] Many of the remains presented here are still unpublished or even undocumented, and those that have been described before have never been put in the larger context in which they actually stand.[22]

---

20 This name occurs in the Māndhātā copper-plates of Jayasiṃha-Jayavarman II, dated *Vikrama saṃvat* (VS) 1331 *i.e.* 1274 CE (eds. SIRCAR 1962, TRIVEDI 1978: 209–227 and MITTAL 1979: 291–314). In a manuscript of the Ṛgvidhāna dated 1707 CE the name 'Māndhātāpura' is found (AUFRECHT 1864: 382(a), No 449), and in an undated *stotra* on the twelve *jyotirliṅgas*, the place is called 'Māndhāttātripura' (WEBER 1853: 347, No. 1242).

21 NEUSS 2013: 118–121.

22 Comparatively few artefacts or monuments from OM have been published in a couple of more general architectural or iconographical studies (see NEUSS 2013: 120, fn. 17). For a list of known historic photographs of OM and its remains, see Appendix 1, Tables 3–7, p. 112ff. The largest number (76) of photographs from OM are held by the American Institute of Indian Studies, Gurgaon (AIIS), see Appendix 2, p. 117ff. The collection is accessible at the 'Digital South Asia Library', http://dsal.uchicago.edu/images/aiis (search term 'Mandhata').

In the course of a survey of the Paramāra temples of Mālvā in the season 1985–86, a team of the ASI Bhopal headed by B.L. Nagarch also visited OM. But during this survey only temples already known were visited and no new discoveries reported (*IA–R* 1985–86: 134–135).

More recently, the DAAM, Bhopal, has published *Known and Unknown*, a three-volume work which professes in its subtitle to represent an *Encyclopaedia of Historical Monuments of Madhya Pradesh*. Volume II (RAG 2012) also covers the present Khaṇḍvā district and contains information on some monuments at OM. Far from being comprehensive even the sparse information given on the few monuments dealt with is almost worthless. The texts contain, I am compelled to state, much irrelevant nonsense, grave mistakes and misrepresentations and at times do not even correspond with the attending illustrations. Nevertheless, as some of the monuments that I describe below are mentioned here for the first time, I shall give respective references to this volume at the appropriate places.

Physical features of OM and distribution of monuments

Let us begin with a bird's eyes view of the island and its surroundings. Map 1.1 served as the guide for my survey and forms the basis of almost all the maps found in this work. As already stated, it shows OM on March 17, 2001, in the dry season.[23] At that time, about two thirds of the total settlement area was located on the south bank of the river Narmadā in the village known as Godarpurā (Plate 1.1), a name which is nowadays very rarely used. The village is regarded to fall into two parts that are divided by a ravine through which a small stream, the Kapilā, flows. This rivulet forms a famous confluence or *saṅgam* with the Narmadā where even the Paramāra king Arjunavarman took a holy bath in 1215 CE.[24] The part to the east of this ravine is called Brahmāpurī, and that to the west Viṣṇupurī. The remaining one third of the settlement was situated on the rivers' north bank along the south-western slope of Māndhātā hill, *i.e.* one of three hills which the island comprises, and is now called Śivpurī (Plate 1.2, Map 1.2).[25] Another small settlement is found at the so-called *saṅgam* at the extreme western end of Māndhātā island, where the two branches of the Narmadā river join.

The physical features of OM were summarized by James FORSYTH some time in the 1860s thus:[26]

> The island covers an area of about five-sixths of a square mile. Towards the northern branch of the river the slope is not very abrupt in most places, but its southern and eastern faces terminate in bluff precipices 400 or 500 feet in height. It is cleft in two by a deep ravine running nearly north and south, the eastern end containing about one-third of the whole area. The southern bank of the Narbadá opposite Mándhátá (called Godarpurá is as precipitous as Mándhátá, and between them the river forms an exceedingly deep and silent pool, full of alligators and large

23 In the field I used b/w paper copies comprising ten A4-Sheets (2x5), resulting in a total map size of 55x94 cm.

24 See NEUSS 2013: 131.

25 The settlement pattern has changed considerably in recent years and many areas on the island (mainly those adjacent to the circumambulatory path, the *parikramāpatha*), which appear rather deserted in this map are now populated. Moreover, large patches of land on the island have apparently illegally been encroached upon by pseudo-religious organizations which have constructed rather extensive conglomerates of temples, monasteries and auxiliary buildings, gardens etc., all neatly fenced in. Most of these have in 2014 again been demolished by the Government for illegal construction. As to be expected, the debris has unfortunately not been removed, but just been left in place (*cf.* Plate 44.2).

26 Though published in 1870, FORSYTH's account was probably written on a long tour in the Central Provinces during 1862–64.

> fish, many of which are so tame as to take grain off the lower steps of the sacred gháts. The rocks on both sides of the river are of a greenish hue, very boldly stratified, and said to be hornstone slate. (FORSYTH 1870b: 257–258).

In view of a structured illustration of the location and distribution of historic remains, I shall follow the traditional division of OM into five major areas which corresponds with the physical characteristics of the island and its surroundings. I shall also retain the traditional designations for these areas, as shown in Map 1.3.[27] Given the amount and extent of the remains and the immediate task at hand of cataloguing them, this approach appears to me as the most practicable one. At the same time, however, it should be borne in mind that certain monuments in different areas may genetically be linked, by chronology, dynasty, style and workmanship, ritual or otherwise. In the prevailing absence of detailed comparative studies which lie beyond the scope of this work, this is perhaps most obvious in the case of the extensive remains of fort walls, which are found both on Māndhātā and Mucukund hills as well as at Godarpurā and to the west of it (Map 1.4).

27 A remark on these names seems appropriate here. Two of them have now become obsolete; while the name 'Mucukund', attested to by FORSYTH (1870b: 261) is now forgotten, although the ruins of a small tribal fort on a hill situated on the north bank of the Kāverī (which is in reality the older northern channel of the Narmadā, see *ibid.*: 258–259) is locally called *mucukund kā qilā* (Mucukund's fort), the name 'Godarpurā' is still known, but not in use any more. The designation 'Panthiā' refers to a vanished village on the north bank of the Kāverī, whose original site is now occupied by the power house of the Oṃkāreśvar dam.

Catalogue of monuments

1. Godarpurā

I shall begin my account with Godarpurā (Map 2.1), because Amareśvara, apparently the most ancient shrine at OM, was located here.[28] As already mentioned, Godarpurā is divided by local tradition into two parts, the western 'Viṣṇupurī' and the eastern 'Brahmāpurī'. Both are situated on elevated plateaus intersected by a ravine in which a small river, the Kapilā, flows (Plates 2.1–4). While the Brahmapurī plateau is precipitous at the west and north and gently slopes down to its eastern and southern sides, the Viṣṇupurī plateau is quite precipitous on its eastern and southern sides and merges with the surrounding terrain only towards the south and west. At the south-east, the old link road connects OM via Sanāvad and Morṭakkā to the Indore-Khandwa highway.

1.1. *The Kapilā ravine*

Nowadays, the Kapilā is concealed by the Māmleśvar *bāzār*, a narrow market street leading from the harbour to the Amareśvara temple complex, and adjacent buildings. At its confluence with the Narmadā, the Kapilāsaṅgam (Plate 3.1), it finally issues out of an old gargoyle (*praṇāla*) with a head of a crocodile (*makara*), commonly believed to represent a cow's head (*gomukha*). Here, the Paramāra emperor Arjunavarman took a bath in 1215 before he made a grant to a *brāhmaṇa*.[29]

1.1.1. Fortification walls

The most impressive remains of old fortification walls at Godarpurā are found to the western and southern sides of Brahmāpurī. They run inside the Kapilā ravine and enclose the Amareśvara temple complex (Map 2.2, No. 1). It is here, that an old portion of this wall is best preserved (Plate 3.2). It is about 2 m strong, up to 4 m high and made of large blocks of almost black stone laid without mortar, resembling the massive walls on the north side of Mucukund hill (*cf.* Plate 56.2). Further to the north, a large

28 See Neuss 2013: 144–145.

29 Sehore Copper Plate Grant of Arjunavarman, see Hall 1860: 30.

portion of this wall has been reconstructed in more recent times. Here, the size of stones differs considerably, they are set with mortar and even parts of some old sculptures have been used (Plate 3.3). Other remains of fortification walls in the Kapilā ravine (Map 2.2, No. 2) are only traceable in the vicinity of the Kapileśvara temple, but here, their original course is largely indeterminable.

1.1.2. Temples

All the temples in the Kapilā ravine are built on terrain considerably elevated above the normal water level of the Narmadā presumably to avoid damage by the annual monsoon floods, which submerge varying portions of the ravine each year.

1.1.2.1. The Amareśvara temple complex

The original Amareśvara *liṅga* and its surrounding area was apparently the most ancient religious centre at OM.[30] Inscriptional evidence proves that at least from about the middle of the eleventh century a stone temple of Amareśvara existed at Godarpurā. The temple seems to have enjoyed popularity over a long period, as HIRALAL reported an inscription, dated 1562 CE, on the left door jamb which still contains the name Amareśvara.[31] However,

> Amareswar was altogether lost during the wars of the seventeenth and eighteenth centuries, the south banks having been deserted and overgrown with jungle, and when, towards the close of the eighteenth century, the Peshwá[[32]] desired to rebuild the temple, neither the Linga nor its old temple could be found. The temple was, however, built, together with a group of smaller ones, from slabs brought chiefly from the ruined temples on the island [...]. (FORSYTH 1870b: 258; footnote in square brackets mine).

The present Amareśvara temple complex (Fig. 1, Plate 3.4) comprises seven temples and one separate *maṇḍapa* in front of the Amareśvara temple housing a stone bull which faces the Amareśvara temple's *liṅga*. Although FORSYTH claims that these temples were built from material "brought chiefly from the ruined temples on the island" it is evident that much old

30 See NEUSS 2013.

31 HIRALAL 1916: 72.

32 If FORSYTH's assertion is correct, the Peśvā referred to must have been either Mādhav Rāv II (1774–95) or, more likely, Bājī Rāv II (1796–1818).

material found *in situ* has also been used, such as the stone slabs which now form the inner north and south walls of the *antarāla* which certainly belonged to the original Amareśvara temple. This is proved by several inscriptions engraved on them in VS 1120, *i.e.* 1063 CE.[33] Their presence alone puts some doubt on FORSYTH's assertion that the original temple could not be found at the time of its restoration. Rather, it seems that three of the temples, Amareśvara, Vṛddhakāleśvara, and, perhaps, Kuntī, have been reconstructed on pre-existing, old temple bases of Paramāra times. At the same time, a considerable variety of material and divergent styles found in these buildings lend credit to FORSYTH's claim that a lot of material had been brought from other sites. Despite its proven antiquity, the Amareśvara temple complex was declared a monument of national importance only in 1967.[34]

1.1.2.1.1. The Amareśvara temple

The Amareśvara[35] temple is the main shrine of the complex and the only one which opens to the west, all the others facing east (Fig. 1, Plate 4.1).[36] The building looks very heterogeneous today, marking different phases of restoration,[37] but the extant plinth (*vedībandha*) and parts of the wall

33 NEUSS 2015 and 2013: 125–130. Whether the present arrangement of the inscribed slabs reflects in any way the original one is uncertain.

34 The proposal under section 4 of the Ancient Monuments and Archaeological Sites and Remains Act, 1958, was announced in *The Gazette of India*, June 4, 1966, pp. 1485–1487 and its execution declared in *The Gazette of India*, May 27, 1967, pp. 1836–1838.

35 The temple and its *liṅga* is currently called 'Māmaleśvar'. It is not clear, when and why this corruption of the original 'Amareśvara' occured, but that seems to have taken place quite recently, because even as late as 1989 TRIVEDI uses the original name in his edition of the Halāyudhastotra (TRIVEDI 1989: 604–611). In this paper I shall retain the original designation 'Amareśvara' throughout.

36 AIIS Acc. Nos. 81914–81923, 81944 (proposed date: "ca. 1000–1099 CE").

37 The following works have been reported: "Mamalesvara Temple, Mandhata, District East Nimar. – Apart from providing barbed-wire fencing, removal of modern accretions, double-shutter wicket gate was provided and boundary walls of the fallen portions of the temple were restored." (*IA–R* 1977–78: 104); "Mamaleshwar Temple, Mandhata, District East Nimar. – The damaged and decayed stone pillar was replaced by a new one matching the original." (*IA–R* 1982–83: 185); "Mamaleshwara Temple, Mandhata, District East Nimar. – The bulged out stones of *sikhara* have been reset, and the fresh fine chiselled ashlar stones were provided to replace the damaged and missing stones. The stone flooring of inner side of the temple has been reset and pointed. The work of providing and laying flagstones flooring on lime concrete base is in progress." (*IA–R* 1984–85: 216–217); "Mamlesvara Temple, Mandhata, District Khandwa – M.S. grill over Compound wall for security purpose was mounted." (*IA–R* 1998–99: 277). In 2002, I witnessed extensive restoration work in the course of which the towers of the Amareśvara and Vṛddhakāleśvara temples were renovated.

(*jaṅghā*) belong to the original Amareśvara temple (Plates 4.2–3). Krishna DEVA, dated this 'original nucleus' to the latter half of the tenth century and regarded the original Amareśvara temple to represent the earliest specimen of *bhūmija* temples,[38] while other parts of the *jaṅghā* indicate that the temple had already been rebuilt in the late eleventh century.[39] While DEVA's dating is based on stylistic considerations, his claim that the temple belongs to the *bhūmija* mode[40] is based on two arguments: a) a supposed stellar ground plan, and b) pilasters crowned with representations of square pavilions (*kūṭastambha*), which adorn the *jaṅghā*. Both arguments are, however, problematic, because a) the plan of the temple is not stellate, but orthogonal in essence, and b) the existence of *kūṭastambhas* does not *per se* mark the temple as belonging to the *bhūmija* mode.[41] This, however, does not necessarily mean that DEVA's classification is false, but that this question requires further investigation.[42]

The extant structure consists of the main shrine (*mūlaprāsāda*) housing a Śiva *liṅga* and crowned by a completely restored, modern tower (*śikhara*), a vestibule (*antarāla*) and a pillared hall (*maṇḍapa*) with three entrances in the cardinal directions. Another, apparently modern, square *maṇḍapa* which houses a sculpture of Śiva's bull facing the *liṅga*, stands detached

38 For his account of *bhūmija* temples, see DEVA 1975. Since then much fresh research on *bhūmija* temples has been published by Adam HARDY who has more recently argued that the earliest specimen of Bhumija temples may be found at Bilotā near Āśāpurī (HARDY 2014: 36; 2015b: 345).

39 DEVA 1975: 92–93, 100–101.

40 I follow here the basic typological framework of 'language', 'mode', 'type' and 'style' proposed by Adam HARDY (2012: 104–106).

41 See TICHIT *2010 (I): 81–82.

42 One of the most characteristic features of *bhūmija* temples are their spires (*śikhara*) which have four spines (*latā*) between which, in the four quadrants, varying numbers of horizontal and vertical rows of miniature *śikharas* (*śṛṅga*) are arranged. Unfortunately, the *śikhara* of the Amareśvara temple has completely disappeared and even among the fragments found in the compound I have noticed just one or two such *śṛṅgas*. One is lying among a heap of stones on the south side of the temple and may or may not belong to the temple. That there are not more such pieces is quite astonishing as there is another temple of comparable style, the Vṛddhakāleśvara, found in the compound (see below, **1.1.2.1.2.**, p. 10). If both temples originally had such *bhūmija śikharas*, one would expect to find a lot more of such *śṛṅgas* than just one or two in the area of the compound or around it. While it is also possible that they have been removed and cut to size for use in later reconstruction work such as, for instance, the northern reconstructed portion of the enclosure wall or the comparatively modern Candramauleśvara temple (see below, **1.1.2.4.**, p. 14) etc., their conspicuous absence and the demonstrable use of such *śṛṅgas* in *śekharī śikharas* at OM (see, for instance, the Brahmeśvara temple, below, **1.2.2.1.**, p. 15) leave doubts that the temples were indeed originally built in the *bhūmija* mode.

immediately in front of the temple (Plate 7.1, right side). As already stated, the *mūlaprāsāda* has an orthogonal ground-plan with five offsets (*pañcaratha*) and is *nirandhāra*, *i.e.* without ambulatory around the sanctum (*garbhagr̥ha*).[43] Its tower (*śikhara*) is completely lost and portions of its base (*pīṭha*) apparently lie underground, as the lowest visible mouldings are the *kumbha* of the *vedībandha* with a horizontal band of *kīrttimukhas* (*grāsapaṭṭī*) beneath it at the south side; on the north side also the top-most layer of the *pīṭha* (*kapotikā*) is exposed (Plate 4.2). The *jaṅghā* is devoid of niches (*devakoṣṭha*) in the central offsets (*bhadra*), except for a single one on the south side, which contains a fine relief of an eight-armed Andhakāri (Plate 4.3).[44] This striking irregularity (*i.e.* the presence of only one *bhadra* niche)[45] shows that the *jaṅghā* cannot be original in its present composition, though almost all of its parts are made of the same kind of whitish stone. There are a few more sculptures fixed into the modern *maṇḍapa* walls[46] and an extensive inscription is found on the inner north and south wall of the *antarāla*.[47] The entrance leading from the *antarāla* into the *garbhagr̥ha* is surrounded by an old *pañcaśākhā* doorframe with five figures including Gaṅgā and Yamunā standing in miniature shrines at its base on both sides (Plate 4.4).

---

43 DEVA thought that this was a feature invariably found in *bhūmija* temples, as, according to him, a *sāndhāra* ground-plan is incompatible with a *bhūmija śikhara* (DEVA 1975: 91). HARDY (2014: 40; 2015a: 69ff.), however, argues that the Śiva temple at Bhojpur was planned to be a *sāndhāra bhūmija* temple – the only known example for such a construction. As the temple was left unfinished, this is, however, not entirely certain.

44 AIIS No. 81944. This sculpture was published, but not identified by DEVA (1975: Pl. 23) and PASRICHA (1972: 43, upper Plate), the latter attributing it falsely to a "Birdheshwar Temple" (=Vr̥ddheśvara, *i.e.* Vr̥ddhakāleśvara, see below, **1.1.2.1.2.**, p. 10). ALI (2002: 48, Pl. 8B) erroneously identified it as 'Tripurāntaka' and wrongly locates it on the north side of the temple. The correct identification as Andhakāri is found in MELZER *2002: (I)102–103, (II) Pl. XIV–A83, but her description of the sculpture is slightly inaccurate, apparently due to the poor quality of DEVA's reproduction of the sculpture on which it is based.

45 The placement of Andhakārī in the south *bhadra* niche may, however, reflect its original situation, as this is its place in most of the *bhūmija* temples listed by TICHIT (*2012: Plates 146–147). The only apparent exception is the Udayeśvara temple, Udaypur, where a comparable icon is found on the south *kapilī*. (See *ibid.*: Plate 146 and TICHIT 2012: 10).

46 Photos are found AIIS Nos. 81917 (Cāmuṇḍā), 81918 (amorous couple and a standing female), 81919 (Naṭeśa) and 81920 (Tripurāntaka); also TICHIT *2010 (II): Plate 94, Fig. 1 (Naṭeśa), Plate 106, Fig.1 (Andhakāri), Plate 117, Fig. 1 (Cāmuṇḍā), Plate 135, Fig. 1 (Tripurāntaka).

47 For a summary of the previously published portions of this inscription, see NEUSS 2013: 123–124 and 125–130. For a previously unpublished portion of it and other unreported short ones, see: NEUSS 2015: *passim*.

1.1.2.1.2. The Vr̥ddhakāleśvara temple

The Vr̥ddhakāleśvara temple[48] stands at a little distance to the southwest of the Amareśvara (Fig. 1, Plates 5.1–2). Like the latter, the present building comprises an orthogonal *pañcaratha mūlaprāsāda* and an *antarāla*. The *garbhagr̥ha* is *nirandhāra* and contains a *liṅga*. The original *śikhara* is lost, but was replaced by a modern construction. The *maṇḍapa* is missing. The ground-plan is comparable to that of the corresponding parts of the Amareśvara temple. Of the original temple, only the lower part of the *jaṅghā* and the *vedībandha* are preserved, which in this case are built from yellow-red sandstone. As in the Amareśvara temple, the lowest visible mouldings are the *kumbha* with a *grāsapaṭṭī* beneath it, suggesting that the *pīṭha* portion of the temple lies underground. The *antarāla* represents a fairly modern reconstruction built around some old pillars and beams in the front wall. Although not explicitly mentioned, DEVA dates the old core of this temple to the late eleventh century.[49] The entrance to the *garbhagr̥ha* is flanked by an elaborate *saptaśākhā* doorframe. The lintel is, however, missing, but has been replaced by another one (Plate 5.3). In front of the *antarāla*, to the north and south of its entrance respectively, lie two large old sculptures, one depicting a bull and the other one a lion killing an elephant (faintly visible in Plate 5.1). In the northern niche of its reconstructed front wall, a relief slab depicting Lakṣmīnārāyaṇa is placed (Plate 5.4). At present, the temple functions as a store-room for about 26 interesting sculptures placed along the inner walls of the *garbhagr̥ha* around the temple's *liṅga*. These include the remainder of the so-called *caubīs avatāra*s (Plate 5.6).[50]

---

48 AIIS Nos. 81926–81932 (proposed date: "ca. 1000–1099 CE"). The temple is mentioned as 'Vrihadeshwara' in RAG 2012: 218, but the description is useless and the corresponding picture shows only the *maṇḍapa* of subsidiary shrine No. 1 (see below, **1.1.2.1.4.**, p. 11).

49 I assume that the "nearly half a dozen Bhūmija temples" (DEVA 1975: 100), which he dates to this period, also include the Vr̥ddhakāleśvara temple.

50 These stylistically identical, rectangular slabs of a dark greenish stone uniformly show standing figures of Viṣṇu. They were brought from the Caubīs Avatāra temple located in the former Panthiā village (see below, **3.1.1.**, p. 85). It is, however, doubtful whether they ever comprised twenty-four; at least there is considerable confusion about their number in historical records. When Henry COUSENS visited the temple in December 1893, he found only 17 of these reliefs with the remaining seven 'missing' (COUSENS 1894: 4). In 1908, Theodor BLOCH (1908: 27–28) reported altogether only nine of them, plus the well-known zoomorphic Varāha sculpture which is made of the same greenish stone (published in RANGARAJAN 1997: 128–130 and Figs. 110–117), a relief of Śeṣaśāyin (still found in the temple, Plate 5.5) and one of Lakṣmīnārāyaṇa (perhaps the one in the northern niche of the *antarāla* front wall, Plate 5.4). Stunningly, when the Caubīs Avatāra temple was dismantled and rebuilt in the wake of the

1.1.2.1.3. The Kuntī temple

The Kuntī temple stands to the north-west of the Amareśvara temple (Fig. 1, Plates 6.1–2). It is a small building consisting of a *mūlaprāsāda* with three offsets (*triratha*), an open *antarāla* and a *maṇḍapa*. The *garbhagṛha* is *nirandhāra* and houses a *liṅga*. The current name of the temple stems from a large mutilated sculpture of a seated goddess made from white stone and fitted into the eastern *latā* of the *śikhara*, above the entrance (Plate 6.3).[51] The *śikhara*, though reconstructed, seems to contain some old parts (especially in the *latā*s). It seems to belong to the *śekharī* mode,[52] albeit of a late type, with two *uraḥśṛṅga*s. In the construction of the *śikhara*, the ribbed, disc-like cornerstones (*āmalaka*) are replaced by representations of water-pots (*kumbha*).

On the reconstructed front wall of its *antarāla*, the temple has two niches, the southern one containing a small relief of Gaṇeśa (Plate 6.5)[53] and the northern one a small slab of Lakṣmīnārāyaṇa (Plate 6.6). The short side walls of the *antarāla* each have a niche on the inside, which contain a dancing Gaṇeśa in the southern and Brahmā with consort in the northern one.[54] The doorframe of the *garbhagṛha* is of a rather late and simple style, with only one flanking figure at its base to either side (Plate 6.4).

1.1.2.1.4. Subsidiary shrines

At the western side of the compound, between the Vṛddhakāleśvara and Kuntī temples stand four more small shrines (Fig. 1, Nos. 1–4; Plate 7.1). They all consist of a square sanctum containing a *liṅga* with a *maṇḍapa* in front. The outer walls of their *mūlaprāsāda* are completely plain and made entirely of cubic rocks laid with mortar, except in the case of No. 3, which has a moulded base. Barring the latter, all structures including

construction of the Oṃkāreśvar dam, a loss of some of the sculptures was reported, the remaining number given as eighteen (SHAINI 2006). From my photographs taken in 2013 at the Vṛddhakāleśvara temple, which cover all the different pieces stored, I count twelve *avatāra* slabs.

51 The figure seems to have been four-armed, but the upper hands are broken. The lower right is held in the gesture of protection (*abhayamudrā*), with a 'rosary' (*akṣamālā*) held by the bent thumb, and the left hand which is also broken off, apparently held a water flask (*kamaṇḍalu*), which is visible about the middle of the leg.

52 For a detailed analysis of the *śekharī* mode, see HARDY 2002.

53 TICHIT *2010 (II): Plate 112, Fig. 3.

54 AIIS Nos. 81924 and 81925 respectively, but erroneously assigned to the Vṛddhakāleśvara temple (proposed date: "ca. 1000–1099 CE").

their *śikharas* represent comparatively recent constructions, although in all their *maṇḍapas* old material (mainly pillars, brackets and doorframes) of various types and styles have been used. Nos. 1 and 2 have been rebuilt on pre-existing platforms that rise above the compound's ground level, the front pillars of their *maṇḍapas* being mounted on older pillar fragments. No. 1 houses a couple of sculptures, the most remarkable of which are the head of a large *kīrttimukha* placed to the north of its entrance, which also has an old, simple doorframe (Plate 7.2). The *garbhagṛha* houses, among others, small reliefs of Sūrya surrounded by figures of eleven Ādityas, and of Varāha (Plate 7.3).

1.1.2.1.5. Hero stones

There are three hero stones found in the compound. The more interesting one stands close to the south-eastern corner of the *mūlaprāsāda* of the Kuntī temple (Plate 6.1, left side). It carries the usual symbols of sun and moon on its northern, the figure of a warrior holding sword and shield on its eastern, a short inscription giving the date *saṃvat* 1320 (*i.e.* 1263 CE) on its southern, and the figure of a craftsman apparently dressing a contemporary pillar on its western face (Plates 8.1–4). The remaining two hero stones stand close to the south-western corner of shrine No. 2.[55]

1.1.2.2. The Viśvanātha temple

According to FORSYTH, the Viśvanātha temple (Plate 9.1),[56] which stands to the south-west of the Amareśvara complex, was built some time in the first quarter of the nineteenth century by the then Rāv of Māndhātā, Daulat Siṅgh, allegedly over the original Amareśvara *liṅga*.[57] The temple contains no old fragments and the claim about the originality of the *liṅga*

55 Their faces show the following motifs: a) N=sun/moon; E=warrior; S=seated male worshipping *liṅga*, W=the same male kneeling and worshipping a standing two-armed male holding a full-blown lotus (right) and a sugarcane rod (left). — b) N=sun/moon; E=warrior; S=seated male worshipping a *liṅga*; W=person lying on a bed (deathbed?) with standing female.

56 First published in RAG 2012: 221.

57 "[...] some time afterwards [...] the old {Amareśvara} Linga was found standing on four arghás, one above the other, showing that it had existed through the four ages of the world. It was also pronounced to be the true one by the Benares pundits, in consequence of being situated in a line with Omkár and the Kapila Sangam, where a small stream joins the Narbadá. Ráo Daulat Singh, the last rájá of Mándhátá, built a temple over it; but its honours and name were gone, and it has now been dubbed Viswa Náth, to distinguish it from its fraudulent rival." (Forsyth 1870b: 258; addition in braces mine).

in its sanctum is highly questionable. Close to the north wall of the temple stands a weathered foundation stone with an almost completely illegible inscription engraved on its north face (Plate 9.2).[58]

1.1.2.3. The Indreśvara temple

The Indreśvara temple,[59] which serves as the local seat of the Jūnākhāṛā, stands to the north-east of the Amareśvara complex, on a small plateau which seems to have been excavated and levelled prior to its construction. The temple opens to the west and consists of an orthogonal *pañcaratha mūlaprāsāda*, an *antarāla* and a *maṇḍapa* with three entrances in the cardinal directions (Plates 10.1–2).

The *garbhagṛha* is *nirandhāra* and contains a *liṅga*. It is entered through a *pañcaśākhā* doorframe (Plate 10.3), which looks as if composed of older fragments in its lower parts and more modern ones above. At the extreme left and right side two slabs depicting deities are found, which seem a bit out of place; while I cannot from my photographs identify the one on the left side, the other one on the right is a representation of standing four–armed Viṣṇu holding *cakra* and *śaṅkha* in his upper hands.

The *jaṅghā* has *bhadra* niches on all three sides but their sculptures are missing (Plate 10.4). From the outside, the temple, which is certainly much later than Paramāra times – it may perhaps have been built in the fifteenth or sixteenth century – looks quite homogenous although some old fragments seem to have been incorporated in the construction at some time. The *śikhara* is certainly not entirely original and may probably have been reconstructed in the seventeenth or eighteenth century. It is composed of many miniature *śikhara*s (*śṛṅgas,* some of them of typical *bhūmija* style) in the four quadrants between the central offsets, the latter being composed of four *uraḥśṛṅga*s each (Plate 10.2). The features of the *śikhara* characterize the temple as belonging to the *śekharī* mode (type 4). Many of the elements in the *śikhara* appear to have been re-used, some have even been re-cut from diverse sorts of stones. HARDY has pointed to a considerable predominance of the *śekharī* mode in recent centuries asserting that "Rajput rulers of the seventeenth and eighteenth centuries saw the *śekharī* as the most appropriate form for a Hindu shrine".[60]

58 According to RAG 2012: 221 the inscription is dated VS 1829 (ca. 1773 CE).

59 AIIS Nos. 81895–81897. Here the temple is called Dattātreya temple (proposed date: "ca. 1100–1125 CE").

60 HARDY 2002: 82.

Thus it is conceivable that the present form of the *śikhara* may not be the original one. It is, however, more likely that the constructional features of the remains determined the type of superstructure and that the original tower was indeed built in the *śekharī* mode (compare the tower of the Brahmeśvara temple, below, **1.2.2.1.** p. 15).

1.1.2.4. The Candramauleśvara temple

This rather modern temple stands on a high, free standing platform to the north-west of the Indreśvara (Plates 11.1–2). It faces north and was probably built in the late nineteenth or early twentieth century by the *mahārāja* Hoḷkar of Indore, of whom an old stone label is fixed above the entrance to the *garbhagṛha*. To the right of that entrance another inscription on stone is found which states that the temple's idol was (re-)consecrated and the temple dedicated to the public on March 4, 1981 on the occasion of *mahāśivarātrī*. Except, perhaps, for the platform whose lower portion seems to have been built around the same time when the northern portion of the fortification wall (Map 2.2, No. 1) was reconstructed, this temple is of no significance in the present context.

1.1.2.5. The Kapileśvara temple

This temple is located to the south-west of the Candramauleśvara and stands on a small levelled plateau about half way up the eastern slope of the Viṣṇupurī hill (Plate 12.1). The extant building faces east and consists of a square main shrine with a *liṅga* and a closed, rectangular hall with arched doorways opening to the south and north. Attached to this hall in the east is another small, pavilion-like structure which houses a fine old sculpture of a bull with a separate *liṅga* in front. All three structures have flat roofs crowned by a low, stunted cupola.[61] These as well as all the inner and outer walls are covered with plaster. The cupolas as well as the arch of the doorway in the pavilion-like structure suggest that the extant building was reconstructed in the seventeenth or eighteenth century incorporating parts of the *mūlaprāsāda* of a much older temple, whose remains are best preserved on the west and south and, to a lesser extent, on the north sides (Plate 12.2–3). These apparently comprise, as far as they are exposed, parts of the *vedībandha* and *pīṭha*. The lower courses of the latter seem to lie

---

61 A similar cupola is found on the shrine of Dvārkādīśa in the Ṛṇamukteśvara temple, (see below, **2.4.2.**, p. 67). A similar one once crowned the *garbhagṛha* of the Siddhanātha temple, but was removed by the Archaeological Survey of India around 1904, apparently on order of Lord Curzon (see MARSHALL 1909: 6–7).

underground as is suggested by the location of an old *praṇāla* on the north side (Plate 12.4) which probably corresponds (approximately) with the floor level of the *garbhagṛha,* which is accessed through an old doorframe, of which only the lower portion is preserved (Plate 12.5). The *jaṅghā,* if preserved at all, is almost completely hidden behind a thick layer of plaster.

The exposed portions of the *pīṭha* and *vedībandha* show that the temple had a stellate ground-plan and was very elaborately moulded and decorated (Plate 12.6). Even the corner *kūṭastambhas* were stellate as can be seen at the south-western corner of the temple (Plate 12.02)

A large number of old *śṛṅgas* and *āmalakas* incorporated in the modern walls of the temple (Plate 12.2, 6) as well as others found scattered all over the site (Plate 12.7) attest to the prior existence of a corresponding *śikhara.*

Moreover, there are a couple of loose sculptures found here which also must have been part of the original structure. One example represents a cornerstone placed outside in front of the temple (Plates 12.8–9). All these remains leave no doubt that this temple represents a specimen of stellate *bhūmija* temples.

1.2. *Brahmāpurī*

Brahmāpurī comprises that part of Godarpurā which lies to the east of the Kapilā ravine. The area borders on the Narmadā to the north and forms a kind of plateau which is very steep at the north-western edge gradually sloping down to the south and east.

1.2.1. Fortification walls

The few rather insignificant fragmentary remains of fortification walls at Brahmāpurī (Map 2.2, No. 3) run along the western edge of the plateau (immediately behind the Indreśvara temple) and then turn to the east, running roughly parallel to the eastern fort wall in the Kapilā ravine (Map 2.2, No. 1).

1.2.2. Temples

1.2.2.1. The Brahmeśvara temple

The Brahmeśvara is the only temple at Brahmāpurī[62] in which remains of an old shrine are found (Plates 13.1–2). It was formerly accessed by a

62 Mentioned in RAG 2012: 219.

steep old staircase, now rarely used, which runs up the north-western edge of the plateau overlooking the Narmadā, on which it stands.

The temple faces west and consists of an octagonal *saptaratha mūla-prāsāda*, an *antarāla* and a small, open *maṇḍapa*. The temple has recently been completely coated with a thick layer of yellow paint which makes it very difficult to discern the different phases of reconstruction. While the *jaṅghā* seems to be almost entirely modern with only its lower-most course partly preserved, the *vedībandha* and *pīṭha* of the *mūlaprāsāda* are old, as is the doorway to the *garbhagṛha* (Plate 13.3). The faces of the *kumbha* of the *vedībandha* carry small sculptures of female deities sitting in stylized miniature shrines all around the *mūlaprāsāda* (Plate 13.2).[63]

Like the *jaṅghā*, the front wall of the *antarāla* with its arched entrance (Plate 13.1), the *maṇḍapa* and the *śikhara* appear comparatively recent. The latter looks somewhat similar to that of the Indreśvara temple, suggesting that both towers may have been rebuilt at the same time in the *śekharī* mode. But unlike in the case of the Indreśvara temple, we find here a considerable number of *bhūmija śṛṅga*s incorporated in the lower *bhūmi*s of the *śikhara* especially in the north-west and south-east quadrants. These *śṛṅga*s represent *bhūmija* spires (Plate 13.5)[64] typically used in *bhūmija śikhara*s and are placed in their appropriate original positions.

An interesting four-armed sculpture of Viṣṇu is found in a niche in the reconstructed upper portion of the southern *kapilī* (Plate 13.4).

1.3. *Viṣṇupurī*

Viṣṇupurī represents what was formerly called Godarpurā[65] and is the most densely populated area of OM. It is limited at its northern, eastern and southern sides by steep precipices which form a kind of plateau which gradually slopes down to the south-west. Here, the village is linked to the old road to Morṭakkā where the Oṃkāreśvar Road railway station on the old Akola–Ajmer metre gauge line is located. Of all parts of OM, Viṣṇupurī has seen the most extensive settlement activity during the latter half of the twentieth century. All public institutions and offices as well as numerous *dharmśālā*s established and run by different castes (*jātī*) are situated here.

---

63 The figure on the northern *kapilī* represents Gaṇeśa. Similar figures in the same position are found on the Viṣṇutemple, below, **1.3.2.1.**, p. 18

64 The design is quite similar to those found at Bijamandal, see TICHIT *2010 (II): 159, Fig. 2.107.

65 The name derives from the Godarākhāṛā which formerly possessed most of the area and still has its seat here.

It may therefore be assumed that considerable portions of old remains, as far as they existed, may either have been dismantled and reused in modern construction work or now lie buried under modern buildings.

1.3.1. Fortification walls

There are remains of a long stretch of a fortification wall running roughly north-east to south-west right through the modern village (Map 2.2, No. 4). Original portions can nowadays only be traced at very few locations as most parts are now inaccessible and concealed by modern structures. The few original remains comprise just one to three layers of large stone blocks laid without mortar comparable to the remains to the west of the Amareśvara temple complex. It is impossible to determine whether this wall originally continued along the precipices on the south and west side to enclose the adjoining area completely. It is equally difficult to determine whether this wall was in any way connected to the remains of fortification walls running along the ridge of a deserted hill to the west of Viṣṇupurī (Map 2.3).[66]

Though these latter walls have almost completely collapsed, their course is, at least in the dry season, comparatively easy to follow (Plate 14.1). They form an enclosure within which a number of settlement structures are found at different places (Plate 14.2). Most prominent among these is a large rectangular structure towards the north-east, clearly visible in Map 2.3, but much less identifiable in the field. The outer fortification wall forks into two in the north-west to enclose another small hill close to the bank of the Narmadā. This hill may have been of strategic importance as it offers a panoramic view far down the river. Another strategically important feature is a passage through the Narmadā which lies close by, just down the northern slope. This is the only place where the river could be crossed, at least on horseback, in the dry season. These strategic advantages suggest that the area may have been of predominantly military use. It must be noted that the walls enclosing this area seem to have largely been built from smaller blocks of stone as those found, for instance, in the northern walls of Mucukund hill or in those near the Amareśvara temple complex. Although this enclosure appears to close off access to Māndhātā island from the south bank of the Narmadā, the differences in style and workmanship may probably point to a later date.

66 This, however, appears unlikely, as these structures appear to be of a later date.

1.3.2. Temples

As already stated, a large number of religious establishments are nowadays located at Viṣṇupurī, often with small temples attached to them which, however, are mostly of recent origin. There are only two temples which can be said to be of antiquity.

1.3.2.1. The Viṣṇu temple

The Viṣṇu temple[67] stands on a large platform at the north-eastern side of Viṣṇupurī, overlooking the Kapilāsaṅgam (Plate 15.1). It opens to the east and faces the Brahmeśvara temple. The temple consists of a *saptaratha mūlaprāsāda*, an *antarāla* and a *maṇḍapa* with three entrances in the cardinal directions which all stand on an original raised common platform. This is one of the instances, where the temple base is exposed almost in its entirety.

The *śikhara* as well as parts of the *antarāla* and *maṇḍapa* have been reconstructed probably in the eighteenth century. The temple was recently renovated and is covered by a thick layer of whitewash which obstructs many sculptural details. The *maṇḍapa* floor has been refurbished with polished slabs of dark red stone and the *garbhagṛha* completely tiled. However, as in all the other temples described so far, remains of the original construction are still found. Thus, the *pīṭha, vedībandha* and *jaṅghā* of the *mūlaprāsāda*, all elaborately moulded, are apparently completely preserved (Plate 15.2). The small *bhadra* niches of the *jaṅghā* are, however, empty. Similar to the Brahmeśvara temple, the faces of the *kumbha* of the *vedībandha* carry small sculptures of female deities sitting in stylized miniature shrines, albeit only on the southern and western sides; on the north side we find a diamond-shaped geometrical figure instead.

The inner pillars of the *maṇḍapa* are very elaborately carved with bands of standing and seated figures (Plate 15.3). The remainder of the pillars appear also old but are carved in various styles. The doorframe of the *garbhagṛha* has a lintel with the *saptamātṛkā*s carved on it (Plate 15.5) and is at its sides partly obstructed by the apparently modern south and north walls of the *antarāla* (Plate 15.4). Four-armed guardian figures flanking the doorway and holding *cakra* (upper left) and *gadā* (upper right) and *śaṅkha* (lower left), and *padma* (lower right) attest to an original *vaiṣṇava* affiliation of the temple. Both side walls of the *antarāla* have a niche each containing sculptures which differ considerably in style. The

67 First mentioned in RAG 2012: 220.

southern one contains a fine sculpture of Lakṣmīnārāyaṇa (Plate 15.6) and the northern one a four-armed standing Viṣṇu made from black stone (Plate 15.7). The rear portion of the *maṇḍapa* is closed to the north and south by modern walls which have two shallow niches on the inside. The southern one contains an interesting sculptured *devapaṭṭa*, originally from Mathurā, which depicts scenes from the life of Kṛṣṇa (Plate 15.8).[68]

There are some more interesting sculptures on the outer walls of the temple and in the compound. Perhaps the most important is a large image of a four-armed standing Viṣṇu which stands opposite to the northern *maṇḍapa* staircase leaning against a wall (Plate 15.9). Remarkable too, is the existence of an erotic sculpture on the modern south wall of the rear portion of the *maṇḍapa* (Plate 15.10).

1.3.2.2. The Nāga temple

The Nāga temple stands to the north-west of the Viśvanātha temple, on top of the plateau near its eastern and southern slopes. It is in a photo from the middle of the 1970s (Plate 2.3, upper right corner) that old remains of the Nāga temple can be seen standing in an open ground. The whole area is nowadays covered with houses. The Nāga temple still exists, but has been completely rebuilt and does not show any old feature today.

2. Māndhātā island

As mentioned before, the island comprises three hills in south-east to north-west succession, *i.e.* the Bīrkhalā hill, the Māndhātā hill proper, and the Mucukund hill (Map 1.3). The island is commonly considered holy because its shape (or that of the fortification walls) is popularly believed to represent the symbol ॐ – albeit a pious misconception. Therefore it is circumambulated on a footpath, the *parikramāpatha*, stretches of which apparently still follow routes that already existed in the ancient fort.

I shall begin my account with the Bīrkhalā hill, the smallest and eastern-most of the three hills on Māndhātā island.

2.1. *Bīrkhalā hill*

The Bīrkhalā hill is a small precipitous hillock at the south-eastern end of the island (Plate 16.1). It figures prominently in one of the earliest references to Māndhātā of colonial times presently available to me, a letter

68 A more detailed discussion of this *devapaṭṭa* is found in NEUSS 2016.

dated November 29, 1822 written by a certain Captain Douglas, Political Assistant in Nimar, to the Resident at Indore.[69] The letter gives an eyewitness account of the religious suicide of a young man, who hurled himself down in the same year from the Bīrkhalā hill onto the Bhairavaśilā, nowadays held to be situated at the south-western foot of the hillock right on the bank of the Narmadā (Plate 16.2).[70] The starting point for the suicidal leap is unknown today, but is said to have been located straight up the hillock, where remains of an old temple are found.[71] The Bīrkhalā hillock is the only hill on the island which is not enclosed by remains of fortification walls.

2.1.1. Temple remains

Few local names for individual temple remains on the Bīrkhalā hillock and elsewhere on the island are known today. In such cases, I shall number monuments or find-spots consecutively. On the Bīrkhalā hillock I shall describe the remains from west to east, as shown in Map 3.

2.1.1.1. Temple B1

The remains of temple B1 are found near the western corner of the Bīrkhalā hill close to the southern precipice falling down to the Narmadā. The surrounding area is full of architectural fragments from the almost completely collapsed temple (Plate 17.1–2). FORSYTH description of the temple differs considerably from its present condition:

> The oldest Sivite temple in the place is probably that on the Bírkhalá rocks, at the extreme eastern point of the island. It consists of a sort of closed court-yard with a front verandah, through which apparently was a passage to the shrine which has now completely disappeared. It is totally different in plan from any of the other temples which consist of the ordinary shrine and porch. The stones are of great size, the verandah and colonnades of the court-yard being supported on massive pillars very plainly carved in rectilineal figures. (FORSYTH 1870b: 260).

69 See FORSYTH 1871: 173–176.

70 The present Bhairavaśilā shown in Plate 16.2 appears to be much too small a target for a lethal leap from the top of the hill. The original rock must have been considerably larger if not to be missed. If it was really situated at this place, it must now be covered with rocks deposited by the annual monsoon floods. Although the ritual suicides were banned by the British in 1824, the rock is still smeared with vermillion and plastered with silver foil which attests to the still living local veneration of Bhairava.

71 However, it seems almost impossible to jump from that place straight down onto the rocks because the hill is far too curved at the upper end.

There are nowadays no traces of a 'closed courtyard', only parts of the verandah or *maṇḍapa* remain. These comprise seven pillars with brackets and beams, but no roof slabs. The two front pillars are shorter than the rest and mounted on a kind of balustrade which is moulded and ornamented. This and the other, 'regular' pillars stand on a high platform with elaborately carved mouldings parts of which are exposed only on the eastern, southern and northern side (Plate 17.3–4). To the south-west of the *maṇḍapa* remains of the base of the collapsed rear part of the building are found (Plate 17.5). The exposed parts probably represent the top of either the *kumbha* or *kalaśa* mouldings of the *vedībandha* of a shrine with a typical *pañcaratha* ground-plan. At one corner of the *bhadra*, four *akṣaras* are found inscribed which are palaeographically similar to those in other records of Paramāra times (Plate 17.6).[72] Shape and size of this structure suggest that it represents the base of the *mūlaprāsāda* with the *garbhagṛha* oriented to the east. Though FORSYTH claimed the temple to be *śaiva*, there is no indication to that effect found here now. Instead, there is a large mutilated sculpture of Viṣṇu, with its head missing, leaning on the platform at the south-eastern side of the *maṇḍapa* (Plate 17.7), but it is unclear whether it originally belonged to the temple or was brought from elsewhere. Mention may further be made of a hero stone found toppled at the southern side (Plate 17.8) which may perhaps, at this particular place, commemorate an old-time human sacrifice.

2.1.1.2. Structure B2

This structure stands to the east of and on a slightly lower level than temple B1 (Plate 18.1). It does, most likely, not represent an original construction, although it contains some old fragments. The most interesting one is an old doorframe (Plate 18.2). The walls of the building are composed of a variety of material and stand on natural rock without any trace of an old platform. To the west of the temple is a mound overgrown with shrubs, where a number of carved stones are partly exposed.

2.1.1.3. Platform B3

To the east of B2, down a staircase made from old stones, and on a yet lower level a small modern platform made from concrete with a *liṅga* is found (Plates 19.1–2). It is surrounded by a few old temple fragments, most notably a door lintel (Plate 19.3).

---

72 The legible *akṣaras* read *de vā i ta* or *de va* | *i ta*.

2.1.1.4. Liṅgas

Further east, down a very steep precipice are said to be two more ancient *liṅgas* in a small natural cave in the rock. I did not visit these *liṅgas*, because the very narrow footpath is extremely steep and dangerous.

2.2. *Māndhātā hill*

Māndhātā hill proper is that part of OM where, at least on the surface, the largest number of antiquarian remains are found. It roughly covers about one third of the total area of the island. We shall consider here only the area inside the old fort on top of the hill, where two of four 'protected' monuments listed by COUSENS in 1897,[73] including the more famous Siddhanātha temple, are situated. The foot and slope of the hill along the south-western side, *i.e.* the modern settlement of Śivpurī, will be dealt with separately (see below, **2.5.**, p. 73), as the ancient remains found there have in the course of time been disturbed and altered on such a massive scale that the site stands somewhat apart from the rest. The Oṃkāreśvara temple, for instance, though containing Paramāra components, was re-built, more or less in its present form, at about the same time when the extant Rājmahal was constructed which is said to have been inaugurated by Rāv Daulat Siṅgh Cauhān in 1657.[74]

2.2.1. Fortification walls

Let us again begin with FORSYTH's observations:

> The walls of the different forts, two of which enclose the two sections of the island itself, and two more the rocky eminences on the southern banks, display some excellent specimens of the old style of Hindú architecture. They are formed of very large blocks of stone without cement. The stone is partly the basalt of the hill itself, and partly a coarse yellow sandstone which must have been brought from a considerable distance.[75] The gateways are formed with horizontal arches, and ornamented with much fine carving, statues of gods, &c. The best are those on the eastern end of the island, or Mándhátá Proper which also appears to be the only part that has ever received any repairs. It is easy to distinguish these from the old works, some being even as recent as the Mohammadan period,

73 COUSENS 1897: 40–41.

74 According to personal information from Devendra Siṅgh Cauhān, senior member of the Cauhān family and managing trustee of the Śrī Oṃkāreśvar Jyotirliṅg Mandir Ṭrasṭ.

75 This is probably not the case, as such a variety of sandstone is found on the south-eastern side of the Bīrkhalā hill.

> as at the Bhímárjuní gate (opposite the Bírkhalá rocks), where there is a distinct pointed archway laid in mortar. (FORSYTH 1870b: 259–260; fn. in square brackets mine).

The plateau on Māndhātā hill is enclosed on all sides by a massive inner wall running along the edge of the hill top (Map 4.1). The course of this wall can easily be determined for most parts, except for some portions at the south-eastern, southern and south-western sides of the hill, where it has almost completely disappeared. Another outer wall, running about 15–20 metres below and approximately parallel to the inner one, is almost completely destroyed apart from a few extant fragments at the eastern end of the hill. Therefore its exact course cannot be conclusively determined today. However, large amounts of stones fallen down the hill especially on the northern side, as well as some other indicators like the existence of the Outer north gate (see below, **2.2.2.5.**, p. 31), suggest that it once formed a complete second enclosure. The absence of remains of the outer wall and large portions of the inner one on the south side of the hill is certainly due to the reuse of the material in later buildings like, for instance, the present Rājmahal of the Cauhān family (see below, **2.5.1.7.**, p. 81). At the eastern end of Māndhātā hill the course of the inner wall is almost completely untraceable, too. But this is probably due to the fact that the surrounding area was last extensively disturbed when, about four decades ago, many stone slabs were used to built a long footpath along the south-eastern and further along the eastern slope of the hill leading up to the tower-like pumping station of the municipal water supply which was implemented some time in the 1980s (see Map 4.3). This path is lined with a large number of old stone slabs, some of them sculptured, and ends in a steep staircase made of similar slabs. All of them seem to have been brought from structures around Area A (see below, **2.2.4.1.**, p. 36) and adjoining remains of the inner fort wall which were the nearest and most conveniently exploitable deposits of suitable material for the task.

2.2.2. Gateways and staircases

There are altogether six extant gateways in different states of preservation found on Māndhātā hill (Map 4.1), four of which stand in the course of the inner wall, roughly in the cardinal directions, and represent what Parul Pandya DHAR calls *pratolī*.[76] Only one gateway originally standing in the course of the outer fortification wall ('Outer north gate') is preserved at a

76 DHAR 2010: 172.

little distance from the North or Cāndsūraj gate of the inner fortification wall. One more gateway ('Inner or Huṇḍī-kuṇḍī gate', see below **2.2.2.6.**, p. 31) stands somewhat isolated in the midst of the enclosure near a central crossroads apparently in the course of an intermediate wall that is hardly traceable in the field now, but which must once have divided the settlement into a western and eastern (or inner and outer) section.

At all the extant gates it is evident that a considerable amount of remains are still buried underground. Five of the six gates stand on the verge of the hill and must originally have been accessible by staircases. Nowadays there are six staircases leading up Māndhātā hill (Map 4.2), but only the staircases leading to the East and North or Cāndsūraj gates can with certainty be stated to be original ones. The staircase leading through the Inner and Outer north gates has been refurbished a few years ago with red stone slabs, but it still follows its original course. The remaining four staircases are all situated at the south-western end of the hill, around the Rājmahal and the Oṃkāreśvara temple which is the most populated area on the island today. As the most extensive settlement activity with frequent restorations and alterations has taken place here in more recent times, it is difficult to tell which portion of the footpaths and staircases in this area might belong to or reflect the situation in Paramāra times. A photograph of Māndhātā shot some time in the 1880s by the Indian photography pioneer Lala Deen Dayal does not show any intact staircase around this area.[77]

The South and West gates, however, would necessitate staircases to access them, too. Hence, the long staircase leading up to the West gate may also, at least partly, be original. The staircase nearest to the South gate lies a little bit to the west of it and the gate is now bypassed by the existing footpath. The other remaining staircase which leads up the hill between these two is situated immediately to the east of the Rājmahal and reaches the summit of the hill, where Dayal's said photograph shows another dilapidated gate which is now completely gone ('South-west gate'). This suggests that this staircase, too, may follow the course of an old one. The footpath leading from the North or Cāndsūraj gate to the centre of the hill and the central stretch of another footpath crossing it near the Inner gate which leads today from the West gate to the Siddhanātha temple probably indicate the original course of the two ancient main roads within the enclosure on Māndhātā hill.

77 The photograph is held by the British Library (BL), Curzon Collection, Shelfmark Photo 430/21(14), accessible at: http://www.bl.uk/onlinegallery/onlineex/apac/photocoll/n/019pho000430s21u00014000.html [last retrieved on November 26, 2016].

The gateways are interesting regarding their architectural features and the sculptures found on or around them which may bear clues regarding their historical sequence. However, most parts of the original gateways are lost either due to destruction or decay. In a few cases original parts have been replaced in the course of later renovations. Other gates, that must originally have existed with some certainty have completely vanished.[78]

2.2.2.1. The North or Cāndsūraj gate[79]

The North gate, locally called Cāndsūraj gate,[80] is located about the middle of the northern stretch of the inner fortification wall on Māndhātā hill (Map 4.1, Plates 20.1–2). The gate is shown in one of a series of seven photographs from OM that were shot between 1850 and 1870 by an unknown photographer, and are now held by the Victoria and Albert Museum (V&A), London (Plate 20.3).[81]

---

78 Such as other corresponding gates in the outer wall and another, inner gateway ('South-west gate') at the top of the staircase which now leads down to Śivpurī at the south-western side approximately midway between the extant South and West gates.

79 AIIS Nos. 81901–81911 (proposed date: "ca. 1100–1150 CE").

80 I shall retain the traditional names of the gates on Māndhātā hill to distinguish them from those located on Mucukund hill.

81 V&A No. E.208:2177–1994. The photo is accompanied by the following information:
"Francis Frith was one of the most successful commercial photographers from the 1850s and 1860s. He also established what was to become the largest photographic printing business in England. This image is part of the V&A's Francis Frith 'Universal Series' archive which consists of over 4000 whole-plate albumen prints predominantly of historical and topographical sites. Images such as these were highly desirable throughout the 1850s and 1860s. It is now known that nearly all of the works bearing the F. Frith and Co. stamp were not taken by Frith himself, but by one of his travelling employees. (...)
In addition to hiring his own photographers, Frith also bought the negative stocks of established photographers such as Roger Fenton and Francis Bedford. The images that make up the V&A Frith 'Universal Series' are file prints acquired from F. Frith & Co. Ltd of Reigate, Surrey. Mounted on brown card, with the place name and stock number usually handwritten on the print itself, they were most probably used as place-markers within the company's filing system, allowing for easy retrieval of stocks of unmounted prints." ('Summary' found at: http://collections.vam.ac.uk/item/O216507/mandhatta-jain-templephotograph-francis-frith/; last retrieved on March 1, 2017).
The seven prints are numbered 4423–4429 and the hand-written title 'Mandhatta. Jain Temple' is uniformly found on all of them, although six were taken at other locations. Three were shot at the Siddhanātha temple, but even these are not consecutively numbered. Obviously the person who sorted the photographs at Frith Co. had no knowledge neither about the photographs nor about OM itself. Hence, the OM series was most likely not shot by one of Frith's associates, but was bought from another company.

The Cāndsūraj gate represents the only entrance to the enclosure from the north side of the hill. It stands close to the precipice where a steep staircase leads through the Outer North gate down to the ravine which separates Māndhātā and Mucukund hill on which another staircase ascends again up to the latter's now almost completely vanished East gate. This path represents a sole direct link between Māndhātā hill proper and the Gaurīsomanātha plateau on Mucukund hill.

Though COUSENS reported the Cāndsūraj gate to be "in a very ruinous condition"[82] and hence considered it unnecessary to be preserved,[83] it was declared a 'protected monument' in 1912 by the Chief Commissioner of the Central Provinces and confirmed by the Governor in Council in 1925.[84] Most parts of the extant massive walls of the gatehouse have been erected around six old pillars to prevent the gatehouse from collapsing. All parts of these walls are made from stones laid with mortar and are certainly the result of subsequent conservation work undertaken especially in more recent times.[85] Their course seems to be largely oriented at the original one, especially in the northern part, as is indicated by the four niches which are probably in their original position; this is certainly the case with the two large north-facing ones. Thus, the northern part of the structure in front of the gatehouse passage seems to give a more realistic impression of the original arrangement, whereas the remaining portions of the extant structure appear rather disturbed.

Only the inner part of the original gatehouse has survived. It is composed of eight pillars, four each standing in two east–west oriented rows (Fig. 2). The four pillars to either side of the passage stand at the corners of large raised recesses in the lower storey of the gatehouse. On both sides of the passage was a second storey, of about half the height of the lower one, as is indicated by an old doorframe in the west face of the building which is accessed by a damaged staircase at the south-western corner (Plate 20.4).

82 COUSENS 1897: 41. The condition of the gate at that time is documented in one of eleven photographs (No. 1388) taken by Henry Cousens in 1893–94 for the ASI, now held by the BL (Shelfmark Photo 1003/1268; see below, Appendix 1, Table 3, p. 112).

83 He classified it as to fall into category III, *i.e.* "Monuments which from their advanced stage of decay, or comparative unimportance, it is impossible or unnecessary to preserve." (COUSENS 1897: ii).

84 See *CPG* 1912, Jul–Dec (Pt. I), p. 957 and *CPG* 1925, Jan–Dec (Pt. I), p. 483.

85 At least one such instance is documented: "Chand Suraj Gateway, Mandhata, District East Nimar. — The damaged and missing stone flooring was restored and area fenced with G.I. barbed wire on angle iron posts to check encroachments." (*IA–R* 1987–88: 181).

The structure of the pillars are the most prominent feature of the gatehouse and expose a rather peculiar and delicate construction of the latter. The lower pillars are crowned by cross-shaped brackets carrying stones shaped like miniature shrines. These are again topped by rectangular stones which end in elephant heads protruding into the passage. On top of these are placed short pillars forming the low upper storey which are crowned by cross-shaped brackets supporting the architraves. On their inner faces, *i.e.* those facing the passage, exquisitely carved stones resembling *toraṇa*s are attached.[86] Most of these elements appear to be detached from the pillars and have apparently been put in place separately, as is suggested by the figures in the upper rear parts, whose heads had to be chiselled off in order to fit the stones in (Plate 20.5). Remains of a comparable *toraṇa* an the south-eastern side of the passage suggest that the gatehouse originally contained at least one more such pair of pillars flanking the passage (Plate 20.6). The doorframe of the western entrance to the upper storey stylistically matches the *toraṇa*s and is probably in its original position (Plates 20.4, 7).

As already mentioned, the northern portion of the gate in front of the actual passage has four niches. Two inner niches flank an open space in front of the gatehouse to the east and west. They are placed in line with the course of the inner fort wall (Fig. 2). The eastern niche faces west and contains an eight-armed image of Mahiṣāsuramardinī[87] (Plate 20.8). The western one, facing east, contains a sculpture of a six-armed Gaṇeśa[88] (Plate 20.9). Both niches are completely preserved including socle, pilasters, architrave and nicely carved *toraṇa*s above that have in the centre an identical four-armed goddess inside a miniature shrine, seated in *lalitāsana*.

Two more, much larger niches are found to the west and east on the outer or north face of the fortification wall flanking the gateway. The western one is better preserved than the eastern one, of which only parts of the socle remain (Plates 20.1, 10). This niche was originally flanked by pilasters and contained a large sculpture of a male *śaiva* deity, probably Bhairava, parts of which lie half-buried in front (Plate 20.11). The figure holds a *khaṭvāṅga* in its upper left hand which is the only attribute discernible. The western niche contains a large, probably twelve-armed, but

86 The arrangement of the pillars represents what DHAR (2010: 172–78) designates *pratolī toraṇa*.

87 AIIS No. 81908, TICHIT *2010 (II): Plate 137, Fig. 5.

88 AIIS No. 81907, TICHIT *2010 (II): Plate 112, Fig. 4.

badly mutilated sculpture of Cāmuṇḍā[89] (Plate 20.12). It was also flanked by pilasters, a broken fragment of which is lying nearby.

Among stray finds in the vicinity of the Cāndsūraj gate, most notable are four loose sculptures kept in the large recess on the western side of the passage (Plate 20.13). These comprise a hero-stone, a male three-headed bust, a stone with sculptured niches in its four sides, one side containing an image of a four-armed Maheśvarī and a worn-off relief of a seated male.

2.2.2.2. The East or Bhīmārjunī gate[90]

This gate is located at the south-eastern corner of Māndhātā hill (Map 4.1, Plate 21.1–2). At least since FORSYTH's time it is locally known as Bhīmārjunī gate, because the large sculptures flanking the entrance are held to represent Bhīma and Arjuna. The gateway has been rebuilt some time probably by Muslim masons as is attested by the arched doorway which incorporates an old core of Paramāra times. Remains of the latter are found in the outer structures flanking the gateway as well as in the niches and sculptures in the south wall. The original gatehouse had two storeys (Plate 21.2) and was probably part of a larger structure (Fig. 3). At the north side of the gatehouse the fort wall turns to the east almost in a right angle and runs as a comparatively high wall around the ridge of a ravine up to an originally probably tower-like square structure, of which only the base is preserved, before it merges into the surrounding area (Plate 21.3).

The original gateway was flanked by a probably double-storeyed gatehouse whose original plan and structure are now difficult to determine. There are neither original pillars or pilasters, nor are there remains of original brackets supporting the architraves of the gatehouse left along the passage. A fragment of an old door lintel, probably a part of the original lintel of the outer gateway, is found half-buried in front (east) of the gate. Its *lalāṭabimba* shows a nicely carved figure of Gaṇeśa (Plate 21.4). Old pillars are found only in the northern part of the upper storey (Plate 21.5). Whether the original gatehouse contained *pratolī toraṇa*s comparable to those found in the Cāndsūraj gate is uncertain, but their original presence is suggested by two stylistically comparable architectural elements. They probably represent socles of niches, and are found facing each other on the north and south sides of the entrance in the upper storey (Plate 21.6).

89 AIIS No. 81906, TICHIT *2010 (II): Plate 117, Fig. 2.

90 AIIS Nos. 81898–81900 (proposed date: "ca. 1100–1150 CE").

The main niches in the front wall and their sculptures which flank the gateway apparently belong to the original construction, as is borne out by the socles beneath the sculptures (Plates 21.7–8). Both are of similar design but differ in their lower portions. The niches were originally framed by pilasters whose bases are still found on the socles. Those in the northern niche are much worn off, but the single base in the south niche contains on its front face a four-armed goddess seated in *lalitāsana*.[91] The outer superstructure of the niches is lost, but both contain large images (ca. 140x230 cm) of eight-armed standing figures of male *śaiva* deities, probably variant forms of Bhairava. The southern one stands in a dancing posture, the northern one in a static position. The latter is apparently accompanied on its proper left by a dog. The attributes in their hands, (as far as preserved) are as follows:

South niche[92]		North niche[93]	
ḍamaru	[broken]	sword	shield
[broken]	[?]	[broken]	[broken]
[broken]	cut-off head	[broken]	[broken]
triśūla(?)	*khaṭvāṅga*	[?]	[?]

2.2.2.3. The South gate

The South gate (Map 4.1, Plates 22.1–2) is located at about three-quarters to the west in the southern course of the inner fortification wall, on the verge of the hill at the eastern end of Śivpurī. As mentioned before, the southern stretches of the inner and outer fortification walls represent their worst preserved portions. Accordingly, the South gate stands somewhat isolated, with few remains of the adjoining walls preserved to either of its sides. Except on the south side, where it stands very close to the slope down to the Narmadā, the surrounding area reaches up almost to half of its own height, indicating that the gate has remained abandoned for a rather long period. A modern plaster coating of the extant ceiling may perhaps represent the floor of a more recent, now vanished, dwelling, rather than

91 Comparable figures are very commonly found at OM, for instance in the *toraṇas* above the smaller niches of the Cāndsūraj gate (Plates 20.8–9), or in the lintels of the Dhavalīmaṭh (see below, **2.4.3.1.**, p. 69 and Plates 62.20–21).

92 AIIS No 81899. The sculpture is locally identified as Bhīma, borne out by modern painted labels below reading "*bhīm mahārāj*" and "*bhīm mahārāj kī jay ho*".

93 AIIS No 81900. This image is locally believed to represent Arjuna as is likewise attested by modern painted labels below reading "*arjun mahārāj*" and "*arjun mahārāj kī jay ho*".

remains of conservation work, as the existence of the gate has not been previously brought to notice. The building is much damaged, but the inner gatehouse is preserved including its ceiling, probably thanks to the plaster coating. Also preserved are four niches with sculptures and a few pillars and architraves of a second storey on the structure's eastern side.

The gateway is somewhat similar in plan to the Cāndsūraj gate, albeit of a much smaller size (Fig. 4.). Like the latter, it has two larger outer and two smaller inner niches flanking the gatehouse in similar positions. However, the gatehouse probably never had *pratolī toraṇa*s as is indicated by the position of the architraves which are placed immediately on comparatively simple pillar brackets as well as the limited overall size of the passage. The outer niches are found on the outer south face of the fortification walls flanking the passage and are in different states of preservation. In the western one the socle is well preserved, but the pilasters and the superstructure have vanished (Plate 22.3). The niche contains an eight-armed, probably male sculpture of a *śaiva* deity standing in a similar pose as the sculpture in the southern niche of the Bhīmārjunī gate. Most of its arms are broken off, but the only discernible attribute is a shield in the figures own upper left hand. The outer eastern niche is even more damaged (Plate 22.4). Here, the socle is completely gone but one pilaster is preserved, albeit much worn-off. The niche contains another badly mutilated eight-armed sculpture of a male *śaiva* deity. Its legs and arms are all broken off, but on its own left side a *khaṭvāṅga* is visible which may probably have been held by its own lower left hand. Like in the Cāndsūraj gate, two inner niches flank an open space in front of the gatehouse. Both niches are preserved except for their superstructures. The western inner niche contains an eight-armed sculpture of Mahiṣāsuramardinī[94] (Plate 22.5), the eastern one a badly mutilated image of a standing eight-armed female deity. Its legs and all its arms are broken off, but in its own upper right hand it holds an object which appears to represent a *cakra* (Plate 22.6).

2.2.2.4. The West gate

The West gate stands at the extreme western end of Māndhātā hill (Map 4.1, Plate 23). The entrance is very narrow, allowing the passage of only few persons at a time. Though much damaged, the gate appears to have been entirely constructed from stone slabs without pillars or pilasters.

94 TICHIT *2010 (II): Plate 137, Fig. 6.

The outer door lintel is placed on top of two bracket stones supported by the walls of the passage. The gate is in such a bad condition that it may collapse in the near future.

2.2.2.5. The Outer North gate

This is the only (extant) gateway in the course of the outer fortification wall on Māndhātā hill (Map 4.1, Plate 24.1–2). It stands about a hundred metres to the north-west of the Cāndsūraj gate down the northern slope of Māndhātā hill in line with the outer wall, whose course can be traced to the east of the gate along the slope, despite its almost completely ruined condition. Contrary to the inner gateways, this gate does not face one of the cardinal directions of the compass, but is oriented west north-west.[95]

The gatehouse is in a much ruined condition. It contains four pillars each to either side of the passage which stand on a raised platform (Plate 24.3). While the eastern row of these pillars stands in line with the inner wall of the recesses to either side of the passage, the western row of pillars stands a little removed from the recesses' western inner walls which have no pillars, but brackets built into the wall supporting the architraves (Plate 24.4). The gate is in acute danger of collapse; its passage has recently provisionally been blocked, the pilgrim's path now bypasses the gate along its eastern side.

2.2.2.6. The Inner or Huṇḍī-kuṇḍī gate

This gateway, locally known as Huṇḍī-kuṇḍī gate, stands a little bit to the west of the middle of Māndhātā hill (Map 4.1, Plates 25.1–2). Most parts of the gatehouse have collapsed though the gate was renovated in comparatively recent, perhaps Marāṭhā, times, as a panel with a royal emblem fixed into the south side of the gateway as well as the use of mortar, suggest. A few pillars, brackets and beams from Paramāra times are found incorporated in the construction, but some of them are in odd positions. The door lintel on the east side, is probably also old and carries a small figure of Gaṇeśa in its centre which, however, is not as exquisitely carved as the one on the original lintel of the South gate (*cf.* Plate 21.4).

95 Presumably, there were more gates in the outer wall, but as no traces whatsoever of any other such gateway are found, their number and positions are presently impossible to determine.

An old sign-board in Hindī[96] gives Huṇḍī-kuṇḍī *dvār* as its name and states that the extant structure represents a gate of a defence wall belonging to the twelfth century. The gate is oriented east–west and probably stands in the course of an inner wall, originally running north–south. However, the course of this wall can hardly be traced in the field, especially on its north side, where the area is difficult to access. To the south-east, in the immediate vicinity of the gate, the area is open and somewhat elevated compared to the surrounding surface level. It is here, that the course of the wall can be traced in satellite images, where it appears to run due south. It probably forms the western limit of the area just referred to. Immediately to the south-east of the gate lie a number of rough stones, pillar fragments and a half-buried large old broken sculpture of Gaṇeśa (Plates 25.3–4). It is doubtful whether this gate already existed in Paramāra times. The few old fragments incorporated in the extant structure could as well have belonged to a temple to which the architectural remains lying around this place, as well as the Gaṇeśa sculpture, and a broken pair of door guardians, probably part of an old doorframe, seem to fit much better. A giant statue of Hanumān (ca. 3,40 x 1,20 m) which is broken into two parts at the legs, stands at the north-east in front of the gate (Plate 25.5). It is much larger in size than the Gaṇeśa sculpture and appears to be considerably younger, ruling out the possibility that both represent a pair originally standing in two flanking niches of the gate. This Hanumān statue is completely smeared with vermillion with a couple of patches of silver foil attached, indicating that it is still under local worship.

2.2.2.7. Non-extant gateways

2.2.2.7.1. The South-west gate

This gateway has completely vanished today, but its former existence is attested by Deen Dayal's photograph already referred to above (p. 24). In the upper left corner the gate can be clearly seen standing at the head of a still extant staircase leading from the Rājmahal up the hill.

---

96 Such sign-boards, all of the same type and age, are found at a few monuments, *i.e.* the Surakṣācaukī (see below, **2.2.3.**b, p. 33), the 'Kuntīmātā' temple (see below, **2.2.4.1.1.**, p. 36), the temple ruin E1, (see below, **2.2.4.5.1.**, p. 47), the Sitāmātā *mandir* (see below, **2.3.1.3.4.**, p. 59), the western or Dharmrāj gate (see below, p. 64) and the Kedāreśvara temple (see below, **2.4.1.**, p. 66). They appear quite old, and are worn off and are difficult to decipher. Apart from some details about the respective monuments they give as the issuing authority the following: *purātattva evaṃ saṃgrahālay ma° pra° śāsan ke liye ārakṣit*. This, however, proves that these boards can, at least, not be older than November 1956, when the state of Madhya Pradesh came into existence.

2.2.2.7.2. The Outer East gate

This gate, too, has completely disappeared. Its existence can only be postulated on the basis of the course of the outer wall as indicated by respective remains adjacent to the Bhīmārjunī gate. Here, the wall traverses an old and probably original staircase (Plate 21.3) that leads uphill.[97] It may be assumed that there was not just a gap in the wall, but that a gate of perhaps comparable dimension as the Outer north gate once existed at this place.

2.2.3. Other structures in the course of the fortification walls

Apart from the gateways, there are remains of three other buildings in the course of the inner fort wall, all situated within its southern stretch.

a) To the north-east of the Bhīmārjunī gate, at the end of the extant stretch of the inner fort wall adjacent to the gate, is a small platform (Fig. 3) with four supporting beams at the south side projecting above the fort wall (Plates 21.3, 26.1). It is topped by a heap of stone fragments, like pillars and beams (Plate 26.2) which represent the collapsed remains of what may once have been something like a watch-tower. An interesting detail here is a water outlet found projecting on the south face of the fortification wall a few metres to the west of that platform, but at a much lower position (Plate 26.1). This position suggests, that the present ground level behind this part of the fortification wall must originally have been much lower than it is today. The water outlet may either be part of a drainage system in that area, or, perhaps more likely, belong to an old tank situated immediately to the east of the Siddhanātha temple (see below, p. 44, Plate 32.10 and Map 4.7).

Another water outlet in a similar position is found in a stretch of the inner fort wall between the Bhīmārjunī gate and the *'surakṣacaukī'* (Plate 26.3). But in this case, it is more likely that it belongs to a drainage system and not to another tank. And here, too, it may be assumed that the ground level of the surrounding area to the north of the wall (Area B, see below, **2.2.4.2.**, p. 38) was originally much lower than it is today.

b) Further to the west stands a second building in the course of the inner wall. An old sign board[98] labels it *'surakṣācaukī'* (watch-post) and dates it to the twelfth century. What remains of it is a small two-storeyed structure raised on a stretch of the inner fort wall (Plates 26.3–5). The

97 The place is indicated in Plate 21.3 by a small platform with a thatched roof situated at the left hand side of the staircase.

98 See also fns. 96 and 154.

lower storey is rectangular in plan with two rows of four pillars in east–west direction and probably one more row of pillars in front (to the south), of which only a single pillar survives. This part of the building, now almost completely collapsed, was mounted on beams projecting over the edge of the fort wall. Three of these beams with a portion of the original floor slabs remain on the western side. The upper storey of the building is square with four pillars supporting the roof which was apparently once crowned by a small pyramidal tower.

c) The third structure lies again further west about the middle of the course of the southern stretch of the inner fort wall and is represented by the remains of a platform and a doorframe made of just two plain pillars with cross-shaped brackets supporting a damaged beam (Plates 26.6–7). The slope of the hill and the area around this doorframe is strewn with stone blocks, most of them carved without ornamentation. One large slab lying immediately next to the doorframe has a typical ornamental band of rhombuses on its narrow sides (Plate 26.7). It is difficult to say, to which kind of structure this doorframe once belonged or what purpose it may have served.

2.2.4. Inside Māndhātā fort: settlement areas and temples

The Māndhātā hill seems to have remained deserted for a long period and modern settlements are presently confined to two areas. One lies in the western part of the hill with domestic dwellings reaching eastwards up to the modern Āśādevī temple[99] and the municipal water supply's tanks behind the South gate. The other area is situated at the eastern side of the hill, just north of the Siddhanātha temple. Its centre is represented by the modern Śrī Vedmātā Gāyatrī Mandiram which is a monastery with a large *gauśālā* (Map 4.3). Apart, perhaps, from a valley in the north-eastern part near that *gauśālā*, settlements within the fortification on Māndhātā hill seem to have been rather evenly distributed in Paramāra times. This is suggested by satellite imagery and also corroborated by extensive remains of settlements which can be traced all over the hill in the field. The satellite map I had initially prepared[100] shows, apart from the well-known Siddhanātha temple and the modern settlements, sixteen conspicuous mounds at different locations on Māndhātā hill (Map 4.4) which, apart from a single one (B2), could all be traced in the field. Most of these mounds turned out

99 Āśādevī is the family deity of the Cauhān Rāv family.

100 See Introduction, p. 1–2 and Map 1.1.

to represent ruins of temples which all remain unreported till date. They are located off the main footpaths in different areas which are densely overgrown with vegetation and are rarely visited by local people, except for the occasional herdsman in search of cows or goats.[101] Only at the peak of the dry season these areas can be reasonably surveyed and it becomes obvious that, apart from the temple ruins, they bear extensive remains of profane structures buried underground. Going by the distribution of structural mounds, five such areas can be distinguished (Map 4.4, A–E) which are partly separated by old footpaths, some stretches of which presumably go back to Paramāra times, especially the one which leads from the Cāndsūraj gate to the Hūṇḍī-kuṇḍī gate and from there eastward up to the Siddhanātha temple. The distinction of the five areas is, of course, arbitrary and used here only for clarity, as I presently possess insufficient evidence to meaningfully distinguish such areas by settlement patterns or structural function. Two larger areas seem to be devoid of settlement structures. One of these is the shallow valley to the north of Area C, where I only found remains of fortification walls at a few places along its edges. The valley itself seems to be devoid of settlement structures, but possibly a few are only concealed by vegetation. The second 'barren' area lies immediately to the east of and adjacent to this valley. It represents the north-eastern edge of Māndhātā hill which is quite rocky here with a steep precipice falling down to the Kāverī river.[102] Vegetation and the rocky character of the terrain renders exploration difficult. Although this area seems to be devoid of large structures, at least a stretch of the Inner fort wall must once have existed here. If at all, only loose and weathered stones are found here which are mostly difficult to identify as old artefacts. This is probably one of the sites where old material was collected and cut for the footpath and staircase of the pumping station (Map 4.3). At some places, the rocky ground seems to show marks of stone masons' work, at other spots, parts of rock cut architecture seem to be exposed.

101 Despite the fact that there have never been any archaeological excavations on Māndhātā hill except in the close vicinity of the Siddhanātha temple (see NEUSS 2013: 118–121), sign boards installed after 2010 by the DAAM are found at a number of locations. They declare the surrounding area as protected archaeological sites and prohibit any settlement activity within a radius of 100 metres.

102 The arm of the Narmadā which flows along the north side of the island and which marks indeed its older course, is popularly regarded as (the extension of) the Kāverī river which joined the Narmadā about two kilometres to the west of Godarpurā. People say, that if you placed a coconut in the Kāverī, it floated across the Narmadā into that very arm.

2.2.4.1. Area A

This area is represented by a roughly rectangular strip running north to south along the eastern end of Māndhātā hill (Maps 4.4, 4.5). It is confined to the east and south by the (partly proposed) course of the inner fort wall, to the west by the Siddhanātha enclosure and to the north by the rocky terrain adjacent to the valley behind the territory of the modern Vedmātā Gāyatrī Mandiram which obstructs parts of its north-western portion, where it borders or rather merges with Area C.

In Area A we find four mounds (Map 4.5, 1–4) which stand more or less in a line running north to south. All of them contain ruined architectural structures and while much of the collapsed material seems to have been removed in the course of time, much material lies presumably still buried underground. Nevertheless, in all cases (apart from, perhaps, A2) some characteristic architectural fragments of the Paramāra period remain at these sites. Area A was last extensively disturbed when the municipality implemented the municipal water supply about four decades ago (see Map 4.3).

2.2.4.1.1. Temple A1

This temple which is named Kuntīmātā *mandir* and dated to the twelfth century on an old sign board[103] stands near the south-eastern slope of Māndhātā hill under a tree in an area overgrown with vegetation (Plate 27.1). Of the original structure which is oriented to the west, only the platform, of which only the surface is partly exposed, portions of the *garbhagṛha* walls, the *udumbara* (doorsill) and lower portions of the *garbhagṛha* doorframe remain. A large sculpture of a (probably) twelve-armed goddess now occupies the sanctum (Plate 27.3).

As far as it is exposed, the platform is about ten metres wide and nine metres long from the staircase in front up to the *udumbara* at the *garbhagṛha* entrance. The *garbhagṛha* is almost square and adds another three metres to the total length of the platform whose original dimension is difficult to determine as it disappears into the surrounding ground at many places. In any case, the original temple seems to have been quite large .
Both side beams (*dvāraśākhā*s) of the doorframe carry five female figures each at the bottom, the central ones representing four-armed female deities of śaiva affiliation.[104] The remaining figures represent two-armed female

103 See also fns. 96 and 154.

104 The figure on the right side carries *ḍamaru*(?) and *khaṭvāṅga* in its upper hands, the lower hands are broken. Beneath it and to the side of the *udumbara* we find again

attendants. The large female sculpture in the *garbhagṛha* is broken at the knees and preserved (or at least visible) only from its knees upwards. It measures ca. 2,20 m in height and ca. 1,20 m in width. Except the lower two, all of its twelve arms are completely broken off. The fingers of the lower right hand are preserved and stretched out holding an *akṣamālā*. The lower left hand is damaged but holds an object which could either have represented a fruit or, perhaps, a *kamaṇḍalu*. It is unclear whether this statue originally belonged to this (or any other) temple. Judging from its size I would rather assume that it may instead have flanked one of the (vanished?) gateways of the fort.

Many architectural artefacts are found strewn around the site among them fragments of pillars, brackets, beams etc. Especially interesting here is a miniature *śikhara* (*śṛṅga*) which originally belonged to the *śikhara* of the temple (Plate 27.2). Apart from the extant remains, other fragments of the temple now line the modern footpath leading up to the pumping station of the municipal water supply (see Map 4.3).

2.2.4.1.2. Structure A2

This structure stands to the north-west of A1 and to the east of the Siddhanātha temple in an area densely covered with vegetation (Plate 28.1). All that is left of it is a large platform made of raw-cut stones which rises about three to four metres above the surrounding ground level. On its western side it is stepped, perhaps representing the foundation of a staircase and suggesting that the original structure was oriented west. On its eastern side the platform merges into the surrounding terrain and its limits are hard to determine here. As far as I could judge, its whole length may lie somewhere between 12 to 18 metres. Just a few sculptured stones could be found on or near this platform (Plate 28.3), but there are probably more fragments hidden in the vicinity. The site is so thickly overgrown that it would need clearance before any reasonable investigation can be undertaken. Hence, it is presently impossible to determine which kind of edifice this structure originally represented.

the figure of a female deity sitting in *lalitāsana,* but here it is apparently mounted on a large animal (perhaps a lion?). The figure on the left side carries a *triśūla* in its own upper right hand, the other attributes are either damaged or broken off. The figure beneath and to the right side of the *udumbara* represents Gaṇeśa.

2.2.4.1.3. Temple A3

Temple A3 is situated to the north-east of structure A2 and its longer sides lie a few metres removed from the southern limits of the modern Vedmātā Gāyatrī Mandiram enclosure. The site appears as a large rectangular strip of land strewn with stone blocks (Plate 29.1), forming a large rectangular expanse with an even surface in its middle and eastern parts, the latter probably representing the floor of the original building. The whole structure is oriented east to west.

The entire base of the structure seems to lie underground, even though the structure gradually projects above the ground level towards its eastern end. At the extreme western end, traces of an adjoining cross-shaped structure is partly exposed which presumably represents a *maṇḍapa* with three entrances in the cardinal directions. The ground-plan of the structure as well as a large number of sculptured fragments like pillars, brackets, beams, socles etc. (Plates 29.3–4) prove beyond doubt that the whole structure represents the ruin of a rather spacious temple which opened to the west with a *maṇḍapa* in front. A few *śṛṅga*s of the *śikhara* are also found at the site (Plate 29.5). The remains suggest that the whole structure originally represented a *bhūmija* temple of about the twelfth century.

2.2.4.1.4. Temple A4

Temple A4 is represented by a mound under a tree behind the north-eastern corner of the modern Vedmātā Gāyatrī Mandiram (Plate 30.1). Only on closer inspection one notices that the site bears a number of architectural fragments, pillars, brackets, beams etc. which suggest that this mound marks an old temple site. This is corroborated by the remains of the temple base which is partly exposed at the eastern side of the mound, where portions of the *kumbha* and *kalaśa* of the *vedībandha* of a typical *pañcaratha* temple are visible (Plate 30.2). The lotus petal design on the *kumbha* found here is reminiscent of, for instance, the Udayeśvara temple, Udaypur.[105] The temple seems to have been oriented to the west, but this can not be said with certainty.

2.2.4.2. Area B

Area B is represented by a large irregularly-shaped stretch of land representing the south-eastern part of Māndhātā island (Maps 4.4, 4.6).

---

105 See TICHIT *2010 (I): 129, Fig. 2.73.

Its northern limit is marked by a long straight line of earthwork (Plate 31) which perhaps marks the course of an inner wall running parallel to the main footpath leading from the Inner or Huṇḍī-kuṇḍī gate up to the Siddhanātha temple enclosure which it includes. In the east, it merges into Area A. To the south, Area B reaches up to the southern slope of Māndhātā hill from the platform with doorframe (see above, **2.2.3.**c., p. 34) in the west up to the Bhīmārjunī gate in the east, from where it can directly be accessed. The western limit is demarcated by the proposed inner fort wall running from the Huṇḍī-kuṇḍī gate due south.[106]

Area B is densely overgrown with vegetation and its ground level appears considerably elevated above the surrounding terrain. In the field, Area B gives the impression of an old settlement site. Among the dense vegetation one constantly stumbles over old stones, many of which seem to form lines and rows or small rectangular structures. However, an overview of larger structures alone is difficult – a consistent exploration of the layout of settlement structures in this area is probably impossible without prior clearance. Apart from the Siddhanātha temple (Map 4.6, No. 1) which is the only site ever excavated (to some extent) on Māndhātā island at all, my basic map seemed to show two small mounds (Map 4.6, Nos. 2 and 3) further to the west. While it was easy to find the westernmost one in the field, I was even on several occasions unable to trace No.2. Nevertheless, I am convinced that some structure must exist at that place and I am equally sure, that the whole area represents an ancient settlement site.

2.2.4.2.1. The Siddhanātha temple (B1)

The Siddhanātha temple has been regarded the most important historic monument at OM ever since the place was first surveyed by the Archaeological Survey of India in 1893.[107] And although it indeed is one of the most

106 The area further to the west is occupied by the tanks of the municipal water supply.

107 COUSENS had first visited OM in November or December 1892 in the course of the preparation of updated lists of antiquarian remains in Central India, when he earmarked OM for a close survey in the next year that was then carried out between November 1893 and April 1894 (HELD *2015: 28–29). Photos of the Siddhanātha temple are AIIS Nos. 81947–81970 (proposed date: "ca. 1100–1150 CE"). The earliest known historic photographs are: a) three prints from Frith's 'Universal Series' (1850–70; Nos. 4425, 4427 and 4429) held by the V&A (Nos. E.208:2174-1994, E.208:2176-1994 and E.208:2178-1994), and b) two photographs taken by COUSENS in 1893–94 for the ASI (Nos. 1386 and 1387), held by the BL (Shelfmarks Photo 1003/(1265) and 1003/(1266).

remarkable among the extant temples architecturally, it had till recently not found the attention it deserves.[108]

The Siddhanātha temple is a large building of exquisite workmanship with a rather unusual *sarvatobhadra* ground-plan (Fig. 5). The *garbhagṛha* is square and opens to all the cardinal directions with pillared halls in front of each of the four entrances. The temple stands on a large cross-shaped, stepped platform which is adorned at its vertical faces with large relief slabs depicting elephants in various positions (Plate 32.1). A rectangular platform in front of the staircase leading to the western entrance hall suggests the existence of a separate *maṇḍapa* at this side (Plate 32.2). This and a number of inscriptions carved onto the western *garbhagṛha* doorframe and *udumbara* (Plate 32.3) seem to mark the western entrance as the main one.

A first survey of the Siddhanātha or Siddheśvara temple[109] by the ASI took place in 1893–94 and was reported in the respective *PRASWI* volume.[110] In the course of this survey, the ASI prepared four drawings including a general plan of the temple, took two photographs and copied one inscription found on a pillar.[111] Of these, unfortunately, only the photographs are available today.[112] By 1897 the temple had already been proposed for protection by the ASI.[113] A first campaign of restoration work

108 It is not even included in the AIIS' *Encyclopaedia of Indian Temple Architecture.* At least a ground-plan has once been published (SAGAR 1979: 58, Fig. 2). In 2015, Patrick HELD submitted a thesis to the Art History Department, Free University Berlin, which represents a rather exhaustive monographic account and analysis of the extant temple and the loose remains found in the compound (HELD *2015).

109 Siddheśvara seems to be the earlier (original?) of the two designations for the temple. It was first used by FORSYTH (1870a: 20) and adopted by Cousens (1894: 3) in his first report on Māndhātā. In the lists of drawings, photographs and inscriptions of the same report (*ibid.*: 15–17), the temple is, however, for the first time named Siddhanātha.

110 COUSENS 1894: 3.

111 COUSENS 1894: 15–17. It is unknown, whether the ground-plan published by SAGAR (1979: 58, Fig. 2) is identical with the one prepared by the ASI, which seems to be lost (see next fn.).

112 The photographs are presently held by the BL (Shelfmark Photo 1003/(1265) and 1003/(1266). Originally they belonged to the Indian Museum, Calcutta (BLOCH 1900: 54; see also Appendix 1, Table 3, p. 112). According to personal communication with HELD, the curator of the India Office Collection, John Falconer, confirmed in an email that the drawings and impressions were never sent back to England and that their whereabouts (if they still exist at all) are unknown.

113 The Siddhanātha temple was classified by COUSENS (1897: 41) as Class Ib, *i.e.*, "Monuments which from their present condition or archaeological value ought to be maintained in permanent good repair [this defines 'Class I'] which are in the possession or charge of private bodies or individuals [this defines 'b']",(*ibid.*: ii; additions in square brackets mine).

started in 1904[114] with the "removal of the ugly dome, and the substitution of something more in keeping with the old work"[115] as the main objective (Plate 32.4). After a slow start, this first campaign of restoration work was completed in 1906 or 1907.[116] In 1912, John Francis BLAKISTON recorded that conservation work on the temple was well executed, the temple being in good condition and that all loose stones and sculptures that could not be fixed had been collected and placed around the temple to form the compound wall. Additionally, he issued a Conservation Note in which he recommended to re-erect a pillar found unbroken among the fragments and to move all unbroken bases on to the platform and to place them in appropriate positions.[117] Ever since, the temple has been subjected to restorations and alterations time and again. Even though the condition of the temple had already been spoilt on a large scale long before COUSENS' first visit, the fact that conservational measures by the ASI have, if at all, been scarcely documented[118] poses additional problems in interpreting the extant remains. It is, for instance, nowhere recorded that the doorframes of the *garbhagṛha* have been re-erected some time after 1894. This can be observed on the north side and even more clearly on the west side, if the present situation (Plate 32.1) is compared with that depicted in one of

The temple was officially declared a protected monument on November 16, 1912 by the Chief Commissioner of the Central Provinces (*CPG* 1912, Jul–Dec (Pt. I), p. 957). The respective notification was confirmed on April 11, 1925, by the Governor in Council (*CPG*, 1925, Jan–Dec (Pt. I), p. 483).

114 COUSENS 1903: 7; 1904: 20.

115 COUSENS 1906: 57.

116 "Restoring and cleaning etc, of certain temples at Mandhata" [...] "Completed, but some further work remains to be given [...]" (LONGHURST 1907: 8).

117 BLAKISTON 1912: 41.

118 Only since 1960 some brief notices have appeared in *IA–R*: "Siddhesvara Temple, Mandhata, District Nimar East. — The boundary-wall of the temple was restored and the pavement around the main shrine and steps re-laid." (*IA–R* 1960–61: 79); "Siddhesvara Temple, Mandhata, District Nimar East. — The collapsed compound-wall was rebuilt in rubble-masonry in mud-mortar." (*IA–R* 1961–62: 117); "Siddhnatha Temple, Mandhata, District East Nimar. — Restoration of a stone masonry compound wall with departmentally available stone in lime-mortar and watertightening the shrine to check the seepage was attended to and the work is in progress." (*IA–R* 1984–85: 216–217); "Sculptures and Plinth of Siddhanatha Temple, Mandhata, District East Nimar (Khandwa). — Lower mouldings of the *jagati* and a large number of sculptures and architectural fragments datable to the eleventh century were exposed by the Bhopal Circle of the Survey." (*IA–R* 1995–96: 129); "Sidhnatha Temple, Mandhata, District Khandwa — Collection of stone beams and fixing over verandah pillars and repairs to the stones and filling of gaps with stone masonry were done." (*IA–R* 1998–99: 277).

COUSENS' photographs.[119] Here, the lintel with figures of *dikpālas* topped by another beam which presently crown the western entrance (Plate 32.5) are missing. Another comparable lintel with figures of *mātṛkās* was, moreover, ignored and placed among other fragments near the eastern boundary wall (Plate 32.6). Even more serious are probably restorations which have a bearing on the ground-plan like, for example, the distribution of pillar bases (or capitals) on the platform following BLAKISTON's Conservation Note just mentioned. In three of the four corners between the pillared halls (*i.e.* in the north-west, north-east and south-east) the ASI has placed altogether 15 pillar 'bases'. The problem here is that eight of these are in fact not bases, but capitals (marked 'C' in Fig. 5). This arrangement was apparently intended to imitate the situation observed in the south-western corner where four pillars and a base are found in comparable positions among the remains of a second inner platform puzzled together from many heterogeneous fragments about the same time (Plate 32.7). The authenticity of these reconstructions is, however, doubtful – not only in view of the vagueness of a respective statement by BLAKISTON,[120] but especially because none of the aforementioned four pillars stands *in situ*. The arrangement of the ASI suggests that the temple originally contained 76 pillars (including eight pilasters), of which only 47 are preserved, resulting in the relatively high number of 29 missing pillars. If we subtract 20 doubtful pillars indicated by the capitals/bases placed in the corners by the ASI, assuming that they never existed, the amount of missing pillars would melt to a more plausible number of nine, but at the same time we would be left with eight extant bases[121] in excess. Theoretically at least, a ground-plan consisting of either 76, 72, 64 or 56 pillars would theoretically be conceivable. This question is further complicated by the fact that the reported number of pillars of the halls in front of the entrances vary among the early witnesses: FORSYTH stated them to be fourteen in each case[122] and COUSENS speaks of twelve pillars plus two pilasters[123] which

119 Cousens No. 1386 (see below, Appendix 1, Table 3, p. 112) now held in the BL. The photograph is available at: http://www.bl.uk/onlinegallery/onlineex/apac/photocoll/g/019pho000001003u01265 000.html (last retrieved on January 23, 2017).

120 "At the south-west corner is the remains of the old plinth which is the only key to the original plan of the base of the temple. I think it might be possible to select, from the miscellaneous collection of stones round the compound, more of these plinth stones and have them set in their approximate former positions." (BLAKISTON 1912: 41).

121 At least two more bases can be identified among the fragments in the compound.

122 FORSYTH 1870b: 260.

123 COUSENS 1894: 3.

would result in altogether 56 pillars in both cases. However, about 15 years later, *i.e.* about a year after restoration work had been completed, RUSSELL asserts that "[t]he central shrine had an entrance on each side with a porch resting on 18 pillars",[124] resulting in a number of altogether 72 pillars. The ASI reconstructed the ground-plan with four additional pillars in the intermediate directions, increasing the total number of pillars to 76, a solution which has eventually been corroborated by HELD.[125]

This may suffice to demonstrate the difficulties the present condition of the temple poses in view of a reconstruction of its original appearance which we may probably never be able to achieve.

What we can say with sufficient confidence is that the Siddhanātha temple originally belonged to, or was built for the Pāśupatas, as the lintels above the entrances each carry a figure of Lakulīśa in their *lalāṭabimba* (Plate 32.8).[126] The date assigned to the temple by the AIIS of ca. 1100–1150 AD is probably not very far off the mark, though the ASI more recently suggested an eleventh century date.[127] The only inscription which is doubtlessly contemporary with the temple is found on the southern front pillar of the hall in front of the western entrance and reads "*magaradhvaja jogī 700*" (Plate 32.9), a graffiti that is well-known from a considerable number of temples in Central India and beyond.[128] As the person whose visit it apparently documents can hardly be expected to have visited mere

124 RUSSELL 1908: 241.

125 After a detailed discussion of the different possibilities in keeping with the factual remains; see HELD *2015: 118–121.

126 As far as I see, this is the only temple on Māndhātā hill, where Lakulīśa is depicted in such an exposed and significant position. A remark about "Ōṅkāra [...] identical with Paśupati [...] having his temple on the bank of the Rēvā [...] near the junction of the Rēvā and the Kāvērī [...]" (SIRCAR 1962: 143) found in verses 6–8 of the Māndhātā plates of Paramāra Jayasiṃha-Jayavarman II, dated VS 1331 (1274 CE), apparently refers to none other than the Siddhanātha temple. A verse about a group of five *liṅga*s (*pañcaliṅga*) inscribed in the Amareśvara temple and dated 1063 CE, further corroborates that the Oṃkāreśvara *liṅga* belonged to the Pāśupatas (NEUSS 2013: 142).

127 *IA–R* 1995–96: 129. Such an early date seems to be corroborated by the inscription referred to in the preceding footnote which, however, mentions only the Oṃkāreśvara *liṅga* and not a temple of that name.

128 The existence of this graffiti on the Siddhanātha temple has not been reported before. HIRALAL's assertion that the same graffiti is found on the Caubīs Avatār temple at Panthiā is apparently based on a mistake (HIRALAL 1916: 72). When I visited the Caubīs Avatār temple at its relocation site in December 2015, I could not find it and the ASI's attendant confirmed that there is no such inscription on that building. On the distribution of this graffiti and details on this personage, see HIRALAL 1927 and MAJUMDAR/UPADHAYAY 2012.

construction sites, the often repeated view that the Siddhanātha temple was probably never completed is presumably wrong.

Mention should finally be made of one of very few religious sculptures found in the compound. It represents a portion of a doorframe with a large figure of Bhairava(?) framed in a *pratolī toraṇa* (Plate 32.10) and may originally have belonged to a now lost doorframe between the inner pillars of one of the halls.[129]

Another important aspect in the present context is that the ASI's compound wall unnaturally isolates the temple from its surroundings to which it was originally more homogeneously linked. This is borne out by remains of an old staircase in the east, now traversed by the compound wall which leads down from the temple compound to an area enclosed by old walls which seem to mark its original limits (Plate 32.11, Map 4.7). These walls bulge out into a trapezium whose southern limit is formed by the portion of the inner fort wall adjacent to the Bhīmārjunī gate (see Fig. 3). This trapezoidal area probably represents an old tank which would explain its comparatively low ground level as compared to that of the surrounding area as well as the existence of the water outlet built into this portion of the inner fort wall already mentioned above, see **2.2.3.a**, p. 33 and shown in Plate 26.1.

2.2.4.2.2. Structure B2

Structure B2 is visible in Map 4.6. to the west of the Siddhanātha temple and marked by a circular spot, comparable to those which mark other remains. Its shape looks similar to that of B3 suggesting that it, too, may represent an old temple platform. This is one of two occasions where, even on repeated visits to the site, I was not able to locate the object in the field.

2.2.4.2.3. Temple B3

This temple ruin is located still further west (Map 4.6) and rises about one and a half metres above the surrounding terrain which is completely covered with vegetation (Plate 33.1). Around the site several architectural fragments, pillars, brackets and parts of the *śikhara* are found (Plate 33.2). Parts of the *vedībandha* are exposed with a few *akṣaras* ('*śrī vāṭā*') inscribed on the exposed *kumbha* (or *kalaśa*) at the south side (Plate 33.3).

These fragments attest to the existence of a ca. twelfth century temple, probably of the *pañcaratha bhūmija* variety, at this site.

---

129 See HELD *2015: 144.

2.2.4.3. Area C

Area C is a large roughly rectangular stretch of land which is enclosed in the west and south by the footpaths leading from the Cāndsūraj gate southwards to the Huṇḍī-kuṇḍī gate and from there eastwards to the Siddhanātha temple (Maps 4.4, 4.8). In the east it reaches up to the compound of the modern Vedmātā Gāyatrī Mandiram and in the north it is delimited by the respective northern stretch of the inner fort wall. Here, the area slopes down into a shallow valley which seems to be devoid of architectural structures.[130] Area C has the same characteristics as Area B from which it is separated only by the main footpath leading from the Huṇḍī-kuṇḍī gate up to the Siddhanātha temple. This footpath marks its southern limit which is likewise marked by a long line of earthwork running parallel to it, in which stretches of an old wall are still visible at a few places (Plate 35). Area C, too, is densely overgrown with vegetation and its ground level appears as elevated above the surrounding terrain as that of Area B. It also gives the impression of an old settlement site in a similar way as Area B, and, like the latter would need prior clearance in order to render systematic exploration successful. The satellite map shows five mounds (Map 4.8, Nos. 1–5) which all lie in proximity to the flanking footpaths. Between these, loose stone blocks, wall remains and fragments of rock-cut foundations are found at several places.

2.2.4.3.1. Structure C1

Structure C1 is a rectangular platform which rises about two metres above the surrounding ground level (Plate 34.1). It tapers upwards in steps and perhaps represents the core of a temple base. It stands immediately to the west of the modern Vedmātā Gāyatrī Mandiram with its long sides parallel to the footpath. Presently the eastern tip of the platform is occupied by a small *liṅga* with a *pīṭha* (Plate 34.2). Although this is certainly a recent addition, it seems to indicate that the temple originally opened to the west which is further suggested by traces of three staircases found at the north-western, western and south-western ends. Only few sculptured fragments are found around the platform, among them a pillar capital, a bracket and two large sculptured blocks of uncertain function on top of the platform itself.

130 This valley lies beyond the broken line shown in Map 4.8 which indicates the approximate northern limit of settlement structures.

2.2.4.3.2. Structure C2

This is another platform located further to the west of C1. It is of similar dimensions (Plate 35). Here, too, only a few sculptured fragments are found, among them some broken pillars and brackets.

2.2.4.3.3. Temple C3

This temple ruin is located to the south-east of and near to the Cāndsūraj gate (Plate 36.1). It is represented by a low platform and many sculptured fragments strewn around it which leave no doubt that once a temple stood at this place. Among the diverse fragments is a door lintel with a figure of Gaṇeśa in the *lalāṭabimba* (Plate 36.2), the lower parts of the doorframe with guardian figures (Plate 36.3) and parts of the *śikhara* with *śr̥ṅga*s (Plate 36.4), suggesting again the former existence of a *bhūmija* shrine at this site.

2.2.4.3.4. Structure C4

Structure C4 is found to the south of temple C3 and represents a very low eroded platform (Plate 37). A number of sculptured temple parts are found scattered around this site, too.

2.2.4.3.5. Temple C5

Located still further south, temple C5 is represented by a small platform situated immediately to the east of the footpath leading from the Cāndsūraj gate to the Huṇḍī-kuṇḍī gate. On its northern and western side, moulded portions of the *pīṭha* and *vedībandha* are still preserved (Plates 38.1–2). Diverse fragments are found around the site, among them parts of the superstructure with characteristic *śr̥ṅga*s (Plate 38.3).

2.2.4.4. Area D

Area D is a rectangular stretch of land, much smaller than Areas B and C (Maps 4.4, 4.9). It lies to the west of the footpath that leads from the Cāndsūraj gate to the Huṇḍī-kuṇḍī gate. In the west it merges with the compound of the modern Āśādevī temple beyond which the area is largely disturbed by the modern settlement. In the north it is limited by the inner fort wall adjacent to the Cāndsūraj gate, in the south by the Huṇḍī-kuṇḍī gate and the footpath leading from there westwards to the municipal water supply and the Āśādevī temple. Area D is densely covered with vegetation and the structures which appear to be rather small, are difficult to trace.

All three sites that I could locate are represented by shallow mounds of stones with a variety of sculptured architectural fragments lying strewn around each site, most of them half buried. Even though all these artefacts seem to represent temple fragments, the area is so overgrown with vegetation and the structures so little exposed that it is difficult to determine their dimensions and to decide whether these shallow mounds indeed represent the remains of old shrines. Plates 39.1–5 give an overview of the structures and fragments which would need excavation before they could be discussed in greater detail.

2.2.4.5. Area E

The terrain beyond the western limits of Areas B and D is largely disturbed by modern settlements and structures. However, there is a small enclave to the west of the modern water supply, Area E which contains the ruins of a large temple and another small building (Map 4.10, Plates 40.1–2). At the south-eastern corner of Area E, immediately adjacent to the water supply, remains of the inner fort wall forming a right-angle are found (Plate 40.3). These seem to be part of a rectangular structure the ruin of which can be seen in the upper left corner of Dayal's 1880 photograph already referred to (above, p. 24 and fn. 77) in connection with the vanished south-western gateway.

2.2.4.5.1. Temple E1

Temple E1 is situated near the south-western edge of Māndhātā hill and represented by a huge heap of stone blocks with a large tree growing out of its centre (Plate 41.1). Stunningly, at the western side stands an old sign board which must originally have belonged to the Siddhanātha temple (B1), but now labels this temple erroneously as Siddheśvara *mandir*.[131]

What remains of the temple suggests that it must originally have been a large and magnificent building. This becomes obvious especially in the west, where parts of the *jaṅghā* are preserved. The *kūṭastambhas*, some of which still stand erect here (albeit without the crowning *kūṭas*) are exquisitely carved with figures and ornamental bands (Plate 41.2). Their design is comparable to that found in the twelfth century Siddheśvara

131 Without doubt, the board must originally have belonged to the Siddhanātha temple, because in all the old reports the name Siddheśvara is alternatively used for Siddhanātha, and it is absolutely certain that both names were used exclusively for that most prominent temple on Māndhātā hill (see above, fn. 109). It is stunning that the board was placed here by the DAAM.

temple at Nemāvar,[132] though their style appears somewhat less elaborate. Their apparent *in situ* existence suggests that the temple's *pīṭha* and *vedībandha* which are unfortunately nowhere exposed, are probably entirely preserved. If these are of comparable dimension and style as in Nemāvar they must lie buried to considerable height under the fallen stones. The presence of the *jaṅghā* portion in the west suggests that the temple originally opened to the east, where the ruin has a cavity with straight unsculptured walls at its western and southern sides (Plates 41.3–4; note orientation marks). The original ground level is much lower here than the surrounding terrain and a few heavy pillars with fine carvings are found at the eastern side of this cavity (Plates 41.5–6). This part of the ruin probably represents a hall in front of the sanctum which, once more, suggests that the temple was originally east-oriented. The vertical, moulded stones found at the western side of the cavity seem to represent the remains of a doorframe (Plates 41.4, 41.7). Another fragment of a doorframe is, however, found half-buried near the north-eastern edge of the ruin (Plate 41.8) with a part of an *udumbara* lying nearby (Plate 41.9). These fragments are apparently dislocated and it is unclear where they originally belonged. Given its proximity to the modern settlement sites, it seems rather astonishing that the temple has not been entirely plundered of its material though much of the superstructure, at least, seems to have been removed. I could locate just two fragments (*śṛṅga*s) clearly belonging to the *śikhara*. Unfortunately, the condition of the ruin with many jumbled-up stones prevent a further assessment of its original ground-plan and design, but this temple must originally have been much larger than its current condition suggests. It may also have been connected to other structures in its vicinity like structure E2 or another building of which we now find only traces of its base buried underground a few metres to the north-west of temple E1 (Plate 41.10).

2.2.4.5.2. Structure E2

This structure stands to the south-west of temple E1 (Plates 40.1–2) and presently appears as a chamber with a hall in front (Plates 42.1–2) seemingly oriented to the south. Upon closer examination, however, it becomes obvious that the extant structure represents only a part of an originally larger building. This is clear from the position of pillars and the shape of corresponding brackets (Fig. 6), especially at the western and southern

132 For an illustration see TICHIT *2010 (II): Plate 52, Fig. 3.

side (Plate 42.2–3) and the north-eastern corner (Plate 42.4) which originally must have supported beams, now gone, projecting outward. The extant walls which partly survive only at the east and north side, are built from two parallel rows of stone slabs. While the inner wall faces are left unsculptured, the outer ones are carved with courses of base mouldings in their lower portions, the lowest layers of which are buried underground. Above these mouldings follow two courses of broad stone slabs forming the *jaṅghā* which are carved with ornamental bands in shallow relief. The most prominently visible one in the centre contains a line of *gavākṣa*s showing a linear version of what HARDY typologizes as "the 'pipal leaf' or 'moonstone' motif",[133] topped by another band of *grāsamukha*s (Plate 42.5).[134] Above these slabs follow two narrow rows of stones, the lower one moulded and the upper one carved with yet another ornamental band of *grāsamukha*s.

Considering the beam supports of the extant pillar brackets, we may infer that the building must originally have included at least one more row of pillars/pilasters in the west. The bracket of the north-eastern pillar in connection with the course of the wall remains seems to further suggest that the core building might once have been enclosed by a pillared passage or a verandah, but this is uncertain. Among the fragments found around the site are, for instance, a pillar and a beam and though a lot of fragments may still lie buried underground, much material seems to have been removed from the site. Without further investigation the original function of this structure cannot be determined and it can also not be decided whether this structure has any architectural or functional connection with temple E2 though this may be assumed, given the proximity of both buildings. As for the orientation of the building, it seems likely that it was originally oriented to the west.

2.2.4.6. Stray finds on Māndhātā hill

Besides the remains reported up to this point, there are a lot of stray finds of loose sculptures and architectural fragments at different locations on Māndhātā hill, whose provenance cannot conclusively be determined. One such spot where a number of objects are found lies just to the north of temple E1. A couple of years back, a rectangular building was erected

---

133 HARDY 2007: 75.

134 A similar design is found on the *kūṭastambha*s of the twelfth century Mudhaidevi temple in Vaghli (Maharashtra) though there are no traces of *kūṭastambha*s here. For an illustration see TICHIT *2010 (II): Plate 54, Fig. 3.

here which people say, was to become a museum. It was, however, never finished and stands abandoned since years (Map 4.3). The two roofless rooms are empty barring a few insignificant fragments. If there were ever sculptures stored here, they must meanwhile have been removed to the sculpture store next to the Gaurīsomanātha temple on Mucukund hill (see below, **2.3.1.3.6.**, p. 61). Still, a number of loose sculptures and architectural fragments are found around the building. The most significant of these may be a fragment of a door lintel with *mātr̥kā* figures (Plate 43.1).

Another spot where we find stray sculptures lies at the foot of Māndhātā hill, near the staircase leading up to the Bhīmārjunī gate, near to the spot where the path forks up to the Bīrkhalā hill. Here stand two temporary structures in which a number of broken sculptures are kept (Plates 43.2–3). Presumably most, if not all of them originally come from the Bīrkhalā hill.

A third find spot is located on the southern slope of Māndhātā hill, between the South gate (see above, **2.2.2.3.**, p. 29) and the platform with doorframe (see above **2.2.3.**c, p. 34). Among remains of the inner fort wall (Plate 43.4) we find here a number of diverse architectural fragments, perhaps originally belonging to a temple (Plate 43.5). Their provenance is, however, uncertain as no temple base could be located around this site. One may speculate that these fragments were perhaps dropped here while being transported from somewhere on Māndhātā hill to be reused somewhere else in the settlement area on the south-western slope of the hill, now called Śivpurī.

2.3. *Mucukund hill*

Mucukund hill is the third and largest hill on Māndhātā island. It lies to the north-west of Māndhātā hill proper and its area is roughly three times larger (Map 1.3). Mucukund hill, too, is enclosed on all sides by courses of a fortification wall running along its summit (Map 1.4). But while the fortress on Māndhātā hill shows two parallel courses of stone walls all around, the outer fortification on Mucukund hill is in the form of a rampart made of rubble and earth that runs only along the north side of the hill.

The fort on Mucukund hill is divided into two major enclosures, the 'Outer fort' (see below, 2.3.2., p. 62) and the Gaurīsomanātha plateau (Map 5). The latter represents a large area in the south-east of Mucukund hill which is closed off to the north and west by a massive fortification wall running roughly south-east to north-west. This wall terminates about the middle of Mucukund hill where it branches off in almost a right angle to the south and continues in that direction until it meets the southern course of the fortification wall. Another rampart that runs parallel to this wall is again found only near its northern stretch.

2.3.1. The Gaurīsomanātha plateau[135]

The Gaurīsomanātha plateau occupies the south-eastern portion of Mucukund hill. It represents the most elevated area on the Mucukund hill and is, as already described, enclosed by a massive fort wall. In the west the adjoining area slopes down gently, whereas in the north the slope beyond the wall is more steep. In the south and south-east the plateau borders on a steep precipice. Satellite images taken in 2001 show the outlines of extensive structures buried underground on the plateau which was till recently largely uninhabited, apart from a small settlement close to the Gaurīsomanātha temple (Map 6.1). Unfortunately most of the western half of the plateau was heavily disturbed in recent years by the construction of vast, (pseudo-)religious building complexes (Map 6.2). To the west of the Gaurīsomanātha temple, an organisation called 'Rājrājeśvarī Sevā Saṃsthān Ṭrasṭ' has constructed a large building complex including a hospital, an old people's home, a temple and a giant, full-kitschy concrete statue of Śiva (Plate 44.1).[136] Simultaneously, the area further west was almost completely occupied by the 'Śiva Miśan Nyās', Gwalior[137] which erected a number of buildings including the curious 'Oṃ Namaḥ Śivāya Mantra Bank'[138] and laid out a quite impressive plantation named 'Nakshatra Garden' which included a swimming pool. About the middle of 2014, however, the buildings in the compound were all demolished by the district administration for illegal encroachment (Plate 44.2). The area is now completely messed up, because the buildings were, as usual, crudely demolished with the help of a JCB, and the broken parts just left

135 This is my own arbitrary designation for this area chosen with respect to the most prominent temple it contains.

136 The statue has aroused much scorn and ridicule in the village because it faces north and hence turns its back on the village and the arriving pilgrims.

137 To have an idea of that organization see its homepage under http://www.shivamission.in and that of the associated 'Namah Shivaya Mission', Śivkoṭhī (near OM) under http://www.namahshivayamission.org [last retrieved on February 2, 2015].

138 This 'bank' has set a dubious world record for the largest collection of hand written *mantras*, see: http://goldenbookofrecords.com/largest-collection-of-hand-written-mantra/ [last retrieved March, 20, 2017].

where they dropped. In October 2014 the Rājrājeśvarī Trust complex had still managed to escape the same fate by bribing the authorities, if local intelligence is to be trusted. According to local hearsay, the demolition campaign was initiated by a complaint of a *bābā* who was incited by the water wastage incurred by the Nakshatra garden with its swimming pool. However, it eventually aimed not only at these large and recent illegal establishments, but threatens also common people who have been living on the hill for years or even decades. Rumour has it that the whole of Mucukund hill is scheduled to soon be completely vacated and a number of people already have received notices to leave their homes.[139] Coming back to our point, these recent developments have at best gravely disturbed, if not completely spoilt, this historically extremely interesting and probably highly significant area which represents the citadel of the fort.

2.3.1.1. Fortification walls

The stretches of fortification walls enclosing the Gaurīsomanātha plateau are in different states of preservation. Much of the massive northern stretch is preserved, though damaged at several places. The western, southern and south-eastern portions, the latter two running along the precipice of the hill, have largely collapsed, but their course can clearly be traced for most parts. Only in the south and south-east some stretches have almost completely disappeared. Much of the material has probably been removed to other places for use in new constructions in the adjacent settlement areas.

2.3.1.2. Gateways and staircases

In the course of the fortification wall we can presently trace with certainty four entrances to the Gaurīsomanātha plateau (Map 6.3). However, it is difficult to determine what the gates originally may have looked like as all of the original structures around these entrances are either destroyed beyond recognition or have been rebuilt. Three staircases are preserved in the north-west, south and east which can with certainty be stated to be original. The north-western one links the plateau to the 'Outer fort',

139 This measure also includes the eastern slope of the hill adjacent to the valley running between Mucukund and Māndhātā hill. It is not yet clear what the intention behind the administration's measures is. Some people in OM say that Māndhātā island will become a protected nature resort, others opine that the *parikramāpatha* will be further developed for the pilgrims and only temples and monasteries be allowed to remain.

along the path leading up to the Kāverīsaṅgam in the extreme west of the island. The southern staircase is the longest and steepest of all and runs from the only extant, though reconstructed gateway down to the bank of the Narmadā. The eastern staircase connects the Gaurīsomanātha plateau with Māndhātā hill proper, the path leading directly to the latter's northern gateways. Of the extant main footpaths on the Gaurīsomanātha plateau, those connecting the north-west with the south and east gates seem still to follow their original course. A third path which today branches off to the south-east near the Gaurīsomanātha temple and which traverses the outer wall about the middle between the south and east gates, is certainly modern.

2.3.1.2.1. The North-west gate

The North-west gate links the Gaurīsomanātha plateau with the large western part of the 'Outer fort'. The short steep staircase which runs through the gate is lined on both sides with small shops (Plate 45.1). The space around the opening in the wall is since long occupied by a Bhilālā family running a small restaurant and a temple with free drinking water supply. Their house and restaurant were recently partly demolished by the administration and the family was asked to vacate the place. The temple which appears to be somewhat old is adorned with stucco, and was fortunately spared. It possibly indicates the position of the ruins of the western wing of the original gatehouse over which it may have been built (Plate 45.2). A pillar at the south-eastern corner of the temple is nicely finished with stucco ornaments which perhaps conceals an old stone pillar. Given the present situation it is, however, difficult to say, what kind of gatehouse originally stood here. The fortification walls running to the west and east of the staircase are very massive, at any rate (visible in Plate 45.1, left side).

2.3.1.2.2. The North-east gate

The structures around this gateway are almost completely destroyed with heaps of stones lying strewn all over the site. The remains are largely overgrown with vegetation at and beyond the northern side. Nevertheless, the remains at the site suggest that this was probably the largest entrance to the whole fort (Plates 46.1–3). The massive fortification wall is, however, well preserved and runs right up to both sides of a wide opening (Plate 46.4). At either side, walls branch off at right angles which apparently formed the side walls of a probably very large, now completely ruined gatehouse, delimiting a wide passage. The present situation seems to suggest, that the passage was flanked on both inner sides by large stone sculptures of Mahiṣāsuramardinī in the west (Plate 46.5) and Kātyayaṇī in the south (Plate 46.6).[140] Both sculptures are still extant at the site, but their placement is probably arbitrarily chosen – the former leans against a heap of rubble, the latter is mounted on an old socle and framed in a niche. It is difficult to say, whether the socle and image are in their original positions. The flanking 'pilasters', at least, cannot be original, as they are formed by a motley collection of stones. Beyond the course of the fort walls, *i.e.* to the north of the passage, remains of massive walls are visible which stand in right angles to either side, forcing the passage into a U-turn in front of the entrance. A staircase which leads from near the Mahiṣāsuramardinī relief up to the western stretch of the fortification wall may, at least partly, be original (Plate 46.3). The present condition of the large ruined structures at the site does not allow for further speculation about the original ground-plan and shape of this gateway and the surrounding structures.

2.3.1.2.3. The East gate

The East gate stands further to the west, not far from the North-east gate, near the extreme eastern corner of the Gaurīsomanātha plateau. Its remains stand like two broken teeth to either side of an opening in the fortification wall (Plates 47.1–2) which is situated at the head of a steep staircase which descends down southward along the slope of the hill into the valley separating Mucukund and Māndhātā hills. At its end it takes a sharp turn and merges with the staircase leading northward up Māndhātā hill and ending there at the Cāndsūraj gate. This path represents the only direct link between Māndhātā hill and the Gaurīsomanātha plateau.[141]

On the northern side of the gatehouse, a recess with two pillars still survives (Plate 47.3) while the corresponding recess at the south side is almost completely destroyed (Plate 47.4). Given the usually elevated position of such recesses found in the other gatehouses, it may be assumed that the bases of these structures lie buried considerably below the present surrounding ground level.

140 For the sculpture of Mahiṣāsuramardinī see also SEARS 2014b, Fig. 7.2.

141 Therefore one may assume that this ruined gate corresponded in a certain way with the Cāndsūraj gate on Māndhātā hill. This gateway may perhaps once have been of corresponding dimensions and similar design even though, admittedly, its present condition does not furnish much evidence in support of this assumption.

2.3.1.2.4. The South gate

This gateway stands in the course of the southern fortification wall at the southern end of the path coming from the Gaurīsomanātha temple and at the head of a long and steep staircase leading down to the bank of the Narmadā (Plate 48.1). It is the only access to the fortification on the Gaurīsomanātha plateau that has an intact gatehouse. It is an old, but not an original construction and must have been built before the end of the nineteenth century, because the gatehouse is visible in its present form in another photograph taken by Deen Dayal in the 1880's.[142] The pillar which now supports the arch (Plate 48.2) is a later addition, as it is missing in Dayal's photograph.

2.3.1.2.5. The West gate

The wall at the west side of the Gaurīsomanātha plateau, though very massive in the northern part, is much damaged with many fallen stones lying along its course. The farther south, the more it looks like a rampart. Apparently this area has been another site from which stones were removed for construction purposes. It is in this stretch that another gateway may probably have existed, but the extant remains make it difficult to determine its exact location or dimensions as nothing seems to be left of it apart from a few foundation stones (Plate 49.1–2).

2.3.1.3. Settlement areas and temples

As already mentioned, we find the outlines of large, partly buried structures in the formerly unoccupied portions of the plateau (Maps 6.1, 6.4) which are now largely obstructed especially in the eastern part where vast areas have been severely disturbed by encroachments. Though settlement activities had also taken place since long in the western part of the plateau, these were never as severe with regard to archaeology. They were of a much smaller scale mostly confined to small dwellings and *āśrams*. In the patches which have been left unoccupied I have found four sites with remains of old temples and/or other structures (Map 6.4, Sites 2–5). But first we shall turn to the Gaurīsomanātha temple (Site 1), the central, most impressive and best preserved monument on the plateau.

---

142 BL Shelfmark Photo 430/21(13). The photograph is available under: http://www.bl.uk/onlinegallery/onlineex/apac/photocoll/m/019pho000430s21u00013000.html [last retrieved on March 20, 2017].

2.3.1.3.1. The Gaurīsomanātha temple

The Gaurīsomanātha temple stands in the western half of the Gaurīsomanātha plateau about half-way between the North-west and the South gates (Map 6.4, Site 1).[143] At first glance it appears to be the best preserved one of all the temples at OM with the *pīṭha*, *vedībandha* and *jaṅghā* of the *mūlaprāsāda* apparently intact (Plate 50.1–4).

The temple is oriented to the east and originally consisted of the *mūlaprāsāda*, an *antarāla*, and a *maṇḍapa* with three entrances in the cardinal directions (Fig. 7). Of these, only the *mūlaprāsāda* and the *antarāla* remain. The temple stands on a large, slightly staggered, unsculptured platform (*pīṭha*) which seems to have been reconstructed around an old core. At the eastern side in front of the temple stands, on a modern platform with a roof, a big bull (Plate 50.5) which was perhaps carved from the same black stone as the giant *liṅga* in the sanctum. However, this platform and the bull are quite recent additions as FORSYTH's description of the site differs considerably from the present condition.[144]

The *mūlaprāsāda* of the Gaurīsomanātha temple has a stellate *saptaratha* ground-plan and is *nirandhāra*. A staircase is found in the south side leading to the two upper storeys of the tower which is accessed by a small entrance in the south-eastern wall (Plate 50.4). While the original *maṇḍapa* is completely gone, the front face of the *antarāla* and the seven-storey *śikhara* have been completely reconstructed.

Only at the north-eastern side of the *mūlaprāsāda*, a number of sculptures are found at the aedicules of the *jaṅghā* which fit perfectly into the space they occupy (Plate 50.6). If in their original positions (but not necessarily *in situ*) they would indicate that the temple originally contained a band of sculptures running all along the *jaṅghā*. The remainder of these on the other sides of the temple must then have disappeared which in

143 AIIS Nos. 81912–81913 (dated ca. 1100–1199 CE). COUSENS (1897: 41) classified the temple to category IIb, *i.e.* "Monuments which, it is now only possible or desirable to save from further decay by such minor measures as the eradication of vegetation, the exclusion of water from the walls, and the like" which are "in possession or charge of private bodies or individuals" (*ibid.*: ii).

144 "An immense Nandí (Siva's bull), of a fine green stone, lies headless in front of the shrine, and about a hundred yards in front of the door is an overthrown pillar which has been nineteen and a half feet high with its capital, and stood on a raised platform of basalt blocks. For the first six and a half feet it is two and a half feet square—thence polygonal, with occasional round belts to the capital which is square—and furnished with five holes in the top, either to hold lamps or the fastenings of some figure." (FORSYTH 1870b: 261.) Fragments of this pillar are still found in front (to the east) of the temple.

turn would suggest that the walls of the temple, too, were reconstructed on a larger scale. Indeed, most of the aedicules in the *jaṅghā* appear to be assembled from fragments which have been cut to fit each other. This is indicated by white vertical lines of lime. At many places they have moreover been rather oddly put together as obvious asymmetries and conflicting designs show. So, in fact, the only portions of the temple which can be said with some certainty to be largely original are the *pīṭha* and the *vedībandha*.

Though it is unknown when and on whose order these restoration works were undertaken, it may be assumed that they have taken place prior to the middle of the nineteenth century, because FORSYTH remarks that the temple "appears, however, to be an old shrine rebuilt with lime".[145] Probably these works, too, were commissioned by the Peśvā about the end of the eighteenth century, at about the same time as those on the temples in the Amareśvara complex, as comparable style and workmanship in the lower parts of the *śikhara* seem to suggest.[146] In contrast to most of the other reconstructed *śikhara*s at OM (see especially Indreśvara and Brahmeśvara temples), here the masons seem to have imitated the *bhūmija* mode. Although the central offsets resemble *uraḥśrṅga*s in *śekharī* fashion, the quadrants in between are arranged in vertical bands, resembling *kūṭastambha*s, a distinct *bhūmija* feature. But, stunningly, not a single original *śṛṅga* has been incorporated, although a large number of such are still found in the vicinity of the temple. The upper portion of the *śikhara* looks like having been added at a still later stage, but this is not certain. At any rate, the extent and quality of the reconstruction which can especially be observed in the *jaṅghā* points to a considerable local importance of the shrine which is in *pūjā* till date.[147]

Apart from the sculptures already mentioned, some fine reliefs are preserved in most of the *bhadra* niches on the *jaṅghā* of the *mūlaprāsāda* and in the corresponding *kumbhaka*s below, as well as in the *kumbhaka*s of the *kapilī*. It is difficult to decide whether the sculptures on the *jaṅghā* are in their original places (*in situ*), because they apparently represent loose slabs, and the niches in which they stand show traces of later repairing work (Plate 50.6, upper right). The sculptures in the *kumbhaka*s are,

145 FORSYTH 1870b: 261.

146 Compare the upper portions of the Vṛddhakāleśvara temple, above, **1.1.2.1.2.**, p. 10.

147 A short note on the temple is found in *IA–R* 1985–86: 135, but to the best of my knowledge, there is no notice on any conservation or reconstruction work found in archaeological literature.

however, certainly *in situ* as they are carved directly onto the *kumbhaka* blocks. The distribution of sculptures is as follows:[148]

	North	West	South
mūlaprāsāda, jaṅghā	Brahmā	Śiva	Kubera
mūlaprāsāda, kumbhaka	Sarasvatī	Pārvatī	Goddess holding *cakra* and *gadā*
kapilī, kumbhaka	Pārvatī		Gaṇeśa

As stated, the figures in the *kumbhaka*s are certainly *in situ* but the figures on the *jaṅghā* need not be, though they correspond well with the former except, perhaps, in the south, where the attributes of the goddess in the *kumbhaka* suggest that it represents some form of Viṣṇu's consort (Plate 50.7).

2.3.1.3.2. Site No. 2 and its surroundings

To the north-west of the Gaurīsomanātha temple runs the path down to the North-west gate. It is enclosed by old city walls built from stone blocks laid without mortar (Plate 51.1). To either side of the path, satellite images show many structural walls running in right angles (Maps 6.1, 6.4). Stretches of these walls are still traceable on the surface today, but in the eastern part modern settlements partly obstruct their course. The area in the west is mostly unoccupied and here we find, close to the north-west corner of the extant fortification wall (Plate 51.2), remains of a large platform which merges with the surrounding terrain (Plate 51.3). At its western end, it is partly paved with stone slabs and here we find a complete *udumbara* of Paramāra times, a *liṅgapīṭha* with a *bāṇaliṅga* and a *pratolī* among a few other fragments (Plate 51.4–5). In the surrounding area a few more fragments are found, most notably a fragment of a base moulding carved with a band of *haṃsa*s and a *śṛṅga*, with only the central *latā* ornamented.

2.3.1.3.3. Site No. 3 and its surroundings

This area lies to the south-east immediately adjacent to the North-east gate (Map 6.4). It borders on the premises of the now demolished 'Oṃ Namaḥ Śivāya Mantra Bank' and has hence suffered severe disturbances

148 For a comparison with other contemporary temples, see TICHIT *2010 (II): Plates 146–148.

in recent times. Nevertheless, a few old structures and a number of loose fragments have still survived here. Apart from traces of the lateral buildings flanking the passage of the North-east gate, we find mainly two structures here, both situated to the south-east of the gateway (Plate 52.1) and adjacent to either side of the *parikramāpatha*. The 'structure' which stands on the north side of the latter, is represented by an old incomplete doorframe and remains of walls adjacent to it. These walls are apparently built from stones collected from different locations, among them temple fragments, and hence cannot represent an original construction (Plate 52.2). Inside the 'structure', behind the doorframe stands a *liṅga* on a *pīṭha*, and a few temple fragments and sculptures are incorporated into the ruined walls or lean on them, among which is a sculpture of Gaṇeśa and one of a three-headed figure. Though the 'structure' now appears like an independent building, it is doubtful if it ever was one. It may originally have been just a portion of the gatehouse and it seems that most of the old fragments found in it originally belonged to an old shrine which stands only a few metres further south, just across the *parikramāpatha*.

At the site of this temple we find a comparatively high platform with a staircase at its northern side and two fragments of heavy pillars in front (Plate 52.4). The top of the platform is covered with a cement flooring around a modern *liṅga* in a *pīṭha* which sits about its middle (Plate 52.5). The cement floor as well as the staircase which is made from old stone slabs laid with cement are modern works, indicating that the platform has been in recent use. The step just before the summit of the platform, however, carries a *grāsapaṭṭī*, a typical base moulding (found, for instance, in the Amareśvara temple, above, p. 9), which may probably be still *in situ* (Plate 52.6). Architectural fragments are scattered around the site, among them *śṛṅga*s, fragments of pillars, parts of the temple base and slabs with carved figures (Plates 52.7–8). All these remains bear ample testimony to the former existence of a temple at this place.

2.3.1.3.4. Site No. 4 and its surroundings

Site No. 4 lies immediately to the west of the East gate. Adjacent to the remains of the northern gatehouse stands the ruin of a building which probably represents just a part of an originally larger structure (Plate 53.1). An old and almost intelligible sign board gives 'Sitāmātā temple' as its name.

The rear or northern side of the building has a central passage with large slabs of stone standing upright behind the flanking pillars (Plate 53.2).

The lateral walls in the east and west of the building are still standing, but the large blocks of stones they are composed of are left unsculptured. The extant pillars carry the typical heavy, three-stepped beams with a central *kīrttimukha* so commonly found in the buildings at OM.

The southern side of the building is also much damaged, but the central passage already observed on the rear side, is here flanked by two dwarfish pillars which are mounted on large blocks of stone. The eastern one is elaborately carved on its front face with small pillars of which only the top-most portions are visible, the rest lying underground (Plate 53.3). The arrangement looks as if it may once have formed a kind of balustrade, composed, perhaps, of horizontal seat-slabs (*āsanapaṭṭa*) and vertical outward-sloping backrests (*kakṣāsana*). Inside of the building we find a number of pillars with their lower parts including their bases buried. At the north side many scattered fragments of the original superstructure are found (Plate 53.4). The extant structure appears as representing just the upper part of a hall preceding a temple, with its lower part being buried underground to a considerable extent. On the basis of these remains, it is impossible to say anything definite about the original plan of the building which, in its present state, seems to have been oriented along a north–south axis.

There are a few interesting sculptures found in and around this structure. At the eastern wall inside of the building we find a stone slab with a probably eight-armed goddess (most arms are broken off) framed by a *pratolī-toraṇa* (Plate 53.5). The slab which leans on the temple at the south-western side (Plate 53.1) shows a badly mutilated image of Mahiṣāsuramardinī (Plate 53.6). Further to the west stands a large slab depicting Hanuman in the open (Plate 53.1). The size of the sculpture suggests that it may perhaps originally have stood in a niche of the gate-house of the East gate.

2.3.1.3.5. Site No. 5 and its surroundings

This area is a large strip of formerly barren land situated on the southern fringe of the Gaurīsomanātha plateau, about a hundred metres to the east of the South gate. The outer fortification wall in this area is almost completely gone. Large portions of this area are now occupied by the Rājrājeśvarī Trust in the north and the Oṃ Namaḥ Śivāya Mantra Bank in the east. In the accessible parts, numerous traces of old walls running in angles can be found, apparently remains of old settlements comparable to those found to the north of the Gaurīsomanātha temple. The spaces between these walls are strewn with stones (Plate 54.1–2). Apart from these settlement remains I have located one spot (Map 6.4, No. 5) where a few architectural fragments are found, but as there is no visible trace of a platform (at least, the site is not notably elevated against its surroundings) it is difficult to decide to which structure these fragments originally belonged (Plate 54.3).

2.3.1.3.6. The sculpture store

Immediately to the south-west of the Gaurīsomanātha temple, a large number of figural sculptures (including a few architectural fragments) are kept in a store made up of two long halls which are joined in a right angle (Plates 55.1–2). A similar number of sculptures of which most were mounted on concrete socles were kept out in the open along the walls of the store until 2014, when a roof was built over and another wall around them. The *caukīdār* who keeps the keys, Mr. Devī Siṅgh Solāṅkī, lives in a small house nearby and opens the doors on request.[149]

I estimate that altogether between 150 and 200 sculptures, most of them fragments, are now kept in the store.[150] Their exact provenance is, however, undocumented and although they may have been brought from any place on the island, it is probably no coincidence that the store has been erected in the immediate vicinity of the Gaurīsomanātha temple. A number of these sculptures may originally have belonged to the temple just like the numerous *śr̥ṅga*s lying scattered in the compound which certainly belong to the temple's original *śikhara*. Most of the sculptures are rather small and often badly mutilated, but a few fine pieces are found among them, such as, for instance, a sculpture of Naṭeśa (Plate 55.3), Lakṣmīnārāyaṇa (Plate 55.4) and a broken panel depicting Gaṇeśa and the *(sapta-)mātr̥kā*s each holding a child on her hips (Plate 55.5).

Finally mention must be made of a giant sculpture of dancing Gaṇeśa with its head and trunk broken off, standing to the south-east of the Gaurīsomanātha temple (Plate 55.6). Going by its size, one may assume that this sculpture may perhaps originally have belonged to one of the gateways of the Gaurīsomanātha enclosure.[151]

149 It is no problem to see the sculptures, but for taking photographs, one would need a permit of the ASI.

150 It seems odd that not a single sculpture from OM is found in the published catalogues of the Central Museum Indore.

151 The sculpture appears to have been brought here some time after 1860 only, as FORSYTH (1870b: 261) does not mention it in his account of the Gaurīsomanātha temple.

2.3.2. The 'Outer fort'

The Outer fort is a large area that covers about three quarters of Mucukund hill (Map 5). It is by far the most extensive fortified area at OM and is again completely enclosed by massive fortification walls which are largely extant on the northern and eastern sides. The south-eastern and south-western stretches of these walls are destroyed at many locations, but their original course is entirely traceable. Leaving aside the accesses from/to the Gaurīsomanātha plateau, the extant remains show that the Outer fort was accessible from outside at only two places, one at the extreme western and the other one at the eastern end, where remains of large gateways are extant.

Physically, the enclosed area falls roughly into three sections (Map 7.1). The eastern part is dominated by a large plain gently sloping down to the north-east. Remains of long stretches of walls are found here, with a gateway at the south-eastern side. The western part is represented by a long narrow plain which is separated at the eastern side by an inner wall. Although it is almost completely gone, its course can still be traced on satellite imagery as well as in the field. Between these two sections lies an extensive forested and largely uninhabited area which is marked by hills and valleys, particularly to the north of the Gaurīsomanātha plateau. Because of the extent of the Outer fort and physical and structural differences between these three areas, we shall deal with them separately.

2.3.2.1. Outer fort, eastern section

As stated, this area (Maps 7.2–3) is marked by a large plain sloping down to the north and east (Plate 56.1). On these sides it is enclosed by a massive fort wall which is largely preserved (Plate 56.2), while the southern course of that wall originally running along a steep precipice is almost completely destroyed. In the latter stretch, not far from the south-eastern corner of the fortification wall, stand the remains of an old gateway probably representing the main point of outside access to this part of the Outer fort. The structures to either side of the passage which runs roughly east to west have collapsed, except some parts of the eastern side of the gatehouse which are still standing (Plates 56.3–4). The gatehouse originally had two storeys and contains some fragments of a *pratolī toraṇa* comparable in style to similar elements found in the Cāndsūraj gate on Māndhātā hill (see above, **2.2.2.1.**, p. 25). Another opening in the fortification wall in this area is found in the northern stretch, but this seems to have been a rather narrow passage with a (ruined) pillared superstructure, perhaps representing a watch-tower (Plate 56.5).

Most of this section of the Outer fort seems to be structured by courses of intermediate walls which can clearly be seen in satellite images (Maps 7.2–3) but are not easy to trace in the field. Even more difficult to trace are clusters of structures, like the one which seems to consist of sixteen squares arranged in four rows of four squares each. The whole area is strewn with rough-hewn stone blocks, sometimes forming heaps or lines, but in the field it is difficult to make out consistent structural patterns. Apart from the sculptured portions found on the East gate and some pillar fragments lying on top of the small passage in the northern fortification wall, I have found no sculptural remains in this section of the Outer fort.

2.3.2.2. Outer fort, central section

This large area which is dominated by hilly and forested terrain is almost devoid of any structural remains, apart from a squarish structure immediately to the west of the Gaurīsomanāthā plateau and a structure with an apsis at its western side near the northern stretch of the fortification wall (Map 7.4). Both structures are of comparatively large dimensions. While the former is easy to find, the one with the apsis is only shown in satellite images shot on March 17, 2001. In subsequent images, nothing of it is detectable and I was also not able to trace it in the field. Possibly the structure shown in the satellite image represents only a temporary structure.

In the eastern part of the central section, a small portion of the northern stretch of the outer fortification wall traverses a small valley. Though this part of the wall is severely damaged, probably as a consequence of flooding, it seems that it had originally been constructed in a different manner than the rest of the wall (Plate 57.1). It seems to show similarities to another comparable construction found on the south side of Mucukund hill, where the central section borders on the western section of the Outer fort.[152] This construction may perhaps represent a kind of dam, annually flooded by the Kāverī river in the rainy season, and holding back the water in the valley. To this assumption one may of course object that due to the perennial Narmadā river, OM probably never experienced

152 Here, we find at a comparable location, *i.e.* where the course of the outer fortification wall traverses the mouth of a valley, a construction with a long flight of steps at its eastern side which appears to represent something like a dam with a *ghāṭ* to hold back water in the valley (Map 7.5, Plate 58.2).

water shortages and, hence, the construction of dams was unnecessary. However, the river banks are dangerous for animals, and as the central section of the Outer fort was probably used as the grazing land of OM, an artificial lake for domestic animals at this site would have been an essential facility at a convenient location.

2.3.2.3. Outer fort, western section

The western section of the Outer fort is a long narrow plain originally enclosed by an outer fortification wall to the north, west and south of which only the northern stretch is preserved (Map 7.5). However, in this section the wall is not as massively built as are its continuations in the central and eastern sections; it appears narrower and not as tall as elsewhere. At different places, toppled merlons suggest that, at least in this section of the fort, the wall was crowned by crenellations (Plate 58.1).[153] Towards the south-east and east, this section of the Outer fort is separated from the central section by an inner wall whose course is still traceable in the field (Map 7.5). At its southern end this wall meets the southern stretch of the fortification wall and here, we find that stepped *ghāṭ*-like structure already mentioned which may have functioned as a dam (Plate 58.2)

Near the north–western end, an old gateway is found in the course of the outer fortification wall (Plates 58.3–4). This gateway is locally known as Dharmrāj gate[154] and represents the only access to the Outer fort in the west. The path which runs through this gate leads up eastward to the North-west gate of the Gaurīsomanātha plateau. To either side of this path a single row of square structures built from the same roughly hewn stones as those used in the outer fortification wall are found (Map 7.5, Plates 58.5–6). On the north side of the path, these platforms are better preserved than on the south side, where traces of only two such

153 Similar merlons are found at several places on the island, but their total number is extremely small with regard to the total length of fortification walls.

154 Here, too, we find an old sign-board of the ASI which represents a kind of palimpsest. Originally it was written in white paint and in the same hand as the other sign-boards mentioned above, fn. 96. Originally the label read "*bhavānī dvār*", but this was painted over with "*dharmrāj dvār*". Likewise, the subsequent description was considerably altered obviously on the order of the head of the District Magistrate (*zilādhyakṣ*) of Khaṇḍvā who is mentioned at the end as the issuing authority. Unfortunately, the old text is largely illegible, but interestingly, at the beginning huge statues of Mahiṣāsuramardinī and Cāmuṇḍā are mentioned. As no trace of such sculptures are found here, it is evident that this sign-board must originally have belonged to another gateway (the Cāndsūraj gate, perhaps?) and was palimpsested to be reused here.

platforms are still found. However, the symmetrical arrangement of these structures suggests that they formed two parallel rows of possibly equal or near to equal numbers. While this part of the Outer fort, too, is devoid of any remains indicating the former existence of a temple, we do find a few sculptural fragments along the footpath up to the Gaurīsomanātha plateau which I would assume to have been brought from other locations on the island. However, a number of sculptures which originally belong to this area are clustered around the Dharmrāj gate. The most important of these is a large sculpture of Naṭeśa which is now housed in a modern shrine about 20 metres to the west behind this gate (Plate 58.7). The sculpture is coated with a thick layer of orange paint which obscures many of its more intricate details.[155] Given its dimension and its proximity to the Dharmrāj gate it seems likely that the sculpture originally flanked this gateway although no traces of a respective niche survives. Another sculpture of Mahiṣāsuramardinī of comparable dimensions which is found in another modern shrine about 50 metres to the west, near the path leading up to the Dharmrāj gate but outside the fort, may perhaps represent the former sculpture's counterpart originally occupying the other niche flanking the gateway (Plate 58.8).[156]

2.4. *Monuments in the island's periphery*

There are a number of structures outside the fort area which certainly go back to Paramāra times. These include two temples, the Kedāreśvara which stands close to the Narmadā river at the south side of Mucukund hill and the R̥namukteśvara at its extreme western tip and two clusters of structures (Map 8). One of these, the 'Rāṇīghāt cluster' is situated at the north-eastern side of the island exactly at the head of a valley which runs north–east to south–west between the Māndhātā and Mucukund hills. The other cluster is found at the south-western slope of Māndhātā hill proper in the modern part of the town, presently known as Śivpurī, around the Oṃkāreśvara temple. However, this entire area has apparently been restructured time and again, most extensively probably in the seventeenth century, when the extant Rājmahal (inaugurated 1657) was built and the Oṃkāreśvara temple reconstructed.[157] The architectural situation in this

155 For a more detailed description see SEARS 2014b: 118 and Fig. 7.10. SEARS dates this sculpture to the twelfth century.

156 See SEARS 2014b: 117 and Fig. 7.7.

157 This date was cited by Devendra Siṅgh Cauhān, senior member of the Cauhān Rāv family, in a personal conversation on February 12, 2013. He also asserted that the

part of the town is complicated. The area shows several layers of building activity with old structures partly overlapping each other horizontally and vertically. Hence, some of these structures are partly obstructed or inaccessible and, moreover, the fact that this cluster represents the central ritual nucleus of OM, renders systematic and detailed investigations particularly difficult. To entangle the puzzle this area poses and to draw a clear picture of its architectural genesis would merit a detailed study of its own. At the present state of investigations I can only give a brief description of the individual structures constituting this cluster which will follow further below. Let us first turn to the other locations outside the fort areas on the island where the situation is less complicated.

2.4.1. The Kedāreśvara temple

The Kedāreśvara temple[158] stands close to the *parikramāpatha* on an elevation near the bank of the Narmadā river at the south-western side of Mucukund hill (Map 8). It is a rather small shrine with a *pañcaratha* ground-plan which opens to the east. A sign-board near the temple claims that it dates to the fourteenth century but was reconstructed in Marāṭhā times.[159] The latter claim is probably correct, because the walls and superstructure of the temple are doubtlessly reconstructed with the stones set with mortar down to the level of the modern platform surrounding the temple, and the workmanship displayed seems to be comparable to other works of Marāṭhā times at OM (Plate 59.1). As the modern platform obstructs possibly existing lower portions of the temple's base, it is difficult to decide whether a another temple really preceded the present construction, although some parts, like the sanctum doorframe, the *udumbara* and two pillars standing in front of the shrine are certainly old (Plate 59.2).

---

palace was inaugurated by his ancestor, Rāv Daulat Siṅgh, which is corroborated by DELAMAINE (1830: 208). However, the only historically known Daulat Siṅgh is depicted as a middle-aged man in a portrait painted by William Carpenter around March 1851 and mentioned as "the last rájá of Mándhátá" by FORSYTH (1870b: 258). So the ruler in question must be either the father or grandfather of this Daulat Siṅgh. (The painting is held by the V&A, No. IS.110–1881; see: http://collections.vam.ac.uk/item/O108184/daulat-rao-of-mandhata-painting-carpenter-william; last retrieved 01–09–2016.)

158 First mentioned in RAG 2012: 224.

159 As in the case of the sign-board at the West or Dharmrāj gate, this one, too, is a palimpsest made on the order of the District Magistrate (*zilādhyakṣ*) of Khaṇḍvā. Not much can be deciphered of the original inscription other than that it must originally have belonged to the Ṛṇamukteśvara temple.

2.4.2. The Ṛṇamukteśvara temple

The Ṛṇamukteśvara temple is located at the western tip of Mucukund hill, outside the fort area (Map 8).[160] The temple proper stands in the centre of a courtyard enclosed on all four sides by narrow buildings (Plate 60.1). The pillars in the temple are old but the rest of the structure is rather modern. Similar pillars are found in a shrine of Dvārkādīśa which occupies the northern half of the western part of the building surrounding the courtyard (Plate 60.2). Above its cella which contains a modern sculpture of Dvārkādīśa, a round cupola is found on a larger flat roof, indicating that the reconstruction of this temple goes back to Marāṭhā times, too. There are very few old but insignificant sculptures found in the courtyard.

2.4.3. The Rānīghāṭ area

The Rānīghāṭ area is represented by a strip of land, elevated about 15 to 20 metres above the Kāverī river's water level (in the dry season) which runs south to north tangentially along the eastern slope of Māndhātā hill up to the south-eastern corner of Mucukund hill (Maps 8 and 9.1–2, Plate 61.1). On its western side this strip of land opens into a narrow valley which separates the two hills from each other. The area presumably represents the principal point of access to Māndhātā island in ancient times. Near the river, the area is strewn with architectural fragments (Plates 61.1–2), while at its rear side, near the slope of the hills, it is overgrown with thick vegetation which obstructs the remains of a fortification wall which originally ran down from the south-eastern corner of Mucukund hill up to the north-eastern corner of Māndhātā hill (Map 9.2), connecting the fort walls on both hills and traversing the mouth of the valley to ward it off against uncontrolled intrusion. A few small stretches of this wall are preserved near the south-eastern corner of Mucukund hill (Plate 61.3), the rest being almost completely destroyed and identifiable in the field only as a course of overgrown rubble. Its full course is also only partially discernible on satellite images (Map 9.1–2).

As the popular name 'Rānīghāṭ' indicates, the area is marked by a vast flight of steps leading down to the northern branch of the Narmadā popularly held to represent an extension of the Kāverī river which joined

160 Mentioned in RAG 2012: 224. The only early reference is found in RUSSELL 1908: 242: "At the western end of the island is a shrine of Rinmukteshwar to whom a handful of split grain is offered by debtors, and this is said to release them from the obligation of their debts or at least to remove any sin attaching to the non-payment of them."

the Narmadā on the south bank a few hundred metres to the east of the site of the Oṃkāreśvar dam prior to its construction.

The Rānīghāṭ is situated near the landing point of a small motorboat which operates as a ferry between Māndhātā island and Panthiā village on the north bank of the Kāverī.[161] Local people assert that before the construction of the dam, the river could be crossed here even on foot in the dry season.[162] Despite obvious large scale destruction at the site a few structures have survived, among them portions of the Rānīghāṭ itself, and a cluster of architectural remains including, most prominently, the so-called Dhavalīmaṭh (Plate 61.4).

Probably due to centuries of recurring monsoon floods, large portions of the *ghāṭ* steps seem to have been washed away over a long period so that the Rānīghāṭ's original extent is impossible to determine (Plate 61.5). Still, the large number of loose architectural fragments and the remaining structures suggest that the *ghāṭ* must once have been part of an impressive assemblage of structures along the now vanished fortification walls. As already stated, functionally the area represents probably the principal point of entry to the fort linking it to the northern region of Mālvā. The strategic position of the site in conjunction with the amount of architectural fragments strewn around the area and the near total destruction of the fortification walls here and in the vicinity on both hills to either side of the valley suggest that the assault(s) on Māndhātā fort which eventually led to the large scale destruction[163] of the island's monuments may probably have commenced from here.

---

161 On the Panthiā side stands a modern staircase and gateway to the Jain *tīrtha* Siddhvarkūṭ, but its condition has much deteriorated after the old Panthiā village was almost completely demolished and the adjacent area bulldozed into a large raised flat mound to accommodate a huge tin shed colony for the work-force brought in for the construction of the dam.

162 The river bed was dredged in order to enhance the river's capacity to absorb and divert the discharge of water from the turbine house.

163 There are a couple of suspects for the apparent large-scale destruction of monuments and sculptures observed at OM. FORSYTH (1870b: 259) held that "The fanatic Alá-ud-dín passed through this country in A.D. 1295 on his return from his Deccan raid, and as he took A'sírgarh, which is not far off, it is improbable that he would have passed over so tempting an idol preserve as Mándhátá. Doubtless the work commenced by him was continued by the Ghorí princes of Málwá, and completed by that arch-iconoclast Aurangzeb."

H.L. SRIVASTAVA (in BLAKISTON 1938: 81), on the other hand, reports that the Oṃkāreśvara and Amareśvara temples are "stated to have been destroyed by Mohammad Ghazni on his way back to sack Somnath (1024 A.D.)."

In 1820 an anonymous visitor to OM recorded another legend which he had heard: "About 150 years ago, a king of Mandoo came to Uooncan with the intention of

2.4.3.1. The Dhavalīmaṭh

The Dhavalīmaṭh (Plates 62.1–2)[164] is a spacious building oriented to the north. It consists of a closed rectangular hall at its rear or southern end, another rectangular (now open) hall of equal dimensions in front which is preceded by a smaller verandah or *mukhamaṇḍapa* with the entrance to the building at the northern side (Fig. 8.1). The two halls each contain three rows of six pillars in east–west direction. The two adjacent rows of pillars of the two halls are placed close to each other and the spaces between the pillars are filled up with stone slabs thus forming a massive wall between both halls. In north–south direction, passages with doorframes, lintels and *udumbara*s are found in this wall between the two central and two peripheral pillars on either side (Plate 62.3). All the pillars in the building are placed at a distance of 2,10 m from each other, except those flanking the central aisle which stand at a slightly increased distance of 2,20 m from each other. The verandah contains one row of four and one row of two pillars in east–west direction. The two pillars of the front or northern-most row again stand at a distance of 2,20 from their counterparts in the second row. All of the six pillars of this verandah are 'split' in so far as their bases support horizontal *āsanapaṭṭa*s on top of which the upper portions of the pillars are placed (Fig. 8.2, Plate 62.4). These *āsanapaṭṭa*s are carved on their outer vertical faces with a band of semi-circular rosettes. There are no traces of correponding *kakṣāsana* slabs, however. The space between the bases of these 'split' pillars is filled with raw stone slabs which originally were covered on the outside with vertical stone slabs carved with miniature pillars. Only at a few places these slabs are still found *in situ*, especially at the outer north-eastern side of the verandah (Plate 62.5). This type of construction is structurally (but not in detail) comparable to other contemporaneous, similarly built *maṇḍapa*s.[165]

destroying all the temples and holy places about the island; he proceeded in his impious design, and ruined all the minor places of worship: but on his approaching the grand temple, he was struck blind, which he attributed to the anger of the god, and desisted. In the hopes of recovering sight, he made the Brahmins magnificent presents; ordered the temple to be enlarged and ornamented, and rebuilt all the places he had destroyed." (ANONYMOUS 1823: 47).

164 The Dhavalīmaṭh was first mentioned in RAG 2012: 228, but the description is very faulty. The building is locally also known as 'Sūrya temple', but there is nothing in the building that points to a solar affiliation.

165 See, for instance, those found in the Mahākāleśvara temple, Ūn (12th cent., TICHIT *2010/II: Plate 4, Fig. 4), the Siddheśvara temple, Nemāvar (12th cent., *ibid.*: Plate 7, Fig 4.), the Galateśvara temple, Sarnel, (12th cent., *ibid.*: Plate 19, Fig. 4) etc.

Presently, the floor level of the building corresponds with that of the area outside, but as all of the *maṇḍapa*s of comparable construction are elevated and accessible by flights of steps of differing dimensions, it may be assumed that considerable portions of the Dhavalīmaṭh's substructure lies buried underground. This is all the more likely as the area has always been prone to annual monsoon flooding by the Kāverī river.

The superstructure of the building is completely lost, but the architraves which are supported by the usual cross-shaped brackets as well as the roof slabs are largely preserved. The outer eastern and western flanks of the front hall are largely destroyed with the front eastern pillar missing (Plate 62.6) and its western counterpart broken (Plate 62.7). However, unsculptured faces on the remaining pillars suggest, that the front hall must originally have been completely enclosed by walls (Plates 62.6–7). The inner core of the outer walls of the rear hall are for the most part extant, but their outer shell which probably have consisted of sculptured stone slabs is completely gone. This is clear not only from the walls' crude appearance but also from the south-eastern corner of the building, where remains of outer base and wall mouldings are still found (Plate 62.8). These stand removed to a considerable distance from the extant wall remains (Plate 62.9).

As already stated, the two halls are set off against each other by a massive wall with three passages. These passages are the only portions of the whole structure which are adorned with figural sculptures. All three contain doorframes, lintels and *udumbara*s comparable to those found in other temples and shrines at OM, the central one being more elaborately carved in comparison to the lateral ones. While the lateral doorframes consist of three vertical jambs or *śākhā*s, the central one has five. In all cases the central *śākhā* is adorned with pilasters supported by *dvārapāla* figures (Plates 62.10–12). While the *dvārapāla*s on the central entrance are accompanied by four attendant figures, those in the lateral doors have only one attendant each, except for the eastern doorframe, where the left doorjamb has been left incomplete with the attendant figure missing (Plate 62.13). On the pilaster (*stambhaśākhā*) immediately above the *dvārapāla* on the right side of the eastern entrance we find '*kānsa*'engraved in Nāgarī characters (Plate 62.14, 16).[166]

The identification of figures on the basis of iconographic details like, for instance, hand-held attributes or *vāhana*s is generally difficult here,

166 The shape of the characters does not furnish any clue to determine the age of this inscription.

because portions of the sculptures are either damaged or broken off. Additionally, the rock surfaces in the Dhavalīmaṭh are coated with a crust of accumulated mineral deposits which conceals many details beyond recognition.

All the *dvārapāla*s on the doorframes are four-armed and of *śaiva* affiliation, the distribution of attributes as far as these are identifiable is as follows (*cf.* Plates 62.13–15):

Eastern passage

	dvārapāla, east side		*dvārapāla*, west side	
	RIGHT	LEFT	RIGHT	LEFT
UPPER	*triśūla*(?)	*khaṭvāṅga*	*ḍamaru*(?)	[broken]
LOWER	on bull's head	[broken]	[broken]	[broken]

Central passage

	dvārapāla, east side		*dvārapāla*, west side	
	RIGHT	LEFT	RIGHT	LEFT
UPPER	?	*nāga*(?)	*nāga*	*khaṭvāṅga*(?)
LOWER	*khaṭvāṅga*(?)	?	*varadamudrā*	[broken]

Western passage

	dvārapāla, east side		*dvārapāla*, west side	
	RIGHT	LEFT	RIGHT	LEFT
UPPER	*khaṭvāṅga*(?)	*triśūla*	*triśūla*(?)	*khaṭvāṅga*
LOWER	[broken]	[broken]	[broken]	[broken]

In the upper horizontal portions all three doorframes have a central *lalāṭabimba* in a single *śākhā* which all seem to show the same four-armed figure sitting in *lalitāsana*, probably representing Gaṇeśa (Plates 62.17–19). This *śākhā* is topped by a carved eaves-like stone slab on which rests a massive elaborately carved lintel (Plates 62.10–12). The lateral lintels are massive rectangular blocks of stone carved each with five figures sitting in miniature shrines (Plates 62.20–21). The figures seem to have no *vāhana*s – at least none is clearly discernible –[167] and all figures are partly damaged or severely corroded. Hence, identification of attributes is difficult, in the western lintel even almost impossible. The figures in the eastern lintel are all four-armed females sitting in *lalitāsana*, with

167 Doubtful in the eastern lintel. Here, the central figure has certainly no *vāhana*. In Nos. 1–2 the respective portion is damaged, in Nos. 4–5, one might sense something of the kind. In the western lintel, I mean to see a *haṃsa* next to the second figure's right leg.

the exception of the central one which sits in *padmāsana*. The figures in the western lintel all sit in *lalitāsana*, but the first figure is male and represents Gaṇeśa. As far as I can see, the distribution of attributes in the lateral lintels is as follows (from east to west):

Eastern lintel

	1		2		3 (centre)		4		5	
	RIGHT	LEFT	RIGHT	LEFT	RIGHT	LEFT	RIGHT	LEFT	RIGHT	LEFT
UPPER	*padma*?	*padma*?	ladle?	*pāśā*?	*triśūla*	*khaṭvāṅga*	*cakra*	?	?	?
LOWER	*varada-mudrā*	?	*varada-mudrā*	?	?	?	?	?	?	?

Western lintel

	Gaṇeśa		2		3 (centre)		4		5	
	RIGHT	LEFT	RIGHT	LEFT	RIGHT	LEFT	RIGHT	LEFT	RIGHT	LEFT
UPPER	?	?	?	?	*ḍamaru*	?	?	?	?	*khaṭvāṅga*
LOWER	?	?	*varada-mudrā*	?	*varada-mudrā*	pot ?	?	?	*varada-mudrā*	?

The central lintel is not as elaborate as the lateral ones and its carving is generally more shallow. The lintel is a long but narrow beam carved with seven sitting figures in miniature shrines. The figures are smaller than those in the lateral beams, and the shrines in which they sit are less elaborately carved (Plate 62.22a/b). The outer left figure is male and probably represents Gaṇeśa, the central figure seems also to be male and holds a *vīṇā*, perhaps representing Vīṇādhara sitting in *padmāsana*. The remaining five figures are all female and sit in *lalitāsana*. A portion of this beam seems to be missing at its right end (Plate 62.22b).

While all the three entrances with their lintels, doorframes and *udumbara*s appear like *garbhagṛha* entrances, it is doubtful that the rear hall to which they give access ever housed a sanctum. On the one hand, the back wall of the hall has two windows, placed exactly between the lateral and central entrances (Plates 62.23–24). On the other hand, there is no indication, neither on the pillars (such as unsculptured faces), nor on the floor or among the debris, that the hall was ever divided by walls into individual rooms or compartments (Plates 62.25–26). Some of the pillars and pilasters in the rear hall carry short inscriptions with symbols on their top-most brackets, possibly representing either names of donors or, perhaps more likely, masons' marks, such as "*māghā śrī*" with an *aṅkuśa* and "*śrī salaghā*" with a combined *triśūla-aṅkuśa* (Plate 62.27).

Although the figural representations at the entrances clearly point to a *śaiva* affiliation of the Dhavalīmaṭh, its orientation as well as the features of the rear hall suggest that the building does not originally represent a temple, but, as the traditional designation also seems to corroborate, a *maṭha*. Instead we find remains of temples at a short distance to the north of the Dhavalīmaṭh.

2.4.3.2. Further structures near the Dhavalīmaṭh

A short distance to the north, in front of the Dhavalīmaṭh and slightly removed to the west and east of its central axis, we find remains of two or perhaps three more structures, now completely in ruins (Plate 63.1).

The western structure which is situated near the slope on which the wall traversing the mouth of the valley between the Māndhātā and Mucukund hills presumably stood (Map 9.2), is represented by a platform buried underground. It is exposed only at its northern side and only a few insignificant fragments are found at this site which do not reveal much about the original features of this structure (Plate 63.2).

The eastern structure which is located near the bank of the Kāverī river is represented by a larger area strewn with numerous remains presumably of a temple including pillar fragments and parts of the *śikhara* (Plate 64.1). To the south of these fragments the remains of a temple base buried underground are found (Plate 64.2). It is not clear whether the fragments belong to this platform or belonged to another building. That a temple of considerable workmanship must have existed around this site is suggested by many fragments and fine sculptures strewn around the site, a charming example of which is shown in Plate 64.3.

For a similar ensemble of buildings possibly corresponding to the Dhavalīmaṭh, see Gayāśilā (below, **3.4.**, p. 97).

2.5. *Śivpurī*

Most of the historic structures in the Śivpurī area are found clustered around the Oṃkāreśvar temple and the Rājmahal (Map 10.1, Plates 65.1–2). The most fundamental reconstructions in the area occurred probably in the seventeenth century, when Śivpurī was given its still dominating structure. Not only was the present Rājmahal built from old material probably collected from several sites on Māndhātā hill, but also the massive foundations along the river banks supporting the buildings from the Cauhān family's *samādhi* in the west up to the Oṃkāreśvar temple in the east including the staircase leading down to the main *ghāṭ* as well as the *ghāṭ* itself were constructed. About the same time, the Oṃkāreśvara temple, many parts of which go back to Paramāra times, was reconstructed. While some structures in this area have been maintained since then, others have subsequently been abandoned. The historic stratigraphy of buildings in the Rājmahal-Oṃkāreśvara temple area is complicated and the entanglement of its architectural history would merit a specific study because the area seems to bear important clues to the architectural history of OM in general. For now, I must confine my description to a brief overview of the main structures found at Śivpurī.

2.5.1. Monuments in the Rājmahal-Oṃkāreśvara temple area

2.5.1.1. The Kālikāguphā

The so-called Kālikāguphā[168] is located at the foot of the hill on which the Oṃkāreśvara temple stands, at the end of the *bāzār* in the corner where the street forks to the staircase leading up to the Oṃkāreśvar temple and turns south to lead down to the main *ghāṭ* (Map 10.1, Plates 66.1–2). It is commonly held that Govindācārya, the *guru* of Ādi Śaṅkarācārya, lived in this cave and that Śaṅkarācārya received his initiation here. Though there seems to be nothing to substantiate this claim,[169] the *guphā* was reconsecrated on the occasion of Śaṅkarācārya's (alleged) birthday on April 21, 1988, by the head of the Kāñcīpuram Kāmkoṭī Pīṭh, Jayendra Sarasvatī, and is since officially named Govindeśvaraguphā.[170] But despite the name and the tradition, it is doubtful whether this structure originally represents a cave or *guphā* at all. The staircase in front leads down to two entrances leading into a low hall of a square ground-plan (Fig. 9). Both entrances lie to the south of the central east–west axis of the building. The northern one opens into the central aisle (Plate 66.3), while the southern one leads into a southern side aisle (Plate 66.4). These aisles

168 For a tradition regarding the name, see below, fn. 177.

169 I find no trace of a corroboration in the hagiographies (written centuries after Śaṅkara) apart from the Narmadā or Revā just being mentioned in some of them (but curiously said to flow in the Māgadha country; for a list of places allegedly visited by Śaṅkara, see BADER 2000: 142–143). The only place on the Narmadā mentioned in these texts at all is Māhiṣmatī, where Śaṅkara is said to have argumentatively defeated Mandanamiśra, but the source texts are at variance on this claim too (*ibid.*: 157).

170 A stone plate commemorating the event has been fixed near the entrance. However, this claim would push back the date of the *guphā* to a point considerably earlier than Paramāra times, as Śaṅkarācārya's dates fall somewhere within the period 650–800. On the different claims regarding Śaṅkarācārya's dates, see BADER 2000: 18–19.

are formed by old stone pillars and pilasters, probably of Paramāra times which stand in modern support frames made from stone (Plate 66.3). The pillars are adorned with large human figures on all four sides at their bases, as are the pilasters on their exposed faces (Plates 66.5–7). At the centre of its southern wall, the hall opens into a very small, empty room (its entrance can be seen in Plate 66.3) and at its north-eastern end is a small staircase leading up into the inner of the temple mound (Plate 66.8). Unless this exit was broken into the wall at a later date, this suggests that the Kālikāguphā may have been just a part of a larger construction. The *guphā* has been profoundly renovated presumably in the course of its reconsecration in 1988. The walls are all covered with slabs apparently made of the same stone as the support frames for the pillars. Hence, it is difficult to say, whether the Kālikāguphā originally represents a stone or brick building (the outer facade seems to suggest the latter). It appears more likely, however, that it originally was (part of) a (larger) stone building, as the central part of the ceiling which is exposed between the four free-standing inner pillars, consists of geometrically carved stone slabs (Plate 66.9).

2.5.1.2. Between the Kālikāguphā and the Oṃkāreśvara temple

Immediately to the north of the Kālikāguphā is a long staircase leading up to a platform in front of, but still below the Oṃkāreśvara temple (Plate 66.1), from which one may access the temple by yet another staircase. Alternatively, one may also branch off to the north here, to go to the Rājmahal or up Māndhātā hill. It is here that a few old artefacts are found. The first one, found immediately on entering the platform, is a large, loose sculpture of a standing Viṣṇu (Plate 67.1) which was dislocated during large-scale renovation work in this area in recent years. Turning north, one immediately faces a construction with four tall pillars which looks like an isolated *mukhamaṇḍapa*, and now stands against the rear wall of a very recently constructed building housing the office of the Oṃkāreśvar Jyotirliṅg Mandir Ṭrasṭ. The unsculptured faces of the front pillars show, that this *mukhamaṇḍapa* was no isolated structure originally. In front of this *mukhamaṇḍapa* some more ancient fragments, among them parts of a doorframe and a pillar, are found (Plate 67.2).

2.5.1.3. The Pātāleśvara temple

Turning back to the east one finds, after a few metres, a small entrance in the northern side wall of the upper staircase to the Oṃkāreśvara temple, with a label reading *pātāleśvara mahādeva*.[171] Near this entrance, some more old fragments are incorporated into the wall (Plate 68.1). After entering, one finds a narrow staircase leading down a few steps into an extremely small antechamber which has niches in its eastern and southern walls and a broken sculpture of a bull lying on the floor (Plate 68.2). A stone slab inscribed "Maharaja Holkar, Indore State" lies in the niche of the south wall. An old pillar stands in the south-eastern corner and at the western side is a *garbhagṛha* which opens to the east (Plate 68.3). It houses a small *śivaliṅga* (Plate 68.4) and has an old niche at its rear side. The doorframe is *triśākhā* with *dvārapāla* figures at either side of the entrance and a beautifully carved *udumbara* (Plate 68.5). The lintel carries a double *lalāṭabimba*, showing Gaṇeśa below and a seated female deity above (Plate 68.6). Despite its present condition, it may be assumed that the Pātāleśvara shrine was originally a free standing building of which only the *garbhagṛha* is preserved.

2.5.1.4. The Oṃkāreśvara temple

The Oṃkāreśvara temple,[172] as it stands today, is apparently the result of several phases of renovation. Core elements of the temple go back to Paramāra times, but considerable parts of it including the entire *śikhara*, portions of the *jaṅghā* and probably parts of the pillared halls in front have presumably been reconstructed in the first half of the seventeenth century, about the same time when the Rājmahal was built.

In recent times, the gravest a(du)lterations have occurred when the immediate surroundings of the temple were completely reconstructed and the temple interiors extensively renovated by Jay Prakash Associates ('Jaypee'), a private company which built the Oṃkāreśvar dam. From May 2005 to December 2007, Jaypee first renovated the entire main *ghāṭ* to the south and below the temple, and then extensively altered the staircase and the structures to either side of the temple's *maṇḍapa* (Plates 65.2, 69.1–3). Inside and around the temple, Jaypee laid a complete new marble flooring and partly tiled walls, especially in the *antarāla* which serves as an antechamber to the irregularly placed *garbhagṛha*. In the *maṇḍapa*, Jaypee lowered the original ceiling level with the help of false ceilings and applied coatings of plaster and paint which now conceal the original rock surfaces. Steel railings were inserted between the *maṇḍapa* pillars to regulate the rush of pilgrims inside the shrine. In the course of these

171 The temple is mentioned in RAG 2012: 223.

172 AIIS Nos. 81933–81943.

works some pillars and a number of sculptures were removed and placed elsewhere. In a documentary on Oṃkāreśvar aired in 2007 by the Indian TV channel NDTV the journalist and writer Hartosh Singh BAL described the then still on-going works thus:

> [...] that looks like a hotel lobby... all that is happening... defies any kind of sense about how conservation of cultural legacy should go on... Jaypee Associates has not consulted anybody, there is no archaeologist involved... they have people who worked on hotel lobbies, then of course you get a hotel lobby... (BORDIA 2007).[173]

The Oṃkāreśvar temple is tightly enclosed within a number of modern constructions crammed around its northern, southern and eastern sides. The vast roof made of corrugated iron sheets around the temple, the *maṇḍapa* and above the staircases shield off most of the daylight from the interior of the temple. All this renders photographic documentation of the temple's architectural features difficult.

A first notice of the temple is found in an anonymous report about a visit to OM in May, 1820,[174] followed by a brief description of the temple by DELAMAINE a decade later:

> On visiting the temple, it covered and enclosed the original one which is very small and old; the dome or *kulis* appearing only through the platform of the upper *sabha*, or portico of the new temple. To enter, therefore, the *sanctum* below, after entering the temple, you turn a little to the right, by which you come into the small original temple which contains the *pindee*. This is extremely worn and furrowed by time, and water found in it. [...] The new temple appears to have been erected by Jy Sing;†[175] the older is lost in antiquity. (DELAMAINE 1830: 208; fn. in square brackets mine).

173 The respective sequence from the Oṃkāreśvara temple is also narrated in BAL 2013: 214–216. When asked about the people responsible for the planning of the restoration, Sachin Gaur, grandson of 'Jaypee' founder Jayprakash Gaur responded ("[w]ith a confidence given to those inheriting a family business..."[BAL]): "Our company is doing it in-house, the entire design is being done by us [...] We are already in the hospitality sector, where we have hotels and stuff, so we are used to doing these kinds of things." (*Ibid.*: 216).

174 "The only thing worth seeing is the Temple which is at least a curiosity; it is built about 200 yards from the river, to which it is connected by a long and regular flight of steps. The weight of it is very great; the platforms of the temple, as they rise over each other, are supported by pillars, thick and placed very close together; [...] the temple, the natives say, has existed since the creation of the world; it has, however, a modern appearance [...]" (ANONYMOUS 1823: 47).

175 DELAMAINE was not sure about the identity of this Jai Siṅgh and gives, in a footnote, two alternatives: "If Jy Sing of Amber, a little more than a century; if Jey Sing of Guzzerat, about 700 years ago."

All that FORSYTH has to say about the Oṃkāreśvara temple is that it "[...] is evidently of modern construction",[176] and COUSENS, who visited the temple in 1893, gave a similar, rather unfavourable judgement on it:

> The great temple of Oṁkâreśvara which claims great antiquity, is for the most part a comparatively modern building, but it is erected in part of material from a much older one. The great columns within all belong to the earlier period, and are coeval with the ruined temple of Siddheśvara upon the top of the hill. The rest is chiefly *chunam* and whitewash. (COUSENS 1894: 3).

The temple faces west and comprises a *mūlaprāsāda* and a double storied *maṇḍapa*. The *mūlaprāsāda* has a high, elaborately moulded base and walls which are exposed to varying heights only on its northern and eastern sides (Plate 69.4–5). On the south side, these parts of the temple are, should they still exist, completely concealed by modern constructions. The *śikhara* of the temple was completely reconstructed probably in the seventeenth century from unsculptured, rectangular blocks of stone and is, apart from a few *spolia*, devoid of any sculptural ornamentation (Plate 69.6).

Inside, the *mūlaprāsāda* bears a unique anomaly. After entering the main entrance, it consists of an *antarāla* which is blocked after a short distance at its rear or eastern side by a wall, just where the entrance to the original *garbhagṛha* must once have been. This wall has been tiled by 'Jaypee' with slabs of grey marble which frame an old lintel with sitting female figures, which seems to be placed much too low as to sit in its original place (Plate 69.7; only faintly visible). On its left side, the *antarāla* has a staircase which is not accessible to the public. On the right side is a chamber, the actual *garbhagṛha*, housing the Oṃkāreśvara *jyotirliṅga*. This chamber is very small and has a second passage on its western side for the devotees to exit. Accordingly, the central cult object, the celebrated Oṃkāreśvara *jyotirliṅga*, is neither placed in the central vertical axis of the *śikhara*, nor does it stand in the central west–east axis of the temple, but is removed to the south side of both. While the temple is oriented to the west, the *garbhagṛha* irregularly faces north in the present arrangement. The reason for this strange anomaly is not publicly known and seems to be rigorously kept secret by the custodians and priests of the temple.[177]

---

176 FORSYTH 1870b: 258.

177 I have never heard a reasonable explanation for this anomaly. Its cause may, however, be reflected in an old legend about the establishment of the Cauhān family's rule. The founder of the dynasty, Bhārat Siṅgh, is said to have been invited by a *gosāī*, Daryāo Nāth, to kill Nāthu, the Bhīl chief of the region and establish himself as the ruler. At that time, Daryāo Nāth "[...] was the only worshipper of Omkár

The large *maṇḍapa* in front of the *mūlaprāsāda* on the ground floor contains six rows of six pillars each of Paramāra times. It is enclosed with high surrounding walls but originally had roofed entrances with two pillars (*mukhamaṇḍapa*s) to all three sides (N–W–S), of which only the western and southern ones remain in their entirety (Plates 69.8–9). The northern one now stands in the small passage along the northern side of the temple, with its north-western pillar and the roof missing (Plate 66.9). The first storey of the *mūlaprāsāda* is preceded by another *maṇḍapa* which contains six rows of three pillars of Paramāra times. This *maṇḍapa* which can be seen in its original state in one of COUSENS' photos (Plate 69.10),[178] has since been extended to approximately the same dimensions as the *maṇḍapa* on the ground floor (Plate 69.11). The central aisle of this *maṇḍapa* leads to another sanctum opening to the west and housing Mahākāleśvara which is at its original and appropriate place in the central axis of the *śikhara* (Plate 69.12). The sanctum has a complete entrance with a *triśākhā* doorframe and an *udumbara* flanked by pilasters of Paramāra times. Different parts of the temple seem to have been constructed on different horizontal levels (*cf.* Plate 69.9).

As mentioned before, the architectural history of the Oṃkāreśvara temple is a puzzle and its documentation a challenge. However, as the pillars inside the *maṇḍapa*s, especially those in the lower one, are among the tallest and most exquisitely carved ones found at OM, the temple (to which they originally belong) must have represented one of the more prominent Paramāra constructions, even if its architectural stratigraphy is yet to be established.

---

on the island which could not be visited by pilgrims for fear of a terrible god, called Kál Bhairava, and his consort, Kálí Deví, who regularly fed on human flesh. Daryáo Náth, however, by his austerities shut up the latter in a subterranean cave (the mouth of which may still be seen), appeasing her by erecting an image outside to receive worship [...]" (FORSYTH 1870b: 259).

If there is any historical truth in this legend, one might speculate that the bracketed statement in FORSYTH's account may be a misinterpretation (he almost certainly hints here at the Kālikāguphā, see above **2.5.1.1.**, p. 74) and that Daryāo Nāth in fact shut up Kālī in the original sanctum of the Oṃkāreśvara temple by sealing it with a wall and establishing the Oṃkāreśvara *liṅga* at its present location. That would explain why the facts are kept secret, the question being commonly treated almost like a taboo. In consequence, this would mean that the present Oṃkāreśvar temple does not represent the original shrine for the Oṃkāreśvara *liṅga*. While this is speculation, too, it is certain that the present Oṃkāreśvara *liṅga* cannot represent the original one, whose existence at OM is attested as early as 1063 CE by the *pañcaliṅga* inscription in the Amareśvara temple (see NEUSS 2013: 146).

178 Shelfmark Photo 1003/(1263). Accessible at: http://www.bl.uk/onlinegallery/onlineex/apac/photocoll/m/019pho000001003u01263000.html [last retrieved November 26, 2016].

2.5.1.5. The Dvārkādhīś Raṇchoṛ temple

Immediately to the north, next to the north-western corner of the lower *maṇḍapa* of the Oṃkāreśvara temple stands this shrine[179] which is a mix of ancient and modern parts (Plate 70.1). The ancient parts comprise the two front pillars, a complete doorframe with lintel, *śākhās* adorned with *dvārapāla* figures (Plate 70.2) and *udumbara,* as well as a few *spolia* in the ceiling. The shrine is completely renovated and covered with a thick coating of paint and the sanctum has been tiled. A painted advertisement on the northern sidewall claims that the cult object in the sanctum, a standing representation of Viṣṇu carved from black stone, is ancient. The sculpture appears, however, to be comparatively modern and is certainly not of Paramāra times (Plate 70.3).

2.5.1.6. The 'Old mahal'

To the north and immediately adjacent to the Dvārkādhīś and Oṃkāreśvara temples lies a large expanse of ruins which reaches up to the Rājmahal in the north-west. Its outer foundations consist of walls built from stone blocks of different dimensions which seem to enclose a platform which carries a vast ruined brick building on top that is now partly overgrown with vegetation (Plates 71.1–3). At the west side is a small passage leading from the Dvārkādhīś temple to a staircase which separates the 'Old mahal'[180] from the Rājmahal (Plate 71.4). Here, the outer wall has an entrance made from bricks now blocked with debris (Plate 71.4–5). Apart from this entrance, the wall is made from stone blocks apparently carved from old material collected from Māndhātā hill as a few incorporated *spolia* suggest. At the extreme western end of this wall stands a sculpture of Śiva, perhaps an old temple icon (Plate 71.6). If the 'Old mahal' is indeed a former palace, then it must be comparatively old, as these structures lie already deserted at least for about two and a half centuries, if the inauguration of the new Rājmahal initiated their abandonment. Interestingly, some ancient structures have either been incorporated in the construction or ancient remains have been reused in it.

At the west side stands a small shrine with the wall of the 'Old mahal' built around it (Map 10.1, 'Temple No. 1', Plate 71.2). The shrine opens

179 AIIS Nos. 81945–81946. The temple is also mentioned in RAG 2012: 222–223.

180 This designation goes back to DELAMAINE (1830: 208), who described the area thus: "The new temple is much disfigured by the ruinous muhals of the Raos of Mandatta, now uninhabited on account of dilapidation and ghosts."

to the west and contains no icon. While the superstructure appears to be of a late date, it has an old doorframe (Plates 71.7–8) with a *lalāṭabimba* showing Gaṇeśa in the lintel and on the right hand side of the entrance a small sculpture of Viṣṇu is inserted (Plate 71.9).

Above this shrine, on the level of the 'Old mahal', is another entrance (Plate 71.1-2, 7) which gives access to a pillared hall of considerable, and, from the outside, unexpected dimensions. The hall is quite spacious and full of garbage and debris, parts of the hall seem to have collapsed (71.10–12). It is very dark inside, but as far as visible, the pillars are of Paramāra times as are other structural elements like, for instance, an old stone screen (*jāla*) (Plate 71.13). There are at least two more entrances in the 'Old mahal' which seem to lead into other, possibly subterranean structures (Plate 71.1). These lie more to the east and on a higher ground level of the 'Old mahal' area and at least the northern one may perhaps give access to other ancient structures.

This short and preliminary account of the monuments in the Oṃkāreśvara temple area show how difficult and complicated the situation regarding the architectural stratigraphy here is. Despite the repeated reconstruction works in this area, and although it falls outside the Paramāra fortification, it is evident that already in Paramāra times the area contained a number of buildings.

2.5.1.7. The Rājmahal

As already mentioned, the Rājmahal (Plates 72.1–2) is said to have been inaugurated by Rāv Daulat Siṅgh Cauhān in 1657.[181] It is an impressive edifice built in typical Rājasthānī style on a platform presumably specially carved out of the rock for the purpose. Probably a large number of stone blocks collected from the ruins on Māndhātā hill and cut to appropriate size were used in its construction, as a number of *spolia* incorporated into the outer walls suggest (Plate 72.3). Immediately adjacent at the western side stands the *cūnāgaṛh*, a building of square ground-plan, in which lime was crushed and the plaster for the walls was mixed. The main entrance to the building is at its eastern side (Plate 72.4). A narrow footpath runs along the northern side of the building where a smaller side entrance is found. Close to the wall stands another inscribed hero stone (Plates 72.5–7).

---

181 See above, fn. 157. The building is briefly described in RAG 2012: 227–228.

2.5.1.8. Temple at the south wall of the Rājmahal

Near the south-eastern corner of the Rājmahal and close to its south wall stands another old temple which is buried almost up to its almost ruined superstructure (Map 10.1, 'Temple No. 2'; Plate 73.1). The temple is in a dilapidated condition. It faces east and is difficult to access because of accumulated debris and garbage blocking its entrance (Plate 73.2). The temple consists of a *mūlaprāsāda* and a small *mukhamaṇḍapa*. The outer pillars of the *mukhamaṇḍapa* are of Paramāra times (Plate 73.2–3). The entrance to the *garbhagṛha* has a *pañcaśākhā* doorframe with *dvārapāla* figures at the bottom (Plates 73.4–5). The lintel shows Gaṇeśa in its *lalāṭabimba* (Plate 73.6). The *garbhagṛha* contains a standing life-size sculpture of a male deity which is so badly mutilated that no attribute is left to determine its identity nor its date (Plate 73.7). An inscription is found on the left inner side of the entrance to the *garbhagṛha*. It is preceded by a curious symbol and written in double outlined ('hollow') characters (Plate 73.8). It is dated in the first two lines *sa[ṃ]vat 1630* and *sāke 1495* which is equivalent to ca. 1573 CE and records the construction of the temple by a person named Lāharāmadāsa. It is not entirely clear whether the temple was only reconstructed or built anew from old material.

It must be noted here that the whole slope along the southern wall of the Rājmahal and to the west of this temple seems to bear old structures. Remains of these can be seen along the southern face, where wall remains are partly exposed.

2.5.2. Monuments in the periphery of Śivpurī

There are a few more historic buildings at the periphery of Śivpurī which merit mention (Map 10.2). All of them were either built or reconstructed probably in Marāṭhā times, and in some of them *spolia* of Paramāra times have been incorporated.

2.5.2.1. The Śiva temple

This small shrine which was probably reconstructed in Marāṭhā times, is located to the north of the Oṃkāreśvara *bāzār*, just behind the northern row of shops and residential buildings (Map 10.2). It opens to the east and consists of a *mūlaprāsāda* and a *mukhamaṇḍapa*, of which only parts of the supporting pillars remain (Plates 74.1–2). It has a *pañcaśākhā* doorframe with figures of *dvārapāla*s at the bottom (Plate 74.3) and a *lalāṭabimba* on the lintel showing a figure which I cannot identify. The *garbhagr̥ha* houses a *śivaliṅga*. On the back wall is an old niche which contains a *mūrti* of Śiva in a miniature shrine with an intricately carved superstructure (Plate 74.4).

2.5.2.2. Shrine No. 1

There are two shrines standing one behind the other on different levels at the extreme south-western end of Śivpurī on the slope of Māndhātā hill (Plate 75.1). Shrine No. 1 consists of a small *mūlaprāsāda* and a *mukhamaṇḍapa* (Plate 75.2). The temple opens east and is badly damaged on the north side. The *garbhagr̥ha* has an old, worn-off doorframe (Plate 75.3) and houses a probably modern *śivaliṅga*. On its back wall is an old sculptured stone slab depicting an emaciated goddess probably representing Cāmuṇḍā, holding *triśūla* and *khaṭvāṅga* within a miniature shrine (Plate 75.4).

2.5.2.3. Shrine No. 2

Shrine No. 2 stands on a lower ground-level behind shrine No. 1. It opens east and consists of a *mūlaprāsāda* and a *mukhamaṇḍapa*. but it has no extant *śikhara* (Plate 76.1). The shrine has a sculpture of Gaṇeśa on the northern side of its front wall next to the old doorframe (Plate 76.2). The *garbhagr̥ha* houses a *śivaliṅga* and has, like shrine No. 1, a sculptured niche inserted in its back wall (Plate 76.3). Unlike the front wall, the inner back and side walls look as if they had quite recently been reconstructed, because the stones are set very evenly in mortar. The temple is used by the neighbouring family as a store room.

2.5.2.4. The Samādhi

This building which looks like a small *śekharī* temple, is the memorial of the Cauhān Rāv family. It stands at the western side of an old high stepped platform which continues eastward along the north bank of the Narmadā up to the Oṃkāreśvar temple. The platform in its present form and the *samādhi* are probably contemporaneous with the Rājmahal.

2.5.2.5. The Hāthīkhānā

This vast but ruined rectangular structure stands half-way up at the north side of Māndhātā hill on the slope of the ravine which runs between the Māndhātā and Mucukund hills (Map 10.2, Plate 78.1). All that remains of this building are its outer walls. At the eastern side is a large opening in the wall in which a modern gate has been fitted (Plate 78.2). A similar opening, but without a gate, is found in the west wall. The southern end of the building forms a steep rock face. The north wall is very long and almost for its entire length, a projection runs along the inside with pillars apparently arranged in pairs, forming what appears to be niches or small rooms (Plate 78.3). The structure is probably contemporaneous with the Rājmahal, but despite its popular designation, it is open to question which purpose it once served.

Further to the west a few remains of a probably similar building of comparable dimensions are found (Plate 78.4).

3. Panthiā

There are some more ancient remains found in a stretch of land along the north bank of the Kāverī river delimited by the now vanished Panthiā village in the south up to the Gayāśilā/Eraṇḍīsaṅgam in the north. The old village of Panthiā was originally situated on the south-eastern tip of the north bank of the Kāverī river, just where it branches off from the Narmadā (Map 11.1). Almost the entire village area has been fundamentally disturbed in the course of the construction of the Oṃkāreśvar dam. The core of Panthiā village has been cleared to make room for the turbine and power houses of the Oṃkāreśvar dam (Map 11.2). The remains of four ancient shrines have been dismantled and relocated to two new sites (Map 11.3). At the same time, a probably considerable number of remains have been lost when temporary workers' quarters, factory sites, and a vast permanent settlement for the technical staff of the dam (to the east of the Siddhvarkūṭ Jain monastery) were constructed. Still, a few archaeological monuments have remained untouched, especially at the so-called Gayāśilā, at the extreme north-western point of this area.

In view of the large scale destruction of monuments and alteration of the landscape at Panthiā, FORSYTH's description of what he encountered here about 1860 is of special significance, as it gives at least an idea of how much has since been lost:[182]

> On the north bank of the so-called Káverí opposite Mándhátá is a series of deserted temples, evidently of considerable antiquity. Mándhátá itself

182 FORSYTH's account of Panthiā which appears particularly detailed as compared to his descriptions of Māndhātā island is all the more important, because it gives a rather comprehensive overview of the monuments at Panthiā, a feature that the later ASI reports, that deal only with the Caubīs Avatār temple and the Mahākālī statue lack.

seems to have been a perfect stronghold of Sivaism, no temple having ever been erected save to the destroyer or his associate deities. Here, however, besides one or two old structures that seem to have been also consecrated to Siva, we find several devoted to Vishnu, and a whole group of Jain temples, the existence of which has only recently been ascertained. Just where the Narbadá forks are the remains of a large Vishnuite erection, of which only some gateways, and a shapeless building formed of the old materials, exist. The former are in the same style of architecture, without cement, as the oldest on the Mándhátá hill. In the latter are twenty-four figures of Vishnu and his various avatárs, carved in good style in a close-grained green stone, including a large varáha or Boar avatár, covered with the same panoply of sitting figures as that at Khandwá. Jain-like sitting figures also appear in the other carvings of Vishnu, illustrating the intimate connection between the two religions. The date 1346 appears on an image of Siva in the same building, but there are no legible dates on the others. Further down the river bank are some very old remains, formed of huge blocks, and apparently from the carvings, Sivite. Of one, a portion of the dome is standing, formed in the same manner of blocks crossing each other at the angles. (FORSYTH 1870b: 261).

3.1. *Relocated remains from Panthiā village*

3.1.1. The Caubīs Avatār temple

In the latter part of this account, Forsyth apparently describes the Caubīs Avatār temple which, prior to its relocation, represented the northern member of a group of three temples which stood in close proximity to each other (from north to south: Caubīs Avatār, Sarasvatī and Paśupatinātha temples, Map 11.3a). Despite its being a 'shapeless building', the Caubīs Avatār temple is the only monument on the north bank of the Kāverī which ever received attention by the ASI after 1893, when Henry COUSENS first visited Panthiā on his second tour to Māndhātā. It was on this occasion that he discovered in the Caubīs Avatār temple seventeen "[...] images of Vishnu where the standing figure is alike in each [...]",[183] with label inscriptions on their socles, of which he deciphered nine.[184] These are the sculptures which account for the traditional name of the temple, even though there is no proof that they ever belonged to a series comprising twenty-four images. COUSENS observed that

183 COUSENS 1894: 3. H. L. SRIVASTAVA (in BLAKISTON 1938:81) dates these sculptures to the eleventh century.

184 Obviously the temple was in such a bad condition that in 1903–04 he proposed to remove some of the images to the Nāgpur Museum (COUSENS 1904: 20), a plan which was later dropped "on account of local objection against it" (BLOCH 1908: 28).

> [t]he four hands each contain a separate symbol – the *konch*, the *chakra*, the *gadâ*, and the *padma* and the variation of the arrangement of these in the several hands give rise to twenty-four different arrangements. [...] There are altogether seventeen of these in the temple; seven are missing. (COUSENS 1894: 3–4).

In 1908, BLOCH reported altogether only nine of them (all with inscriptions).[185] On a visit to OM in November 1911 BLAKISTON counts again nineteen such statues in the temple. For their protection, he recommends "that the temple which is now in rather a dilapidated condition, be put in good order, or sufficiently so, to serve as a proper shelter for the sculptures, and that the building and its contents be declared "protected" under the Ancient Monuments Act".[186] In a note, dated November 16, 1912, the Chief Commissioner of the Central Provinces declared the "Chaubis Avatar Temple with its contents"[187] as protected under the Ancient Monuments Preservation Act, No. VII of 1904.[188] BLAKISTON recommends further restoration work on the Caubīs Avatār temple for the season 1913–14.[189] The last reference to any such activity by the ASI is found in *ARASI* 1921–22, where all restoration work on the monuments at OM are marked as 'completed'.[190] On April 11, 1925, the Governor in Council eventually confirmed the temple's status as a protected monument.[191]

Ever since published information on the Caubīs Avatār temple is extremely scarce. Only about the middle of the 1980s we again find a reference to the temple after it had been visited by members of the ASI under the leadership of B.L. Nagarch in the course of a survey of the temples of

185 BLOCH 1908: 27–28.

186 BLAKISTON 1912: 41–42. When the temple was relocated in 2005–06, the then General Manager of the Narmada Hydroelectric Development Corporation, I.D. Dayal, who supervised the relocation, found eighteen images (probably counting all icons, not only the *avatāra* slabs). In an article in the news magazine *Outlook* published on October 18, 2006, he stated "Of the 24 idols, only 18 remain now. The rest have been stolen." (SHAINI 2006). From my photographs taken in 2013 at the Vṛddhakāleśvara temple which cover all the different icons stored, I count only twelve *avatāra* slabs; see also above, fn. 50).

187 Along with the "Chandsuraj Gateway"and the "Siddhesvara or Siddhnath Temple", see above, p. 26 and fn. 113.

188 The respective notification, signed by G.M. Harriot, Secretary to the Chief Commissioner, Central Provinces, was published in *CPG*, 1912, Jul–Dec (Pt. I), p. 957.

189 As well as on the Cāndsūraj gate and the Siddhanātha temple, see SPOONER 1913: 12.

190 SPOONER 1924: 192.

191 Confirmation published in *CPG*, 1925, Jan–Dec (Pt. I), p. 483.

the Paramāras of Mālvā.[192] About a decade later, a small excavation was carried out near the Caubīs Avatār temple in the wake of its relocation due to the construction of the Oṃkareśvar dam.[193]

The only two photographs of the Caubīs Avatār temple at its original location known to me are one shot by COUSENS in 1893[194] (Plate 79.1) and another, later one, published in the East Nimar District Gazetteer of 1969.[195] The temple has been relocated in 2005–06 to a site belonging to the ASI to the north-east of the Siddhvarkūṭ Jain monastery (Map 11.3b) which has been converted into a garden that is neatly maintained. The building faces east. Apart from a few minor alterations and general improvement of the fabric, the temple seems to have been reconstructed rather true to its original shape (Plate 79.2).

It is, however, by no means clear that the building really represents a temple. The brief description prepared by NAGARCH's ASI temple survey team erroneously states: "The original temple consisted in plan of a sanctum, *antarala*, *sabhamandapa*, and *ardhamandapa*. The sanctum and the *antarala* are entirely lost. The *sabhamandapa* has sixteen pillars which are richly carved."[196] This, however, contradicts SRIVASTAVA's earlier observation that "nothing except the *sanctum* and the oblong *maṇḍapa* have survived."[197]

Plate 79.2 shows that the base of the building which lies completely underground in Plate 79.1 must have been excavated, the slabs being numbered in the same way as the rest of the stones of the building probably for correct placement in the relocation process.[198] Given the extant

192 *IA–R* 1985–86: 135.

193 A very brief excavation report appeared in *IA–R* 1995–96: 47. However, here the Caubīs Avatār is erroneously called a "star-shaped temple" – in reality its groundplan is rectangular. Obviously this refers to the platform of the Sarasvatī temple which now lies immediately to the south of the Caubīs Avatār (see below, **3.1.2.**, p. 89).

194 Photo No. 1395 also held by the BL (Shelfmark Photo 1003/(2623)) and accessible at: http://www.bl.uk/onlinegallery/onlineex/apac/photocoll/g/019pho000001003u02623000.html [last retrieved on November 27, 2016].

195 SHRIVASTAV 1969, opp. p. 471. It is unknown, when this photo was taken. The support wall which is visible here on the right side of the temple seems to have been constructed rather recently. The photograph may perhaps have been taken by the ASI sometime around 1920 (even though there is no respective note in the Annual Reports), as we have no indication that considerable restoration work has taken place thereafter.

196 *IA–R* 1985–86: 135.

197 In BLAKISTON 1938: 81.

198 In a personal email dated October 21, 2016, Brahmacārī Narmadāśaṅkar, the former *pujārī* of the Paśupatinātha temple, however, informs me that the stones were already numbered when he first saw the temple in 1985.

ground-plan of the building (and as it is inconceivable, that the platform portions of a 'lost *sanctum* and *antarāla*' could have entirely disappeared even if their superstructures did), we see SRIVASTAVA's observation confirmed here. At the front of the building is a verandah with a balustrade, consisting of 'split' pillars intersected by *āsanapaṭṭa*s and lined at the bottom with vertical stone slabs carved with pilasters (Plate 79.3). Composition and design are somewhat comparable to those found in the so-called 'Sītāmātā temple' (above, **2.3.1.3.4.**, p. 59) and the Dhavalīmaṭh (above, **2.4.3.1.**, p. 69) and as in these cases there is no trace of corresponding *kakṣāsana* slabs.

The entrance to the main hall has an elaborately carved *saptaśākhā* doorframe (Plate 79.4). The *udumbara* is missing here, but seems to have been erroneously placed in front of the staircase outside in front of the building (Plate 79.5). The *lalāṭabimba* of the lintel carries a figure of seated Gaṇeśa (Plate 79.6). This seems to contradict the common notion that the Caubīs Avatār temple represents a *vaiṣṇava* building.[199] The main hall (Plate 79.7) is rectangular and, apart from the original pillars, has probably lost in the relocation process any distinctive feature which would give a clue to its original function. Nonetheless it is clear that this hall cannot represent the sanctum of a temple. An old stone screen is inserted in the rear wall (and also in the front wall to either side of the entrance), but these need not be in their original positions. Five damaged stone slabs carved with figures stand leaning against the back wall.

The mouldings on the outside walls of the temple (Plate 79.8) seem to be similar to those found on the Dhavalīmaṭh. On the west side of the building the mouldings bulge out as to form another passage into the main hall (Plate 79.9) which, however, is now blocked by its back wall. It is not clear, whether this arrangement is in any way true to the original situation, but if so, it would suggest that there was another adjoining building

199 An inscribed stone outside of the temple states: "The temple of Chaubis-Avatar is a shrine named after the twenty-four incarnations of Vishnu. Images carved in black stone of several of the incarnations are extant. From the remains it is surmised that this was formerly a seat of the cult of Vishnu." SRIVASTAVA (in BLAKISTON 1938: 81) had instead assumed that the images did not originally belong to the temple, but "were brought from the ruins of temples near about and kept here."

A similar supposition had already been expressed by FORSYTH, when he stated: "[...] the writer found a headless sitting image of a Tírthankar, carved in the same green stone as the images in the Vishnuite temple already mentioned [the Caubīs Avatār temple]. Probably all these green stone images were brought from a distance long after the erection of the temples in which they stand." (FORSYTH 1870b: 264; addition in square brackets mine). It is to be noted, that FORSYTH speaks here of 'temples', as if the sculptures were stored in more than one building at his time.

at this side. Similarly artificial appears the entire superstructure of the building above the mouldings, especially since only few of its stone blocks appear to belong to the original construction.

3.1.2. The Sarasvatī temple

Of the Sarasvatī temple, only the star-shaped base of the *mūlaprāsāda* which was found only sometime in the 1990's,[200] survives (Plate 80.1). It has been relocated along with the Caubīs Avatār temple and now lies a few metres to the south of it. It has a square sanctum in the middle with a modern *liṅga* on a floor level about half a metre below that of the surrounding area. The entrance is to the west, with a few steps leading down into the sanctum (Plate 80.2). Apart from the outer stones, the reconstructed parts of the structure are entirely modern and it is unknown how much of the present arrangement corresponds with the original.

3.1.3. Loose fragments in the compound

A fair number of temple fragments are unsystematically placed along the eastern wall of the ASI compound which surrounds the two temple just described. Among them are sculptures (Plate 81.1) as well as architectural remains such as fragments of pillars, *śṛṅga*s and an *āmalaka* of a temple *śikhara* (Plate 81.2). The provenance of these remains is unclear.

3.1.4. The Paśupatinātha and Śiva temples

Although the Paśupatinātha temple originally stood in close vicinity to the south of the Caubīs Avatār and Sarasvatī temples, it has been relocated to a site considerably distant from their new location. The reason for this is that the Caubīs Avatār temple (and the Sarasvatī temple) belong to the ASI whereas the Śiva and Paśupatinātha temples belong to the DAAM, Bhopal.[201] The latter two have been relocated to a site near an old tank at a considerable distance to the east of the Jain monastery and, despite their original situation, now stand in close proximity to each other (Map 11.3b, Plate 82.1). The place is properly cared for by a *sādhu*, with a nice garden around it and the shrines are under *pūjā*.

---

200 According to personal information from Brahmacārī Narmadāśaṅkar.

201 Sign boards near the temples were erected by the Department of Archaeology and Museums, Bhopal. In these it is stated, that the relocation of the temples was undertaken in collaboration with the Narmada Hydroelectric Development Corporation.

3.1.4.1. The Śiva temple

The Śiva temple is a rather small building which opens to the west.[202] Only parts of the base of the *mūlaprāsāda,* a few fragments of the walls (Plates 82.1–4), the doorway to the *garbhagṛha* with Gaṇeśa in the *lalāṭabimba* of the lintel (Plate 82.5), and two pillars, apparently of an original *antarāla* or *maṇḍapa*, are preserved. The shrine remains a fragment and it is difficult to say how true to the original it has been reconstructed. Some structural parts have obviously been misplaced (as, for instance, in the north-eastern corner of the base) and the insertion of a few sculptures in the otherwise entirely modern superstructure appears arbitrary as, for instance, the fragment of a door lintel on the outside of the eastern wall (*cf.* Plate 82.3). The *garbhagṛha* houses a modern *śivaliṅga* and contains a few old fragments, among them an old niche on the back wall, whose originality can not be ascertained (Plate 82.6).

3.1.4.2. The Paśupatinātha temple

The Paśupatinātha temple[203] stands immediately to the east behind the Śiva temple (Plate 82.1). Unlike the latter, it faces east.[204] The shrine is surrounded on all sides by a modern platform with iron poles supporting a roof made from corrugated iron sheets (Plate 83.1). The temple seems to have been entirely reconstructed (Plate 83.2). The only old parts in it are the doorframe of the *garbhagṛha* in the east, again with Gaṇeśa in the *lalāṭabimba* (Plate 83.3), two pillars in front forming a *mukhamaṇḍapa* which contains a sculpture of Śiva's bull, the ceiling slabs of this *mukhamaṇḍapa* (Plate 83.1) and a few fragments incorporated into the modern wall of the *mūlaprāsāda* (Plate 83.4). The *garbhagṛha* of the temple houses a modern *śivaliṅga*. Its floor has been tiled, but the walls are left raw and the back wall is adorned with an old sculptured niche (Plate 83.5).

3.1.5. The Rāvaṇṇālā

Let us begin again with (the sequel of) FORSYTH's observations:

> A little way on is a small ravine running down from the hills, called the Ráwana nálá, in which are some curious remains.
>
> First comes a prostrate figure carved in bold relief on four basalt slabs laid end to end. From head to foot it measures eighteen feet and

202 Mentioned in RAG 2012: 230.

203 Mentioned in RAG 2012: 230–231.

204 A side entrance is found on the south side of the apparently entirely modern *mūlaprāsāda*.

a half in length. It is rather rudely executed; it is much weather-worn, and the legs are gone from the thighs to the ancles. It has ten arms, all apparently holding clubs and pendent skulls, but only one head. One foot rests on a smaller prostrate human figure, in which also are fastened the tigerlike claws of a small figure on the left. A scorpion is carved on the chest of the large figure, and a rat is sculptured on the slab near his right side. The people call it Ráwan,*[[205]] the demon who carried off Sitá, the wife of Ráma, but it is questionable if statues are ever erected to him, nor have the scorpion and rat, it is believed, anything to do with the story of the Rámáyana. The figure was evidently intended to be erected in a mammoth temple which never advanced far towards completion. The adjoining bed of the ravine is strewn with huge basalt blocks, rough-hewn, and slightly carved in some places. They are from ten to fifteen feet in length, and about two feet and a half square; a few intended for uprights are partially cut into polygons and circles. A number of blocks, shaped like crosses, are also to be seen. They are quite rough, five and six inches across each limb, the four projections being of equal size—cubes of one foot nine inches. They were evidently intended to be cut into the bracket capitals of the temple. [...] Numbers of the stones from this nálá appear to have been removed to build the modern town of Mándhátá. The dry bed of the Narbadá, near the fork, is strewn with them, as if they had fallen out of boats in the attempt to transport them during floods. It may be conjectured that the figure is some form of Bhairava or some other of Siva's sanguinary developments. (FORSYTH 1870b: 261–262; fn. in square brackets mine).

The area around the Rāvaṇnālā, too, has been gravely disturbed during construction of the Oṃkāreśvar dam. Today nothing remains of the artefacts that FORSYTH describes except the giant sculpture that he initially "conjectured" to represent "Bhairava or some other of Siva's sanguinary developments". The statue was photographed by COUSENS in November 1893 (Plate 84.1)[206] and briefly mentioned in his report:

205 The asterisk marks a footnote inserted by GRANT (1908: 262) which reads: "*Regarding this figure Captain T. Forsyth, the writer of this article, has contributed the following additional information:—"On a second visit to Mandhátá [sic!] and careful examination of this figure, I am satisfied that it represents the consort of Siva in her more terrible form of Mahákálí. It is certainly a female, has a girdle and necklace of snakes, and is either eight or ten-handed, it is not very clear which. The sword, bell, mace, skull, and head held by the hair in her hands, point, I think, clearly to the dread goddess Kálí."—T. F."

206 Photo No. 1396. The photo is held by the BL, Shelfmark Photo 1003/(2624) and available at: http://www.bl.uk/onlinegallery/onlineex/apac/photocoll/b/019pho00000 1003u02624000.html [last retrieved March 20, 2017].

> A short distance from the temple, nearer the village, and lying full length upon the ground in four separate pieces, is a colossal statue in bas-relief of Mahākāli.[207]

A more detailed description of the figure is found about fifteen years later in RUSSELL's Gazetteer of the Nimar District:

> It is 18 feet long and ten-armed and really represents the goddess Mahākāli — the consort of Siva. She has a girdle and necklace of snakes, and holds a sword, mace and skull in her hands. Her stomach is empty to signify her unslaked longing for human victims, and has a scorpion carved on it. (RUSSELL 1908: 243).

Apparently unaware of these notes, SRIVASTAVA reports in *ARASI* 1935–36 the 'find' of this statue:

> Opposite Mandhata island and close to Panthia village was found lying in a gorge of the Vindhya range a broken image of Charchika erroneously called Rāvaṇa. The image which measures 19' x 5'9" x 2'4" has 10 hands, a rat near the waist, a scorpion (14" long) above the contracted abdomen with the left foot placed on a lion and the right on a prostrate figure of a man. It may be assigned to the 9th–10th century A.D. Close by are seen groups of images of the same period which formed part of a temple. (SRIVASTAVA in BLAKISTON 1938: 81).[208]

The sculpture originally lay on a slope, broken into four pieces, with all the extant parts[209] arranged in due sequence and orientation (Plate 84.1). It has been relocated to a site on top of a partly artificial hill in front of a new school building (Plate 84.2) . But in view of the antiquity of the statue and the nature of the task, this work has been carried out in an stunningly sloppy manner as the four parts of the figure have been placed without any regard for their correct sequence or orientation:

---

207 COUSENS 1894: 4. His concluding remark on the monuments at Panthiā is: "Further up the river, and on the opposite side, is the ruin of an old temple, now dedicated to the bloodthirsty *devi* Kâli, at whose shrine goats are still sacrificed, and heaps of cocoanut shells attest to the number of devotees who worship at it." (*Ibid.*)
The context seems to suggest that COUSENS speaks of a shrine along the Kāverī river, but I suspect that he refers here to the erstwhile Saptamātr̥kā temple at Koṭkheṛā (popularly known as Sātmātrā), about 2 km north of Godarpurā on the south bank of the Narmadā (see below, **4.2.**, p. 101). This temple, too, lay within the submergence zone of the Oṃkāreśvar reservoir and has been relocated to a site a few kilometres to the south-east of its original location.

208 It is unclear to which sculptures SRIVASTAVA refers to here, as there is no other reference to such artefacts.

209 FORSYTH had already noticed that a portion between the thighs and the lower legs including the knees, was missing: "legs are gone from the thighs to the ancles".

210 As shown in COUSENS' photo No. 1396, (Plate 84.1).

Original situation[208]	After relocation
1. the head up to the chest	1. the head up to the chest, but turned 90° counter clock-wise (Plate 84.3)
2. the abdomen	3. the thighs, but upside down (Plate 84.5)
3. the thighs	4. the lower legs and feet, but upside down (Plate 84.6)
4. the lower legs and feet	2. the abdomen (Plate 84.4)

The Mahākālī statue is probably the tallest of the numerous large ferocious icons at OM. Given the location of most, if not all, of such statues, one would conjecture that this sculpture, too, was not meant to be housed in a temple as FORSYTH assumed, but that it may rather have flanked a doorway to a fortified enclosure originally. The "huge basalt blocks, rough-hewn, and slightly carved in some places" that FORSYTH mentions seem to fit much better to such a structure than to a "mammoth temple". Unfortunately all of the apparently vast remains which FORSYTH witnessed and which could furnish a clue in this regard are irretrievably lost.

3.2. *The Siddhvarkūṭ Jain monastery*

Although the Siddhvarkūṭ, *i.e.* the hillock on which the Jain monastery[211] stands, lies outside the area which has been most affected by the construction of the Oṃkāreśvar dam, almost nothing of antiquity seems to have survived in this large monastic complex. If it stands at the place of the old Jaina remains at all, which seems to be the case though, it must have been built completely anew as it now gives an entirely modern impression with all the shrines, rooms and halls neatly plastered and painted (Plate 85.1).[212] The complex comprises altogether 13 temples, halls and rooms for the accommodation of pilgrims and ascetics, a *bhojanālay* etc., enclosed by a modern compound wall. On the inside, all these edifices are adorned with numerous colourful paintings illustrating diverse Jaina legends. To the visitor it is nowhere apparent that this is really a place of antiquity. Hence, for an appraisal of this monastic complex in a historic perspective we have, once again, to turn to (the sequel of) FORSYTH's

211 Mentioned in RAG 2012: 229–230.

212 I have visited the monastery thrice and could not find anything of ancient provenance. However, I was always guided by some clerk of the monastery and could not freely move about the premises.

report, which is the only eye-witness account left to us. In this case it is rather lengthy and surprisingly detailed:[213]

> The most curious of all the remains along this branch of the river is the group of Jain temples. They cover an elevation overlooking, but a little retired from, the river. The building nearest the figure just described appears rather to be a monastery than a temple. It may be described as a quadrangle, measuring outside 53 feet east and west, by 43 1/2 north and south. The western extremity is, however, rounded off at the corners, so as to make a sort of bow-face towards the river. In the centre is an open courtyard 23 1/2 feet by 14 feet. The whole of the rest, except in three places, has been roofed by flat stone slabs, resting on numerous carved pillars, with bracket capitals which differ only in the style of ornamentation from those of the neighbouring old Hindú temples.
>
> There are four main rows of these pillars running round the building, and they stand about ten feet apart. They are also about ten feet high, and the building is therefore wholly wanting in external architectural effect. But the three spots now uncovered were evidently at one time covered by domes or spires. Two of these were of small diameter, on either side of the main entrance, at the eastern end of the building. Of one of these a portion is still standing, and it seems to have been of a ribbed pyramidical shape. The third must have been a large dome, over an octagonal opening in the centre of the western or rounded end of the building. It appears to have been built of large flat bricks, some of which are still *in situ*. The building appears to have been closed by walls on all sides except that towards the river. The eastern wall is still complete. The carving is mostly in the form of circles of foliage, quadrated lozenges, and variations on the square, polygonal, and circular sections of the pillars. It is all done in the same yellow sandstone as the Hindu temples, and is of greatly inferior execution to the Jain remains at Khandwá. The building seems to have been left almost entirely devoid of external ornament. To the right of the eastern entrance have been two chambers projecting into the building, and immediately under the small spires already mentioned. That to the left is, with its spire, in ruins. In that to the right the writer found a greatly mutilated image of one of the Tírthankars; but neither on it, nor any where in the building, was there any trace of an inscription. Immediately to the right and left of the doorway, on entering, are two figures carved on slabs about two feet in height. That to the left might be taken for Bhawání, the consort of Siva, with her tiger and usual accompaniments, except that she has a sort of corona, or canopy of radiating foliage, and holds in one of her four hands a sort of triple-knotted rope, both of which emblems are often seen in Jain carvings. That to the right is palpably an adaptation of a Tírthankar to Sivite ideas, and may be considered a most curious exemplification of the proneness of the later Jains to adopt

213 This attests, presumably, to the deep impression the ruins had left on FORSYTH.

the Hindú mythology of the sect that happened to be most in fashion in their neighbourhood. It is a pronouncedly naked (Digámbar) figure, with a single cord round the waist, and pendent ends which alone would stamp it as Jain. It has also large circular ear-rings and plain round anklets. It is standing in an easy attitude, one leg encircled by a long loop, seemingly part of a snake which also passes along the left side, through the left hand, and up behind the head, where it ends in three-hooded snake-heads, forming a canopy over the head. So far it might all be Jain (the serpent making it out as Pársvanáth); but beyond this it has four hands, one occupied, as stated, by the snake, while two hold a sword and buckler, and the fourth Siva's drum or hour-glass (damaru). These and the Tírthankar already mentioned seem to be the only images now left in the building, though the usual Jain figures are carved all over the ornamentation of this and the other two buildings now to be mentioned. It should be added that this building is erected on a platform of basalt blocks five or six feet high.

A little to the north of the last building is the second, a great part of which is a ruin. This ruin seems to have been the temple proper, and to have been formed of a pyramidical shape with numerous smaller spires. The building still standing is its anterior porch, closely resembling that of A'mwá near Ajanthá, figured in Fergusson's Architecture, vol. II. p. 626, except that the plinth extends much further out all round, forming in fact a wide open terrace about sixty feet square in front of the porch, and cut down the centre into a long flight of steps. In form it is a square of fifteen feet and a half, worked into an octagon by large slabs thrown across the corners, on which appears to have rested the dome, now quite gone. From each side of the square projects a recess or alcove about six feet square. At each angle is a carved pillar, the intervals being filled up with dressed sandstone blocks. The pillars are richer than those in the monastery, and the ceiling in particular appears to have been exceedingly richly carved in concentric circular patterns of foliage. The main entrance is to the east, opposite the steps. The northern alcove is closed by a wall; and in it the writer found a headless sitting image of a Tírthankar, carved in the same green stone as the images in the Vishnuite temple already mentioned. It bears a Sanskrit inscription on the pedestal, stating it to be Sambhúnáth. It has not yet been properly deciphered, but the date appears to be illegible. It is very correctly carved, but does not appear to be of any very great age. Probably all these green stone images were brought from a distance long after the erection of the temples in which they stand. The recess in the southern face may have been either a doorway or another image chamber, and is now quite ruined. The doorway from the porch into the ruined shrine is covered with ornamental carving, chiefly sitting female figures like that on the left of the entrance to the monastery, with friezes of elephants' heads, and figures of goats with human heads. No doubt the most interesting part of the building is the shrine, now buried beneath the ruins of its dome.

> The third building is merely a small temple, nineteen feet square, built on the top of a pyramid of basalt blocks, about twenty-five feet high, and with very steep sides. The dome must have been a very high one, judging from the quantity of ruins, and it appears to have had no porch of any sort. It has an image recess in the southern face which is now, however, empty. The sitting figures over its doorways and other carvings are precisely similar to those in the two larger buildings. It is probable that these buildings date from the same period as the other Jain remains of Nimár at Wún, Barwání, Hasúd, and Khandwá, viz. a.d. 1166 to 1293; but excepting those at Wún, they are the only remains of the sort at all in decent preservation. The hills adjoining these temples are like Mándhátá itself covered with remains of habitations and walls of stone, and no where is there any trace of the use of lime in the building. It seems therefore that the whole of the section of the Narbadá valley, in which Mándhátá stands, was at one time the seat of a populous community. It is now unoccupied except by the attendants of the temples and the Rájá's people. (FORSYTH 1870b: 262–264).

The only photograph which very probably shows a part of the Jain ruins FORSYTH refers to here is another one of the Frith series (Plate 85.2). It shows a conglomeration of buildings which cannot be identified otherwise and which are definitely not extant today.[214] Only the tripartite sculptured stone above the doorway in the middle of the photo (under the faintly written number 4426) I believe to have recently seen inserted into a modern wall above an entrance to the 'Śrīśambhavnāth temple' in a *Youtube* video about the Siddhvarkūṭ Jain monastery.[215]

The monastery is managed by the 'Śrī Digambar Jain Siddh Kṣetr Siddhvarkūṭ Ṭrasṭ.' According to a local tradition narrated in the *Youtube* video, the Siddhvarkūṭ *tīrtha* once fell into oblivion. Then, on *kārttik kṛṣṇa* 14, *saṃvat* 1935 (November 24, 1878), a Jain monk from Indore, Bhaṭṭāraka Mahendratīrtha, had a sudden dream about this *tīrtha* and

214 Frith No. 4426, V&A Number E.208:2175-1994. One of the problems regarding Frith's photo is that it belongs to a series of seven, all taken at Māndhātā (Nos. 4423–4429). Five of these are *recto* uniformly labelled 'Mandhatta Jain Temple', even though No. 4425 shows the Siddhanātha temple, No. 4427 one of its porches, No. 4428 the Cāndsūraj gate and No. 4429 again a few of the elephant slabs from the plinth of the Siddhanātha temple. Hence, the labels as well as the numerical sequence can hardly be those of the photographer himself, but must go back to someone, who never visited Māndhātā. As the label 'Jain temple' is so uniformly applied with none of the remaining pictures matching it, it is very likely that No. 4426 indeed shows the then still extant ruins of the Jain monastery. All of Frith's pictures can be found at: http://collections.vam.ac.uk/, search term 'Mandhata' [last retrieved February 22, 2017].

215 The video is available at https://www.youtube.com/watch?v=SdjVseFefpo [last retrieved on November 28, 2016]. The stone briefly appears at time codes 20:17 and 20:37.

after consulting some old treatises, he went to search for it on the banks of the Revā. During his exploration,[216] he saw the ruins of a huge temple and some other Jaina buildings and, while inspecting them, found an ancient image of Ādinātha [with an inscription] of *saṃvat* 11[?] carved from black stone[217] and another one of Candraprabhusvāmī, dated *saṃvat* 1545 (ca. 1488 CE). From *saṃvat* 1940 (ca. 1884 CE) onwards, the temples were renovated and in *saṃvat* 1951 (ca. 1895 CE) the idols were consecrated.[218]

As already indicated, it is not known what exactly happened to the Jain remains that FORSYTH had described. COUSENS, who first visited Panthiā in 1893, (*i.e.* nine years after renovation work is said to have commenced), is conspicuously silent about them in his 1894 report. In 1908, RUSSELL remarks that "[...] on the Sidhwarkūt hill the ruins of a number of old Jain temples formerly existed, but these have now been restored by the Jain community and have a modern appearance. Some images found in the old temples bear the date of 1488 A.D."[219]

3.3. *Further remains*

To the east of the new colony built for the staff of the Oṃkāreśvar dam exists a probably old, large pond. At its western side stand a few huts and houses to both sides of a footpath running roughly north to south. Though the area has been disturbed during the construction of the new colony, some old fragments are still found at the south-western corner of the pond (Plates 86.1–2).

3.4. *Gayāśilā*

FORSYTH has just one sentence to say about the area around and beyond the Siddhvarkūṭ hill which concludes his remarks about the remains at Panthiā: "The hills adjoining these [the Jain] temples are like Mándhátá

216 The legend suggests that Mahendratīrtha was the person who rediscovered the Siddhvarkūṭ monastery in 1878. However, this claim is in conflict with FORSYTH's assertion that the existence of "a whole group of Jain temples [...] has only recently been ascertained" (FORSYTH 1870b: 261; see above, p. 85).

217 The image including the inscription appear in the same Youtube video at time code 18:00 ff. The video is not really clear, but the date seems to be actually written as a four-digit number.

218 Apparently a great portion of the expenses were borne by Seth Hukumchand Jain (Kasliwal) of Indore (1874–1959), who was one of the wealthiest Indians of his times. His portrait along with those of Seth Kasturcand of Indore and Seth Kalyan Mal of Indore are found painted on the walls of the Śāntināth temple.

219 RUSSELL 1908: 243.

itself covered with remains of habitations and walls of stone, and no where is there any trace of the use of lime in the building."[220]

The Gayāśilā lies about one kilometre as the crow flies to the north-west of Siddhvarkūṭ. It represents a plateau about 20–30 metres above the river just at the northern corner of the Eraṇḍīsaṅgam, the confluence of an old *nālā*, the Eraṇḍī which is now dry for the most part of the year, with the Kāverī river (Maps 11.1, 12).[221] The gorge of the Eraṇḍīnālā separates Siddhvarkūṭ hill from the surrounding hills further to the north.

The Gayāśilā is accessed from the mouth of the *saṅgam* walking about 50 metres up the dry bed of the *nālā*. Here one must turn north and climb up the slope of the hill and walk into the forested area for about another 50 metres. The structures found here can hardly be detected from the *nālā*, because they are concealed by trees and overgrown with vegetation. Before approaching the buildings described below, one comes across the remains of old walls running along the southern side of the slope which are exposed at only a few places (Plate 87). The style of these walls is very similar to that of the fortification walls on Māndhātā island, but it is uncertain whether these, too, represent fortification walls or only served as reinforcements against floods. At some distance to the north of these wall, the remains of a *maṭha*, of temples and loose sculptures are found.

3.4.1. The Gayāśilāmaṭh

The largest and most prominent edifice at Gayāśilā is the Gayāśilāmaṭh (Plate 88.1).[222] The building faces south and seems originally to have been a rather spacious construction of which only rear portions are preserved. The only reasonably intact portion is a rectangular hall at the northern end which is separated from the collapsed front part of the building by a wall with a single, centrally placed entrance (Plate 88.2). But even this part of the building has collapsed at its eastern side (Plate 88.3). It is difficult to determine the extent and structure of the hall (or halls) which stood in front of which only two pillars with beams are now standing. However, the remains of a rock-cut platform which is exposed at a distance to the south-west suggests that the building must originally have been

220 FORSYTH 1870b: 264; addition in square brackets mine.

221 This is one of the few cases in which I am unable to exactly locate extant monuments in the satellite images.

222 Mentioned in RAG 2012: 229, from where I borrow the designation which, however, I have never heard from anybody at OM.

of considerable dimensions (Plate 88.4). The whole area is full of loose architectural fragments (Plate 88.5).

The front wall of the extant hall is built from large rectangular and undecorated stone slabs placed upright between the pillars and beams supporting the roof (Plate 88.6). This is an unusual structural feature and may perhaps represent a later replacement for the original wall.[223]

The entrance to the hall has a *pañcaśākhā* doorframe, with *udumbara* and lintel (Plate 88.7). It is devoid of any figures flanking the entrance, but the lintel carries Gaṇeśa in its *lalāṭabimba* (Plate 88.8). Inside, the hall is a plain rectangular structure without windows or ornamentation except those of the pillars and the usual *kīrttimukhas* on the beams traversing the pillar capitals, so uniformly found in all the buildings at OM (Plate 88.9). The *liṅgam* now placed inside the hall is probably modern.

3.4.2. Temple ruin

Remains of what may probably once have been a temple contemporaneous with the *maṭha* are found to the west of it. These are now represented by an overgrown heap of stones (Plate 89.1). On top of this mound a few fragments still stand erect, including the lateral portions of a doorframe (Plate 89.2).

3.4.3. The *phaṃsanā* shrine

At a short distance to the south-west of the *maṭha* stands another small shrine which consists of a square *mūlaprāsāda* with a tiny *mukhamaṇḍapa* in front (Plate 90.1). Both are crowned by a *phaṃsanā* superstructure. The walls of the shrine proper which is devoid of a cult object, are made of single stone slabs standing upright. The central one on the rear or eastern side is missing and those on the northern side have tilted outward (Plate 90.2). The shrine is apparently much younger than the *maṭha* and the temple ruin. The similarity in construction of its walls with that of the extant front wall of the Gayāśilāmaṭh may point to a late contemporaneous usage of both buildings.

3.4.4. Loose sculptures

A few loose sculptures are found among the large number of architectural fragments lying around in the vicinity of this shrine and the Gayāśilāmaṭh.

223 Compare the outer walls of the later *phaṃsanā* shrine nearby which are similarly constructed. The corresponding wall in the Dhavalīmaṭh, for instance, is built from smaller and horizontally placed slabs (*cf.* Plate 62.3).

The most interesting one among them is a large sculpture of Viṣṇu (Plate 91.1) with eleven(!) *avatāras* in miniature shrines placed around the central standing four-armed figure of Viṣṇu whose arms including attributes are all broken off. The distribution of the *avatāras* is as follows:

Buddha	
Bālarāma	Kr̥ṣṇa (with a cow?)
Rāma	Kalkī
Vāmana	Paraśurāma
Varāha	Narasiṃha
Matsya	Kurma

To the side of Viṣṇu's feet stand Cakra- (proper left side) and Śaṅkhapuruṣa (proper right side) and below these, sitting figures of two donors are found. Garuḍa is apparently absent and the sculpture is not inscribed.

The second sculpture is a representation of four-armed Gaṇeśa (Plate 91.2) and a third one is a slab depicting a two-armed female with her left foot placed on an unidentifiable object (Plate 91.3). Finally there is yet another old *liṅgapīṭha* lying nearby (Plate 91.4).

To the south-east of the Gayāśilā and still on the north side of the Eraṇḍī *nālā* at a place called Pāṇḍukaśilā, an old well is found which is said to cure diseases (Plate 92.1–2). In its vicinity, a few remains of walls made of large stone blocks are found which suggest that this area, too, may represent an old settlement site.

4. Beyond Oṃkāreśvar–Māndhātā

There are two more sites with old temples which do not strictly fall into the area of Oṃkāreśvar-Māndhātā, but must be mentioned here, as they have been culturally and ritually connected to the Oṃkāreśvar *kṣetra*.

4.1. The Kuberabhaṇḍārī temple

The Kuberabhaṇḍārī temple stood near the confluence of the Kāverī and the Narmadā rivers about 1.5 km east of Godarpurā (Map 13). While OM itself is almost absent from *paurāṇik* accounts of the Narmadā river,[224] eulogies of the Kāverīsaṅgam and the Kuberabhaṇḍārītīrtha are already

224 See NEUSS 2012a: 157–164.

found in Matsya- and Kūrmapurāṇa.[225] Meanwhile, the Kuberabhaṇḍārī temple has been submerged in the Oṃkāreśvar reservoir.[226] The only known photograph of it is found in RAG (2012: 231) which shows only part of the building where it appears to have been a rather modern reconstruction topped by a round cupola comparable to those found on the Kapileśvara temple (above, **1.1.2.5.**, p. 14) and the Dvārkādīśa shrine of the Ṛṇamukteśvara temple (above, **2.4.2.**, p. 67). The walls were covered with plaster and the only old parts seem to have been the pillars of the front hall (only faintly visible in the photograph) and the doorframe inside the temple, not shown in the photograph at all, but mentioned in the accompanying text. As stated, the temple is lost today, but was replaced by a modern shrine erected on the south bank of the Narmadā near to the Oṃkāreśvar dam.

4.2. The Sātmātrā temple complex

The Sātmātrā (=Saptamātṛkā) temple complex was originally located at Koṭkheṛā on the south bank of the Narmadā opposite Selānī village, about 5 km to the east of Godarpurā. Originally, three shrines, the Sātmātrā, Cakkardevī and Śiva temples were found at this place. A short description of the Sātmātrā shrine was given by Māyānand Caitanya[227] who states that the temple faced north and that the shrine contained nine statues, standing in groups of three at each of its walls, *i.e.* a) east: Bhairavanātha, Kaumārī and Maheśvarī, b) south: Brahmāṇī, Vaiṣṇavī and Indrāṇī, and c) west: Vārāhī, Cāmuṇḍā and Gaṇeśa. Moreover, outside to the west of the shrine statues of Hulkādevī, Mahāvīra, Vāgeśvarī, Kapālabhairava and fragments of other ancient temples were found. As Koṭkheṛā fell into the submergence zone of the Oṃkāreśvar dam, the monuments at the site were dismantled and relocated to a site near Mātāghāṭ about ten kilometres further to the south-east. While it is unknown whether the Sātmātrā and Cakkardevī temples have been relocated in their entirety, al least the ancient rock-cut platform and the *liṅga* of the ruined Śiva temple have been left for unknown reasons at Koṭkheṛā (Plate 93.1), only the

225 Matsyapurāṇa 189.13–20 (attested by an almost literal quotation in Lakṣmīdhara's Kṛtyakalpataru, datable to ca. 1125–50), and Kūrmapurāṇa 38.40. Later, the place figures also in Revākhaṇḍa (Skandapurāṇa) 41 and Revākhaṇḍa (Vāyupurāṇa) 29, (see NEUSS 2012a: 154–155; 2012b: 203).

226 The temple was scheduled for relocation, but local people prevented its being dismantled (see NEUSS 2012b: 203–204).

227 In ĀVṬE 1919: 123.

pillars and beams have been transferred to the new site (Plate 93.6).[228] From the outside, the relocated shrines do not appear to include much old material. Of the Cakkardevī temple, only the doorframe seems to be old. The shrine is mounted on a new platform and a few old sculptures have been incorporated rather arbitrarily into the front wall (Plate 93.2). Similarly, the Sātmātrā temple makes a rather modern appearance from the outside (Plates 93.3–4), but the 16 pillars/pilasters inside, including the beams they support, are old (Plate 93.5). Apparently, the building does not represent a temple, but rather a hall of an old monastery. The images of the *saptamātr̥kā*s are all extant, but worn off and smeared with red paint beyond recognition. Moreover, they are dressed in clothes. All this makes their identification or a judgement about their antiquity difficult (Plates 93.7–10). I believe that they are of rather recent origin in comparison to some other sculptures, also badly damaged which stand outside at different locations in the compound (Plates 93.11–12).

228 See NEUSS 2012b: 212–213.

Concluding remarks

As I have shown elsewhere, OM has yielded six inscriptions of the Paramāras of Mālvā, the second-most number of records of that dynasty found at a single place.[229] These are dated between the middle of the eleventh and the end of the thirteenth century covering about 220 years and were issued during the reign of five of the dynasty's rulers.[230] The most prominent and earliest object of veneration referred to is the Amareśvara *liṅga* which was probably established already in the ninth century as references in *śaiva* literature suggest. Its first inscriptional reference is found in a copper-plate grant of Paramāra Jayasiṃha I dated 1055,[231] in which Amareśvara figures as the central icon of a settlement of *brāhmaṇa*s who are the recipients of the grant. In 1063 a stone building must have existed at that place as the impressive stone inscription dated in that year and preserved in the present Māmleśvar temple proves. The extant inscription comprises six different compositions engraved in four parts, each dated VS 1120 in their last lines, suggesting that these parts were fixed at different places in the respective building.[232] The contents of the inscription further suggest that the building in which the slabs were fixed, was a monastery rather than just a temple, as the personages mentioned in it are all monks of the Pāśupata sect said to reside at Amareśvara. Its highly refined literary portions[233] point to a high level of patronage and integration within courtly culture, although an introductory portion comprising a genealogy of the ruling king, that Tamara Sears describes as typical for a *praśasti* is missing here.[234] Anyway, the concluding prose passage of the record which states some details of the Pāśupata residents, suggests

229 I very briefly summarize here only the main findings from my earlier paper on the subject (Neuss 2013) to which I kindly refer the reader for more detailed information.

230 These rulers are Jayasiṃha I, Vindhyavarman, Arjunavarman, Devapāla, Jayasiṃha-Jayavarman II.

231 Māndhātā Grant of Jayasiṃha I, VS 1112 (1055 CE), eds. Kielhorn 1895, Mittal 1979: 86–91 and Trivedi 1978: 61–64.

232 The present arrangement of the inscribed slabs in the *antarāla* of the Amareśvara temple is certainly not the original one: north wall – Narmadāstotra (1) and Śivamahimnastava (2), south wall – Halāyudhastotra (3), Śivadvādaśanāmastotra (4), a *śloka* enumerating the *pañcaliṅga*s (5) and a prose portion giving details about the resident Pāśupata monks (6). See Neuss 2015: 127, figs 2 and 3.

233 Narmadāstotra, Śivamahimnastava and Halāyudhastotra.

234 Sears 2014a: 50ff. As the inscription is certainly not *in situ* it is entirely possible that it originally included such a portion which has only got lost.

that this inscription was commissioned by the heads of the Amareśvara monastery and not by a member of the ruling dynasty.

A single *śloka* of the same inscription contains a verse mentioning a series of five *liṅgas* (*pañcaliṅga*) including the Amareśvara and Oṃkāreśvara *liṅgas*, representing the first dated reference to the latter. But even though both *liṅgas* appear side by side here, the Amareśvara *liṅga* seems to have held a more prominent position for a considerable period, as the Paramāra king Arjunavarman visited Amareśvara and bathed at the nearby Kapilāsaṅgam on the occasion of a lunar eclipse in 1215.[235] While the contents of a copper-plate inscription of Devapāla dated 1225[236] do not contain any explicit reference to Māndhātā, it is notable that this is the only record found on the island itself, in a stone box near the Siddhanātha temple.[237] It records a grant to 32 *brāhmaṇas* whose actual place of residence is not clearly mentioned, but as the grant was proclaimed by Devapāla at Mahiṣmatī, it may be deemed likely that the donees lived at or near that place. The question arises, why the record was found at Māndhātā. Either the donees indeed lived there and travelled to nearby Mahiṣmatī for the occasion, or (some of) the donees settled at Māndhātā at a later time bringing the copper-plates that attest their shares of the grant with them. Devapāla seems also to have been a royal patron of the Oṃkāreśvara temple which may have been built around this time, as his coinage bearing the *śrī oṃkār* legend on the reverse suggests.[238]

Two inscriptions issued during the reign of the last important Paramāra ruler Jayasiṃha-Jayavarman II record land grants to various *brāhmaṇas* who certainly resided at Māndhātā. His record of 1261[239] was found at Godarpurā and records a grant to three *brāhmaṇas* made on behalf of the ruler by *pratīhāra* Gaṅgadeva, after he, too, had bathed at the Kapilāsaṅgam and worshipped Amareśvara with a *pañcopacāra pūjā*.

---

235 Sīhor copper-plate of Arjunavarman, VS 1272 (1215 CE), eds. HALL 1860: 24–31, MITTAL 1979: 243–247 and TRIVEDI 1978: 168–171. Although generally referred to as 'Sīhor (Sehore) copper-plates', the record was actually found sometime before 1836 at Pipliānagar (HELD *2015: 43–44).

236 Māndhātā copper-plates of Devapāla, VS 1282 (1225 CE), eds. KIELHORN 1908: 103–117, MITTAL 1979: 252–267 and TRIVEDI 1978: 175–185.

237 As it records a grant to 32 *brāhmaṇas* apparently living at Maṇḍapadurga (Māṇḍu), the question arises, why the record was found at Māndhātā. Perhaps some of the donees settled at Māndhātā at a later time and took the copper-plates that attest their shares of the grant with them.

238 See my section on Paramāra *gadhaiya* coinage in NEUSS 2013: 134–140.

239 Māndhātā copper-plates of Jayasiṃha-Jayavarman II, VS 1317 (1261 CE), eds. KIELHORN 1908: 117–123, MITTAL 1979: 271 and TRIVEDI 1978: 200–206.

His second inscription, dated 1274,[240] is the only record which directly refers to the fort on the island and gives its name as Māndhātr̥durga. It moreover contains some interesting details about the fort. For one, it attests to the construction by Cahamāna Anayasiṃha of a temple of Jambukeśvara[241] and a tank near the "temple of Paśupatinātha who is named Oṃkāra here"[242] the latter standing on the banks of the Revā in the vicinity of the Kāverīsaṅgama. In my view this description fits perfectly the present Siddhanātha temple which is the temple standing nearest to the (now vanished) Kāverīsaṅgam. Since this is the only temple at OM which is undoubtedly identifiable as a Pāśupata monument by the Lakulīśa *lalāṭabimba*s on the lintels above its four entrances, I am inclined to identify it with the original Oṃkāreśvara temple. A temple of *sarvatobhadra* ground-plan would certainly suit the veneration of the 'Lord of the (all-pervading) *praṇava*' perfectly. Significantly, we find the signature of *magaradhvaja jogī 700* inscribed on this temple.[243] As already mentioned, the tank Anayasiṃha had excavated may be represented by the trapezoidal enclosed area immediately to the east of the Siddhanātha temple. The location of Anayasiṃha's Jambukeśvara ('Lord of jackals') temple – apparently a temple of Bhairava – remains unclear, though. It may be represented by any of the structures around the Siddhanātha temple, in Area A or B, the most likely candidates being A 1–3 or B 2–3, see above pp. 36ff. and pp. 44ff. respectively.

It is further stated in the plates that Anayasiṃha had a *brāhmaṇa* settlement (*brahmapurī*) built at Maṇḍapadurga (Māṇḍū) which included a wall (*prākāra*), a gateway (*pratolī*), sixteen lofty temples with golden pots (*svarṇakumbha*) as pinnacles, many (private) rooms (*bhūrikakṣa*), an abode for *guru*s and divinities (*gurusurasadana*), and a water well (*ambukuṇḍa*).[244] The next stanza states: "What he established in the fort called *maṇḍapa*, has here too, in this settlement, obtained by the *brāhmaṇa*s on the king's order; in Māndhātr̥durga itself he granted an exactly similar and matchless construction."[245]

240 Māndhātā copper-plates of Jayasiṃha-Jayavarman II, VS 1331 (1274 CE), eds. SIRCAR 1962, MITTAL 1979: 291–314 and TRIVEDI 1978: 209–227.

241 This temple is mentioned in at least one manuscript of the Revākhaṇḍa of the Vāyupurāṇa, see AUFRECHT 1859: 56(b).

242 "...*prāsādo...paśupateḥ so 'yam oṃkāranāmnā*" (SIRCAR 1962: 148).

243 See above, p. 43.

244 "*prākāreṇa pratolyā ṣaḍadhikadasa[śa]bhir maṃdiraiḥ svarṇṇakuṃbhair uttuṃgair bhūrikakṣair gurusurasadanenāṃvu[bu]kuṃḍena yuktāṃ* |" (SIRCAR 1962: 153).

245 "*yo durgge maṃḍapākhe[khye] vyatarad iha purīṃ vrā[brā]hmaṇebhyo nr̥pājñāṃ lavdhvā[bdhvā] māṃdhātr̥durge 'py anupama racanaṃ tadvad eva vyadhatta*" (*ibid.*).

Anayasiṃha's assertion that he built the *brahmapurī* at Māndhātṛdurga suggests that this *brahmapurī* which is doubtlessly represented by the enclosure on Māndhātā hill was built later than the fortifications and structures on Mucukund hill including the citadel on the Gaurīsomanātha plateau. The exact extent of Anayasiṃha's constructions remains, of course, unclear. While the inscription suggests that it included the fortification walls and gates, dwellings, some minor shrines and a pond, the hill was probably not devoid of structures before. At least the Pāśupata settlement with the monumental Siddhanātha temple at its centre is certainly older.

The main object of the inscription is Anayasiṃha's grant of the shares of four villages to fourteen *brāhmaṇas*, who are explicitly stated to reside at the *brahmapurī* at Māndhātā.[246] They all seem to have been persuaded to settle here, as all of them originally hailed from distant places.

The details of the donees given in the copper-plate grants (see Appendix 3) and the quality of literary composition displayed in the Amareśvara stone inscription characterize OM as an important place of religious discourse and learning in the eleventh to thirteenth century. This fits PARGITER's conviction that the Mārkaṇḍeyapurāṇa, and especially the Devīmāhātmya contained in chapters 81–93, were composed here,[247] albeit probably considerably earlier. As Amareśvara on the south bank of the Narmadā was very likely established long before the Paramāras leave their first traces of royal patronage at OM, the settlements on the island and on the north bank may likewise be assumed to predate Paramāra times.[248] It is hardly conceivable that a fortified city like Māndhātṛdurga would have been built at a formerly uninhabited place of no importance, isolated and with no infrastructural ties to its hinterland. The extensive constructions would in any case have necessitated to sustain a considerable work-force over a period of several decades – unthinkable without adequate infrastructure.

The legend about the establishment of the Cauhān family's rule which asserts that the island lay deserted about 1165 and that the worship of Śiva was resurrected by Daryāo Nāth, seems to support this assumption.

---

246 "*māṃdhatṛvra[bra]hmapurīvāstavyebhyo vrā[brā]hmaṇebhyaḥ*" (*ibid.*).

247 PARGITER 1904: viii–xiii, and 333–334, note ‡.

248 At present it is impossible to say when and by whom the fortifications at Māndhātā were built. The earliest historic personage mentioned in connection with building activities at OM is Paramāra Vākpati Muñja (ca. 973 – ca. 995). BHATIA (1970: 58) asserts that this ruler built "temples and embankments at Ujjain, Maheśvara, Oṅkāra-Māndhāta and Dharmapurī." But this is perhaps merely a conjecture, as BHATIA gives no reference to substantiate this claim.

Although the authenticity of this legend and the Cauhān family's genealogy may well be questioned, it is notable, that the donor of the 1274 grant, Anayasiṃha, belonged to the Cāhamāna (Cauhān) clan and that his genealogy given in verses 75–76 of that inscription includes as his great-grandfather a certain Rāṭa to whom the title *rāuṭṭa* is applied which is probably reflected in the hereditary title '*rāo*' still held by the Cauhān family of OM. Accordingly, Anayasiṃha Cāhamāna may represent an early member of this family.[249] This would perhaps explain his explicit involvement in the construction of the *brahmapurī* at OM, *i.e.* the enclosure on Māndhātā hill proper which seems to postdate those on the Gaurīsomanātha plateau and Mucukund hill.

The first wave of destruction of the monuments at OM may have occurred not long after Māṇḍu, refuge of the late Paramāra kings, was conquered by 'Ain-ul-mulk Multānī in 1305. But this is uncertain[250] and the history of OM after the Paramāras lies almost completely in the dark. During the following centuries OM was raided probably more than once, but the place never lost its old fame and the Amareśvara and Oṃkāreśvara *liṅga*s retained their popularity up to the present day. Both are prominent members of the celebrated twelve *jyotirliṅga*s, and OM is especially distinguished by the presence of two *jyotirliṅga*s at a single location.[251] The place was never deserted once and for all, and (re-)constructions seem to have occurred time and again, most profoundly in the seventeenth century, when the Rājmahal was built. The latest assaults on OM occurred demonstrably in the early nineteenth century during the period of civil war preceding the establishment of British rule in Central India. FORSYTH reports that Godarpurā had been deserted for some decades in the late seventeenth century[252] and the settlement on the island was found destroyed by fire in May 1820.[253]

I hope that this report instigates new interest in the vast and complex remains at OM, of which, for obvious reasons, I could give only a brief

249 Albeit apparently of a side branch. If we take the traditional name of the dynasty's founder, Bhārat Siṅgh, for granted and also the date of 1165 when he is said to have established himself at OM, he must have been roughly contemporaneous with Rāṭa.

250 For the views of earlier writers about the destruction of OM see above, fn. 163.

251 For a detailed discussion of the *jyotirliṅga* concept, see NEUSS 2013: 146–160.

252 FORSYTH 1870b: 258.

253 "Uooncan is situated on the south face of an immense rock, rising out of the centre of the river. The town now in ruins (being destroyed by fire previous to our arrival) is a miserable place (...) Immediately opposite to the south bank of the river lies the village of Gojaporah, much superior in its appearance to Uooncan (...)" (ANONYMOUS 1823: 46).

overview in this report. At the present state of knowledge I consider it inappropriate to attempt an analysis of the remains regarding their historic genesis and structural relationship. I hope to have demonstrated the considerable scope and urgent necessity for archaeological investigations at OM which, I am convinced, would certainly yield hosts of structures and artefacts now buried underground and considerably increase our knowledge about this remarkable and unique Paramāra city.

If I were asked to propose sites for excavations, I would suggest that first of all the sites around previously unreported remains, like temple platforms and other structures, should be thoroughly cleared. Larger structures should further be excavated about two meters in circumference down to the lowest course of their bases. This would help to decide on the further course of investigations and probably yield a great number of artefacts that are now buried and, I would predict, more epigraphic and numismatic evidence. The following areas appear to me to be most promising for archaeological excavations:

1. Godarpurā: The area immediately behind or to the south of the Amareśvara temple complex delimited by the fortification walls which is now used as a car-park

2. Māndhātā hill:
   a) The areas to the east and west of the Siddhanātha temple
   b) Trial trenches in areas A, B, C and D
   c) Temple E1

3. Gaurīsomanātha plateau:
   a) The area around the Gaurīsomanātha temple, especially to the north, where old city walls are still extant
   b) to the south-east, where ancient structures lie buried underground
   c) The area around the North-east gate which was probably the main gate for supplies to the citadel

4. Outer Fort Area: The area around the East gate and a trial trench across the structures in its vicinity towards the Gaurīsomanātha plateau

5. Other areas:
   a) The area around the Dhavalīmaṭh/Rānīghāṭ
   b) The area around the Gayāśilāmaṭh

The most important area that should be given priority regarding archaeological investigations is certainly No. 3, the Gaurīsomanātha plateau. Already severely disturbed by encroachments in recent years, this area which represents the royal quarter of the old fort, should be put under strict protection from further disturbances as soon as possible.[254] No. 2a, the areas around the Siddhanātha temple, have not been adequately investigated during the early twentieth century's conservation work and excavations here may be expected to reveal that the temple was not an isolated construction as it appears now, but was the centre of a monastic complex of the Pāśupatas. Trial trenches in the areas suggested under No. 2b would certainly yield clues that would help to obtain a clearer picture about the general layout and functional structure of the *brāhmaṇa* settlement on Māndhātā hill. Systematic archaeological excavations on a larger scale would certainly bring to light a full-fledged network of temples, monasteries and domestic structures that would amply illustrate the living conditions in an environment especially planned for and dedicated to learned *brāhmaṇa*s and (predominantly *śaiva*) ascetics in Paramāra times.

Investigations at No. 4 in connection with No. 3c and No. 5a should furnish insights into the economic conditions, especially the management of supplies and traffic to and from Māndhātr̥durga, as these areas mark the main access to the fort.

No. 5b represents the only undisturbed area on the Panthiā side. It probably represents a monastic complex and is the fort's only extant link to its northern hinterland.

No 1. is the only site on the south bank which may reasonably be considered for excavations. The site may perhaps bear further fragments of the original Amareśvara temple, but this is admittedly uncertain. Should this book help to initiate archaeological investigations at OM, I would be most grateful if I were invited to participate.[255]

In my view, the fort on Māndhātā island bears great potential to furnish crucial information and considerably increase our insights and knowledge about the largely understudied 'early medieval' phase of South Asian historiography in general and important aspects of political and cultural organization in the Paramāra kingdom in particular. A thorough investigation of the structural remains on Māndhātā island would amply illustrate actual town planning as well as religious and residential

254 *I.e.* a ban on any new building activity whatsoever. The people who already live around the Gaurīsomanātha temple must be allowed to stay until excavations would make the shifting of individual dwellings inevitable. In such cases, adequate compensation and resettlement to a nearby location should be a matter of course.

255 My personal pet project would be the excavation and reconstruction of temple E1, No. 2c, which is among my favourite monuments on the island. I think this must once have been a very impressive and beautiful building.

architecture in the Paramāra kingdom. Especially with regard to the latter, Māndhāta seems to be of considerable importance as comparatively large areas of royal and domestic structures seem to be preserved at various locations. If thoroughly excavated, it will be possible to compare these structures with the exposition of residential architecture in Bhoja's Samarāṅgaṇasūtradhāra (SSDh) which has more recently been analysed in detail by Felix OTTER (2010). Adam HARDY and Mattia SALVINI have already amply demonstrated that theoretical instructions of the SSDh have indeed been applied and followed by architects and masons with regard to religious architecture (HARDY 2015a). I am confident that the remains at Mandhātā will provide similar evidence for domestic architecture.

Being located, as it is, in the middle of a forested and hilly tract, Māndhātā must have been of strategic importance especially as it apparently controlled a subsidiary, dry season trade route across the Narmadā river. Certainly Māndhātā played a major role in the trade of local forest produce and was a place of contact and exchange between mainstream and tribal societies.[256] Much of the sculptural remains on the island with a striking preponderance of sculptures depicting ferocious deities, especially on the gateways of the fort, seem to bear witness to this cultural contact. A considerable number of various Bhairava sculptures would certainly merit a fresh appraisal of the iconography of this deity, which apparently plays a prominent role in the religio-cultural life of OM till date. Given the state of preservation of the numerous temples and shrines described in this study, it is presently difficult to establish a reliable historical sequence of their construction. A starting point here could be the stylistic comparison of the comparatively numerous doorframes that are preserved. Here again, only thorough archaeological investigations can furnish a factual basis on which a reliable historical sequence could be established.

256 Here it is of special significance that OM has been and still is the major trading place for the famous *bāṇaliṅgas*. These were traditionally "harvested" by tribal people at Dhavṛīkuṇḍ, a deep pool in the Narmadā river (now submerged) about 15 kms east of OM (see AKTOR 2014: 25-27)

APPENDIX 1 – Historic photographs, impressions, drawings and paintings pertaining to Oṃkāreśvar-Māndhātā

Table 1: List of drawings prepared by the Archaeological Survey Party of Western India during the months November to April 1893–94[257]

Serial No.	*Title of Drawing*	*Scale*	*Drafts-man's Name*	*Date*
1115	Temple of Siddhanâtha, general plan of –	1/100	Sitaram Dinkar	14.–23.11.93
1116	do., elevation, section and plan of doorway of –	1/12	S.J. Pacheco	29.11.–7.12.93
1117	do., elephants on basement of –	1/10	Ghulam Muhammad	29.–30.11.93
1118	do., pillars and ceiling of plan of Gauriśaṁkara temple	1/10 1/100	do. and Jayarao Raghoba	29.11.–2.12.93
1119	Temple of Oṁkáreśvara, general plan of –	1/100	Sitaram Dinkar	3.–8.12.93
1120	do., general plan of upper storey	1/100	do.	9.–12.12.93
1121	do., two pillars from upper storey	1/10	Jayarao Raghoba	8.–11.12.93
1122	do., upper storey, ceiling in porch	1/5	do.	12.12.93
1123	Temple at Pânthia, plan and details of –	1/50, 1/10	do.	4.–8.12.93
1124	do., sculptures from –	1/5	Hari Gopal	8.–12.12.93
1125[258]	do., 18 figures of Vishnu	1/10	do.	29.11.–8.12.93

---

257 COUSENS 1894: 15. According to the curator of the India Office Collection, John Falconer, the drawings and impressions (see Appendix 1, Tables 1 and 2, p. 111f.) were never sent back to England. Their whereabouts (if they still exist) is unknown.

258 In the original, the number is erroneously given as 1135.

Table 2: List of inscription impressions prepared by the Archaeological Survey Party of Western India during the months November to April 1893–94[259]

Serial No.	*Position of Inscription*
1085	Oṁkáreśvara temple, on a stone built into the wall near the Nandi porch
1086	*Do.*
1087	Siddhanâtha temple, on a pillar in the —
1088	Old temple at Pánthia, on the bases of sculptures in the —

Table 3: List of photographs prepared by the Archaeological Survey Party of Western India during the months November to April 1893–94[260]

Serial No.	*Title of Photograph*	*BL Shelfmark*[261]
1386	Temple of Siddhanâtha on the hill, General view	Photo 1003/(1265)
1387	*do.*, pillars in porch	Photo 1003/(1266)
1388	Old gateway on the hill	Photo 1003/(1268)
1389	Temple of Oṁkâreśvara, top storey	Photo 1003/(1263)
1390	*do.*, pillars from	Photo 1003/(1264)
1391	Portion of town on mainland and river, general view	Photo 1003/(1260)
1392	Town on mainland, *do.*	Photo 1003/(1262)
1393	Town, Ghát, and temple of Oṁkâreśvara, *do.*	Photo 1003/(1261)
1394	Old carved doorway of an old temple	Photo 1003/(1267)
1395	Panthiā, old temple, general view	Photo 1003/(2623)
1396	Panthiā, large sculpture of Mahâkâli	Photo 1003/(2624)

259 COUSENS 1894: 17. The whereabouts of these impressions is unknown.

260 COUSENS 1894: 16. The photographs were initially held by the Indian Museum, Calcutta (BLOCH 1900: 54, 98) and later sent to the Office of the Director-General of Archaeology in India, John Marshall, at Simla (HAMID 1921: 74, 151). In the latter work, the two photos from Panthiā (Nos. 1395 and 1396) are erroneously listed under 'Bombay, Districts Dharwar–Hyderabad' (*ibid.*: 74). Presently all these photographs are held in the British Library, London, in the Archaeological Survey of India Collections, Western India 1893–94. The present BL numbers are the same as the original serial numbers in brackets prefixed by 1009/2, *e.g.* 1009/2 (1386) etc. The size of the original negatives is given as 12x10 (inch?).

261 The BL Shelfmark number does not figure in COUSENS' report, but was added by me.

Table 4: Archaeological Survey of India, Eastern Circle – List of photographs taken during field season 1907–08[262]

Serial No.	*Subject*
143c	Image of Varāha in Chaubīs Avatār kā Mandir
144c	Southern Gateway of Ancient Fort at Mândhâta
145c	Temple of Siddhanâtha: General view
146c	Temple of Siddhanâtha: Carved figures of fighting elephants along plinth

Table 5: Archaeological Survey of India, Eastern Circle – List of Photographs taken in 1911–12[263]

Serial No.	*Subject*
212c	Columns of Siddhnath temple
213c	Ditto, eastern side
214c	Chandra Suryya gate

Table 6: Miscellaneous photographs held in the British Library, London

Curzon Collection: 'Views of places proposed to be visited by Their Excellencies Lord and Lady Curzon during Autumn Tour 1902'

Year	*Title*	*Author*	*BL No.*
1880s	Mandhata temple Onkarji	Dayal, Deen	430/21(13)
1880s	Nerbudda River Oonkarji	Dayal, Deen	430/21(14)

Curzon Collection: 'H.E. the Viceroy's Autumn Tour, C.I. 1902'

Year	*Title*	*Author*	*BL No.*
31 Oct. 1902	View of the Temple of Oomkar, Mandhata	unknown	430/23(51)
31 Oct. 1902	Old Sevite Temple on the Birkhala Rocks, Mandhata	unknown	430/23(52)
31 Oct. 1902	Temple of Siddisman Mahadeva, Mandhata	unknown	430/23(53)

262 BLOCH 1908: 10. These photographs are held by the British Library, London, in the Archaeological Survey of India Collections, Eastern Circle 1905–09. The present BL numbers are the same as the original serial numbers in brackets prefixed by 1005/2, *e.g.* 1005/2 (143c) etc.

263 SPOONER 1912: 24. These photographs are held by the British Library, London, in the Archaeological Survey of India Collections, Eastern Circle 1909–13. The present BL numbers are the same as the original serial numbers in brackets prefixed by 1005/3, *e.g.* 1005/3 (212c) etc.

Curzon Collection: 'H.E. the Viceroy's Autumn Tour, C.I. 1902'

31 Oct. 1902	Temple of Ghoree Somnath, Mandhata	unknown	430/23(54)

Curzon Collection: Delhi Durbar Photographs

Year	*Title*	*Author*	*BL No.*
1890s	View of Mandhata from the island in the Narmada,[*sic*!] with the Onkar Temple at the waterside and the Rao of Mandhata's Palace on the hillside beyond	unknown	430/79(395)
1890s	White Jaipur marble Nandi in shrine in the Onkar Temple, Mandhata	unknown	430/79(396)

Curzon Collection: Miscellaneous loose photographs

Year	*Title*	*Author*	*BL No.*
ca. 1900	Mandhata. The Godapura Ghat as seen from the Mandhata side of the Narbadda River	unknown	430/81(109)

Ramsden Collection: Central Provinces views

Year	*Title*	*Author*	*BL No.*
1936	Mandhata	Ramsden, Geoffrey Charles Frescheville	Photo 472/14(7)
1936	Mandhata	Ramsden, G. Ch. F.	Photo 472/14(8)
1936	Mandhata	Ramsden, G. Ch. F.	Photo 472/14(14)
1936	Mandhata	Ramsden, G. Ch. F.	Photo 472/14(15)
1936	Mandhata	Ramsden, G. Ch. F.	Photo 472/14(16)

J. Forbes Watson and John William Kaye – 'The People of India. A series of photographic illustrations, with descriptive letterpress, of the races and tribes of Hindustan. Volume VII' (India Museum, London, 1872).

Year	*Title*	*Author*	*BL No.*
1862	Brahmins of Oomkar. Mundhata. Nimaur	Waterhouse, James	972/7(373)
1870s	Sculpture of an Elephant, said to have come from Mandhata, Nimar District, in the Nagpur Museum	Beglar, Joseph David	1002/25(1252)

Table 7: Photographs held in the Victoria & Albert Museum, London

Francis Frith 'Universal Series' archive

Year	*Serial No.*	*Title*	*Author*	*V&A No.*
1850–70	4423	Mandhatta, R. Nerbuddha	unknown	E.208:2172–1994
1850–70	4424	Mandhatta, Rajahs Palace	unknown	E.208:2173–1994
1850–70	4425	Mandhatta. Jain Temple	unknown	E.208:2174–1994
1850–70	4426	Mandhatta. Jain Temple	unknown	E.208:2175–1994
1850–70	4427	Mandhatta. Jain Temple	unknown	E.208:2176–1994
1850–70	4428	Mandhatta. Jain Temple	unknown	E.208:2177–1994
1850–70	4429	Mandhatta. Carved Elephants Jain Temple	unknown	E.208:2178–1994

Table 8: Paintings held in the Victoria & Albert Museum, London

Date	*Motif*	*Artist*	*Materials; Dimensions (w/h)*	*V&A No.*
March 1851	Daulat Rao of Mandhata	Carpenter, William	Pencil and watercolour on paper; 34x24 cm	IS.110–1881
March 1851	Men playing Pachisi at Mandhata	Carpenter, William	Watercolour on paper; 6.5x5 inch	IS.116–1881

Table 9: Miscellaneous photographs and drawings

Photographs:

Date	*Title*	*Reference*
<1908	Mandhata island	RUSSELL 1908: 6f.[264]
<1908	Mandhata from the island	*ibid.*: 240f.
<1916	Temple of Siddhnath, Mandhata	CHATTERTON 1916: 36f.[264]
<1916	Mandhata island on the Nerbudda	*ibid.*: 120f.
<1916	Onkar Temple and Birkhala Cliff, Mandhata	*ibid.*: 124f.

264 The plates in RUSSELL 1908 and CHATTERTON 1916 are inserted unnumbered between consecutively numbered text pages and carry the signature 'Bemrose, Cello., Derby.'

Drawings:

Date	*Motif*	*Artist*	*Materials and Dimensions (w / h)*
1850–1855	Island of Onkar Mandhata and the Narbada river*	Waddell, Charles Douglas (1821-84)	Pencil; 26.4x15 cm

*Inscribed: 'Sacred Island of Ooncai Mandata on the Nerbuddah above Mundlasur', and on reverse: 'The Sacred Island of Ooncai Mandata in the Nerbuddah above Mundlaisir taken at the flood of the River.' *Reference*: BL, India Office Select Materials, Prints & Drawings; Shelfmark WD4291

Date	*Motif*	*Artist*	*Reference*
<1891	Mandhata island	John Pedder[265]	CAINE 1891: 398

265 John Pedder (1850–1929), was born in Liverpool. He was a landscape artist who painted chiefly in watercolour.

APPENDIX 2 – List of photographs from Oṃkāreśvar-Māndhātā held by the American Institute of Indian Studies, Gurgaon[266]

Acc.-No.	*Neg.-No.*	*Caption / Description*	*Date (CE)*
81895	673.39	Dattatreya temple – Garbhagrha, doorframe	ca. 1100–25
81896	673.40	Dattatreya temple – Garbhagrha, doorframe, right jamb	ca. 1100–25
81897	673.41	Dattatreya temple – Mandapa, pillar	ca. 1100–25
81898	673.75	*Fort, Suraj Gate – A view from the south*[267]	ca. 1100–50
81899	673.74	Fort – South gate, east wing, Bhairava	ca. 1100–50
81900	673.73	Fort – South gate, west wing, sculpture	ca. 1100–50
81901	673.52	Fort, Suraj Gate – A view from the north-east	ca. 1100–50
81902	673.49	Fort, Suraj Gate – General view, from the south	ca. 1100–50
81903	673.45	Fort, Suraj Gate – Entrance, view from the north	ca. 1100–50
81904	673.48	Fort, Suraj Gate – South face, pratoli-torana	ca. 1100–50
81905	673.46	Fort, Suraj Gate – South face, pratoli-torana, view from the north	ca. 1100–50
81906	673.44	Fort, Suraj Gate, north face – north face, Camunda	ca. 1100–50
81907	673.43	Fort, Suraj Gate, north face – east face, Ganesa	ca. 1100–50
81908	673.42	Fort, Suraj Gate, north face – west face, Mahisamardini	ca. 1100–50
81909	673.47	Fort, Suraj Gate – East wall recess	ca. 1100–50
81910	673.50	Fort, Suraj gate – Siva bust, lying near gate	ca. 1100–50
81911	673.51	Fort, Suraj Gate – West wall recess, south pillar	ca. 1100–50
81912	676.61	Gauri Somnatha temple – A view from the south	ca. 1100–99
81913	676.62	Gauri Somnatha temple – A view from the south-east	ca. 1100–99
81914	673.26	Mamlesvara temple – General view from the south	ca. 1000–99
81915	673.24	Mamlesvara temple – Garbhagrha, doorframe, left jamb, base	ca. 1000–99
81916	673.23	Mamlesvara temple – Mandapa, pillar	ca. 1000–99
81917	673.36	Mamlesvara temple – Mandapa, south wall, Camunda	ca. 1000–99

266 The photographs are accessible at http://dsal.uchicago.edu/images/aiis/ (search term 'Mandhata') [last retrieved February 22, 2017]. According to Vandana Sinha, Director Academic, Center for Art & Archaeology at the AIIS, all the photographs were taken in February/March 1988. Errors and inconsistencies are italicized.

267 Wrong attribution, caption should read "South gate, east face".

Acc.-No.	*Neg.-No.*	*Caption / Description*	*Date (CE)*
81918	673.37	Mamlesvara temple – Mandapa, south jangha, detail	ca. 1000–99
81919	673.22	Mamlesvara temple – Mandapa, Natesa in niche	ca. 1000–99
81920	673.21	Mamlesvara temple – Mandapa, Tripurantaka in niche	ca. 1000–99
81921	*A52.54*[268]	Mamlesvara temple – Mulaprasada, pitha and mandovara, view from the south	ca. 1000–99
81922	673.20	Mamlesvara temple – Mulaprasada, vedibandha detail from the north	ca. 1000–99
81923	673.25	Mamlesvara temple – Mulaprasada, south wall, east end	ca. 1000–99
81924	673.34	*South-west shrine*[269] – Antarala, niche, Ganesa	ca. 1000–99
81925	673.35	*South-west shrine*[269] – Antarala, niche, Brahma with consort	ca. 1000–99
81926	673.27	South-west shrine[270] – Partial view from the south-east	ca. 1000–99
81927	673.32	South-west shrine – Vedibandha detail from the north	ca. 1000–99
81928	673.33	South-west shrine – Vedibandha detail from the north	ca. 1000–99
81929	673.29	South-west shrine – Antarala, left pillar, view from the east	ca. 1000–99
81930	673.28	South-west shrine – Antarala, pillars, view from the east	ca. 1000–99
81931	673.31	South-west shrine – Garbhagrha, doorframe, left jamb, detail	ca. 1000–99
81932	673.30	South-west shrine – Garbhagrha, doorframe, right jamb	ca. 1000–99
81933	676.75	Omkaresvara temple – Mandapa pillar	ca. 1100–25
81934	676.69	Omkaresvara temple – Mandapa pillar	ca. 1100–25
81935	676.68	Omkaresvara temple – Mandapa pillar	ca. 1100–25
81936	676.67	Omkaresvara temple – Mandapa pillar	ca. 1100–25
81937	676.66	Omkaresvara temple – Mandapa pillar, detail	ca. 1100–25
81938	676.65	Omkaresvara temple – Mandapa vedibandha	ca. 1100–25

268 Completely different negative number. In the DSAL database, the photograph appears within a mixed series of pictures from Gujarat and Rajasthan.

269 Wrong attribution, caption should read 'North-west shrine', the photos show details from the Kuntī temple, **1.1.2.1.3.**, above, p. 11.

270 From here onwards, "South-west shrine" refers to the Vr̥ddhakāleśvara temple, **1.1.2.1.2.**, above, p. 10.

Acc.-No.	*Neg.-No.*	*Caption / Description*	*Date (CE)*
81939	676.71	Omkaresvara temple – Second Storey, Mandapa of Mahakalesvara, pillar	ca. 1100–25
81940	676.70	Omkaresvara temple – Mulaprasada, pitha and vedibandha detail	ca. 1100–25
81941	676.72	Omkaresvara temple – mulaprasada, II storey, Mahakalesvara garbhagrha, lower doorframe	ca. 1100–25
81942	676.73	Omkaresvara temple – mulaprasada, II storey, doorframe, left	ca. 1100–25
81943	676.74	Omkaresvara temple – Mahakalesvara garbhagrha, mulaprasada, second storey, wall detail	ca. 1100–25
81944	*676.100*[271]	Mamlesvara temple – South bhadra niche, *Tripurantaka*[272]	ca. 1000–99
81945	676.63	Dwarkadhisa temple – Garbhagrha, doorframe	ca. 1100–99
81946	676.64	Dwarkadhisa temple – Garbhagrha, doorframe, left jamb, base	ca. 1100–99
81947	673.70	Siddhesvara temple – General view from the north-west	ca. 1100–50
81948	673.62	Siddhesvara temple – A view from the north	ca. 1100–50
81949	673.53	Siddhesvara temple – Garbhagrha doorframe on west	ca. 1100–50
81950	673.54	Siddhesvara temple – Garbhagrha, doorframe on west, left jamb, detail	ca. 1100–50
81951	673.72	Siddhesvara temple – east doorframe, left jamb	ca. 1100–50
81952	673.76	Siddhesvara temple – doorframe on south, left jamb	ca. 1100–50
81953	673.71	Siddhesvara temple – east doorframe, right jamb, base	ca. 1100–50
81954	673.64	Siddhesvara temple – Jagati, view from the north-east	ca. 1100–50
81955	673.77	Siddhesvara temple – Jagati, detail	ca. 1100–50
81956	673.68	Siddhesvara temple – Mandapa, east entrance, pillar	ca. 1100–50
81957	673.66	Siddhesvara temple – Mandapa, east face, pillar bracket	ca. 1100–50

271 The negative number of this photograph is separated from the otherwise unbroken series (676.61-75) by 25 numbers. A search for Nos. 676.76-99 yields no results in the DSAL database.

272 Wrong identification, the figure really represents Andhakāri, see above, fn. 44.

Acc.-No.	*Neg.-No.*	*Caption / Description*	*Date (CE)*
81958	673.67	Siddhesvara temple – Mandapa, east face, pillar bracket	ca. 1100–50
81959	673.59	Siddhesvara temple – Mandapa, ceiling	ca. 1100–50
81960	*673.70*[273]	Siddhesvara temple – Mandapa, pillars	ca. 1100–50
81961	673.69	Siddhesvara temple – Mandapa, pillars	ca. 1100–50
81962	673.60	Siddhesvara temple – Mandapa, pillar bracket	ca. 1100–50
81963	673.58	Siddhesvara temple – Mandapa, pillar detail	ca. 1100–50
81964	673.56	Siddhesvara temple – Mandapa, pillar detail	ca. 1100–50
81965	673.57	Siddhesvara temple – Mandapa, pillar detail	ca. 1100–50
81966	673.55	Siddhesvara temple – Mandapa, pillars on west	ca. 1100–50
81967	673.63	Siddhesvara temple – North face, eastern end, view from the north-east	ca. 1100–50
81968	673.65	Siddhesvara temple – East face, north end, jagati view	ca. 1100–50
81969	673.78	Siddhesvara temple – Loose sculpture	ca. 1100–50
81970	673.79	Siddhesvara temple – Bhairava bust lying in garbhagrha	ca. 1100–50

273 This is apparently a mistake; the number should be 673.61 as 673.70 already corresponds with Acc.No. 81947, above.

APPENDIX 3 – Residents and/or donees listed in inscriptions found at Oṃkāreśvar-Māndhātā

Māndhātā Grant of Jayasiṃha I, VS 1112 (1055 CE)[274]

*Brāhmaṇa*s of the *paṭṭaśāla* at Amareśvara.

Māndhātā Amareśvara Temple Stone Inscription, VS 1120 (1063 CE)[275]

1) *pāśupatācārya bhaṭṭāraka śrī* Bhāvavālmīka. He originally hailed from Naṃdiyaḍa and lived in the Someśvaradevamaṭha at Bhojanagara.
2) *bhaṭṭāraka śrī* Bhāvasamudra (disciple of 1).
3) *paṃdita* Bhāvavirimcī.
4) *paramabhaṭṭāraka śrī* Supūjitarāsiḥ.
5) Vivekarāsiḥ (disciple of 4).
6) *paṃdita* Gāndhadhvaja (engraver of the inscription, disciple of 5).

Māndhātā Copper-Plates of Devapāla, VS 1282 (1225 CE)[276]

Name	*Surname*	*Gotra*	*Vedaśākhā*[277]	*Place of origin*[278]
1) Gaṅgādhara	Śrotriya	Parāśara	ŚYV Vājimādhyandina	Āśrama
2) Bhadreśvara	Śukla	Pavitra	RV Āśvalāyana	Mahāvana
3) Candrakaṇṭha	Śukla	Pavitra	RV Āśvalāyana	Mahāvana
4) Nārāyaṇa	Dīkṣita	Audalya	ŚYV Mādhyandina	Mahāvana
5) Śūra	Triveda	Kātyāyana	SV	Mahāvana
6) Viśveśvara	Triveda	Bhāradvāja	SV Kauthuma	Ṭakārī
7) Rāma	Dīkṣita	Bhāradvāja	ŚYV Mādhyandina	Ṭakārī
8) Bhṛgu	Paṇdita	Bhāradvāja	*omitted*	Tripurī
9) Nārāyaṇa	Agnihotrin	Kāśyapa	RV Āśvalāyana	Mutāvathū
10) Gosala	Rājan	Parāvasu	*omitted*	Akolā
11) Gose	Mahārāja-paṇḍita	Vāśiṣṭha	RV Āśvalāyana	Mathurā

---

274 Eds. KIELHORN 1895, MITTAL 1979: 86–91 and TRIVEDI 1978: 61–64.

275 An edition of the relevant portion of the inscription is found in CHAKRAVARTI 1948.

276 Eds. KIELHORN 1908: 103–117, MITTAL 1979: 252–267 and TRIVEDI 1978: 175–185.

277 RV = Ṛgveda; ŚYV = Śuklayajurveda; KYV = Kṛṣṇayajurveda; SV = Sāmaveda.

278 For a possible identification of the 'places of origin' see the respective inscription's editions, especially those of KIELHORN.

12) Rāmeśvara	Caturveda	Bhārgava	RV Āśvalāyana	Mathurā
13) Gadādhara	Caturveda	Kāśyapa	RV Āśvalāyana	Mathurā
14) Garbheśvara	Caturveda	Bhārgava	RV Āśvalāyana	Mathurā
15) Lohaṭa	Caturveda	Kāśyapa	RV Āśvalāyana	Mathurā
16) Puruśottama	Caturveda	Gautama	RV Śāṅkhāyana	Diṇḍvānaka
17) Gadādhara	Dviveda	Kāśyapa	ŚYV Mādhyandina	Mutāvathū
18) Udāī	*omitted*	Kāśyapa	ŚYV Mādhyandina	Mutāvathū
19) Kuladhara	Paṇḍita	Gautama	SV Kauthuma	Mahāvana
20) Abhinanda	Āvasathika	Vatsa	SV Kauthuma	Ṭakārī
21) Ananta	Agnihotrin	Mudgala	ŚYV Mādhyandina	Madhyadeśa
22) Sthāneśvara	Agnihotrin	Śāṇḍilya	ŚYV Mādhyandina	Madhyadeśa
23) Ūdha[ra]	Caturveda	Dhaumya	RV Āśvalāyana	Mathurā
24) Kuladhara	Triveda	Bhāradvāja	SV Rāṇāyanī	Mathurā
25) Madhusūdana	Triveda	Bhāradvāja	SV Rāṇāyanī	Mathurā
26) Alli	Caturveda	Haritakutsa	KYV Kaṭha	Sarasvatī
27) Lāhaḍa	Dīkṣita	Kāśyapa	ŚYV Mādhyandina	Madhyadeśa
28) Narasiṃha	Āvasathika	Śāṇḍilya	ŚYV Mādhyandina	Madhyadeśa
29) Mārkaṇḍeya	Āvasathika	Mārkaṇḍeya	ŚYV Mādhyandina	Madhyadeśa
30) Vāyudeva	Pāṭhaka	Bhāradvāja	ŚYV Mādhyandina	Madhyadeśa
31) Rāje	Caturveda	Kautsa	RV Āśvalāyana	Mathurā
32) Kusumapāla	Paṇḍita	Pārāśara	SV Kauthuma	Hastināpura

Māndhātā Copper-Plates of Jayasiṃha-Jayavarman II, VS 1317 (1261 CE)[279]

Name	*Surname*	*Gotra*	*Vedaśākhā*	*Place of origin*
1) Mādhava	Agnihotrin	Bhārgava	ŚYV Mādhyandina	Navagāṃva
2) Janārdana	Caturveda	Gautama	RV Āśvalāyana	Ṭakārī
3) Dhāmadeva	Dviveda	Bhāradvāja	ŚYV Mādhyandina	Ghaṭāūṣari

279 Eds. KIELHORN 1908: 117–123, MITTAL 1979: 279–287 and TRIVEDI 1978: 200–206.

Māndhātā Copper-Plates of Jayasiṃha-Jayavarman II, VS 1331 (1274 CE)[280]

Name	*Surname*	*Gotra*	*Vedaśākhā*	*Place of origin*
1) Padmanābha	Dīkṣita	Gautama	RV	Ṭakārī
2) Mādhava	Caturvedin	Gautama	RV	Ṭakārī
3) Śrīkaṇṭha	Paṇḍita	Bhāradvāja	RV	Ṭakārī
4) Govardhana	Dvivedin	Kāśyapa	RV	Lakhaṇapura
5) Vāmana	Dīkṣita	Candrātreya	ŚYV Mādhyandina	Tolāpauha
6) Ananta	Avasathin	Vāśiṣṭha	ŚYV Mādhyandina	Ṭakārī
7) Hariśarma	Dvivedin	Bhāradvāja	ŚYV Mādhyandina	Ṭakārī
8) Mahādeva	Dvivedin	Kāśyapa	ŚYV Mādhyandina	Ṭenī
9) Harideva	Dvivedin	Kātyāyana	ŚYV Mādhyandina	Ṭakārī
10) Ananta	Dvivedin	Bhāradvāja	ŚYV Mādhyandina	Ṭakārī
11) Yogeśvara	Pāṭhin	Ātreya	ŚYV Mādhyandina	Ṭakārī
12) Nārāyaṇa	Trivedin	Vāśiṣṭha	SV Kauthuma	Ṭakārī
13) Puruṣū	Trivedin	Sāvarṇi	SV Kauthuma	Ṭakārī
14) Vāūṃ	Trivedin	Śāṇḍilya	SV Kauthuma	Ṭakārī

280 Eds. SIRCAR 1962, MITTAL 1979: 291–314 and TRIVEDI 1978: 209–227.

GLOSSARY[281]

abhayamudrā	hand gesture of assurance or protection
akṣamālā	rosary
akṣara	graphic representation of an Indian letter
āmalaka	ribbed crowning member of *nāgara* temples resembling a myrobalan fruit
aṅkuśa	an elephant driver's hook
antarāla	antechamber in front of sanctum door; vestibule
āsanapaṭṭa	seat-slab
āśram (H)	hermitage, dwelling of a *sādhu*
avatāra	divine incarnation
bābā (H)	colloquial for *sādhu*
bāṇaliṅga	conical polished stone from the Narmadā river held to represent Śiva
bāzār (H)	market
bhadra	central offset (wall division); principal projection, usually on a cardinal axis
bhojanālay (H)	a mess, eating hall
bhūmi	tier or storey of a *prāsāda*, horizontal division in a *latina śikhara*
bhūmija	architectural mode of the *nāgara* temple with continuous vertical chains of *kūṭastambhas*; superstructure type with corner and intermediate vertical bands made up of miniature shrines (*śṛṅga*s)
cakra	wheel, discus
caukīdār (H)	watchman, guard
ḍamaru	drum in the form of an hour-glass
devakoṣṭha	niche for a divinity; shrine
devapaṭṭa	a carved slab depicting religious themes
dharmśālā (H)	free-of-charge public lodging
dikpāla	guardian of the compass directions (eight, aṣṭadikpālā
dvār (H)	gate, doorway
dvārapāla	door-guardian
dvāraśākhā	band of doorframe ornament; doorjamb

281 Most of this glossary is compiled from the reference glossaries accompanying some volumes of the AIIS' *Encyclopaedia of Indian Temple Architecture* in combination with the glossary found in HARDY 1995: 387–391. All terms are Sanskrit, except those marked (H) which are Hindī/Urdū.

gadā	mace
garbhagṛha	'womb-house', sanctum, holy of holies
gauśālā	cowshed
gavākṣa	'cow-eye' or 'sun ray' aureole or horseshoe arch gable motif in *nāgara* temple architecture;
ghāṭ (H)	bathing place on the bank of a river or lake
gomukha	cow head
grāsamukha	gorgon face or head; *kīrttimukha*
grāsapaṭṭī	band of *grāsa* heads (*kīrttimukhas*) in file
guphā	cave
guru	(spiritual) teacher
haṃsa	goose, gander (decorative motif)
jagatī	temple platform in *nāgara* terminology
jāla	mesh design, grille, perforated screen
jaṅghā	wall, wall frieze; elevation between *vedībandha* and *śikhara*
kakṣāsana	seat-back, backrest
kalaśa	"pot, pitcher"; jar-shaped pinnacle of *śikhara*; also cushion moulding in plinth; torus moulding
kamaṇḍalu	small water pot
kapilī	walls projecting in front of the sanctum framing a vestibule, sometimes connecting the *prāsāda* to a portico or *maṇḍapa*
kapotikā	minor cyma-eave
khaṭvāṅga	club or staff with a skull at the top
kīrttimukha	'face-of-glory'; face of a monster, *vyāla*, lion; *grāsamukha*
kṣetra	field; area around a religious centre
kumbha	pot; foot moulding of the *vedībandha*
kumbhaka	base of a pillar or a pilaster
kūṭa	crowning pavillion; square aedicula of *prāsāda*; spirelet; representation of a square (occasionally circular, octagonal or stellate) pavilion, with domical roof
kūṭastambha	pillar form (usually embedded, as a pilaster) crowned by a *kūṭa*; miniature curvilinear or pyramidal shrine model placed over a pillaret (decorative motif or in vertical chains in the formation of a *bhūmija* superstructure)
lalāṭabimba	crest figure, central (rarely floral) symbol on door lintel
lalitāsana	posture of royal ease, with one leg folded and the other one hanging down
latā	'creeper'; projecting vertical band in a *nāgara śikhara*; curvilinear vertical band of *śikhara*, usually carrying *jāla*-web pattern

latina	the basic, unitary mode of *nāgara* shrines; North Indian mono-spired curvilinear *śikhara*-type with curved vertical bands (*latā*s) usually carrying *jāla*-pattern
liṅga	phallic emblem of Śiva
liṅgapīṭha	base of a *śivaliṅga*
mahāśivarātrī	annual Hindu festival, celebrated on the fourteenth day of the dark-half of the Hindu month *phālguṇ* (corresponding with February/March)
makara	crocodile-like mythical beast
maṇḍapa	pillared hall of temple, either closed (surrounded by walls), open (without walls, except perhaps at rear, where *vimāna* adjoins), or partially open
mandir (H)	temple
maṭha, maṭh (H)	monastery
mātṛkā	mother-goddess (seven, *saptamātṛkā*)
mukhamaṇḍapa	front hall; entry hall
mūlaprāsāda	main shrine, shrine proper, of a *nāgara* temple (as opposed to subsidiary shrines in a complex)
mūrti	sculpture of a divinity
nāga	snake
nāgara	North Indian temple style
nālā (H)	a ravine, rivulet, canal
nirandhāra	without *pradakṣiṇāpatha* (circumambulatory)
padma	lotus
padmāsana	lotus position, sitting posture with both legs crossed
pañcaratha	with five offsets from corner to corner
pañcaśākhā	having five *śākhā*s, with five jambs
pañcopacāra pūjā	religious ceremony with five offerings
parikramāpatha	circumambulatory path
pāśā	noose
phaṃsanā	shrine mode with pyramidal superstructure of tiered eaves-mouldings; tiered, pyramidal roof-type; 'wedge'; tier of pyramidal roof-type
pīṭha	pedestal or sub-base of a *nāgara* temple
prākāra	(walled) enclosure; enclosure wall
praṇāla	sacred drain; water chute; gargoyle
praṇava	the syllable *oṃ*
praśasti	praise, eulogy;
pratolī	gatehouse
pratīhāra	door-keeper, attendant
pūjā	religious ceremony
pujārī (H)	temple priest

śākhā	decorative door-band; door-jamb
samādhi	tomb
saṅgam (H)	confluence of rivers
śaṅkha	conch shell
saptamātr̥kā	seven "mothers" or mother-goddesses
saptaratha	with seven offsets
saptaśākhā	doorframe with seven jambs
sarvatobhadra	temple-type with four openings at cardinal directions
śekharī	one of the later, composite modes of *nāgara* temples
śikhara	whole superstructure or 'tower, spire' of a *mūlaprasāda*
śr̥ṅga	spirelet
tīrtha	sacred spot (often near water)
toraṇa	arch-like gateway; arch-like motif
triratha	plan/wall with three projections
triśākhā	doorframe with three *śākhā*s
triśūla	trident
udumbara	threshold; doorsill
uraḥśr̥ṅga	half *śikhara* form on the 'chest' (*uraḥ*) of a *śekharī* superstructure; conceptually an embedded, emergent *śikhara*
vāhana	mount
varadamudrā	hand gesture of conferring a boon
vedībandha	moulded base or 'plinth' of a *nāgara* temple
vīṇā	Indian lute

Abbreviations

AIIS	American Institute of Indian Studies.
ARASI	*Annual Report of the Archaeological Survey of India.* Delhi: Manager of Publications.
ASI	Archaeological Survey of India.
BIS	Berliner Indologische Studien (Berlin Indological Studies). Berlin: Weidler Verlag.
BL	British Library, London
CII	*Corpus Inscriptionum Indicarum.* New Delhi: Archaeological Survey of India.
CPG	*The Central Provinces Gazette.* Nagpur: Government Press.
DAAM	Directorate of Archaeology, Archives and Museums, Bhopal.
EI	*Epigraphia Indica.* Calcutta/New Delhi: Government of India Central Publication Branch/Archaeological Survey of India.
IA–R	Indian Archaeology – A Review. New Delhi: Archaeological Survey of India.
PRASWI	*Progress Report of the Archaeological Survey of Western India.* Bombay: Government of Bombay.
SSDh	Samarāṅgaṇasūtradhāra of Bhoja
V&A	Victoria and Albert Museum, London.
VS	*Vikrama saṃvat*

BIBLIOGRAPHY

AKTOR, Mikael

2015 The Śivaliṅga Between Artifact and Nature : The Ghṛṣṇeśvaraliṅga in Varanasi and the Bāṇaliṅgas from the Narmada River. In Knut A. JACOBSEN (ed.) – *Objects of worship in South Asian religions: forms, practices, and meanings*. London: Routledge: 14-34.

ALI, Rahman

2002 *Temples of Madhya Pradesh—The Paramāra Art*. New Delhi: Sundeep Prakashan.

ANONYMOUS

1823 Visit to Uooncan Mandatta. Journal of a visit to Uooncan Mandata, in May 1820. *The Calcutta Journal of Politics and General Literature* (Calcutta), 3.106 (May 3): 46–47. (Reprint 1824 in *The Asiatic Journal and Monthly Register for British India and its Dependencies* (London), XVII.XCVIII (For February 1824): 135–138.

AUFRECHT, Theodor

1859 *Catalogus Codicum Manuscriptorum Sanscriticorum Postvedicorum Quotquot in Bibliotheca Bodleiana Adversantur. Pars I.* Oxonii: E Typographeo Academico.

1864 *Codices Sanscriticos complectens.* (Catalogi codicum manuscriptorum Bibliothecae Bodleianae, Pars VIII). Oxonii: E Typographeo Clarendoniano.

ĀVṬE, Tryambak Harī (ed.)

1919 *Narmadāpañcāṅga*. Puneṃ: Indirā Pres.

BADER, Jonathan

2000 *Conquest of the Four Quarters. Traditional Accounts of the Life of Śaṅkara*. New Delhi: Aditya Prakashan.

BAL, Hartosh Singh

2013 *Waters close over Us. A journey along the Narmada*. Noida: Harper Collins/Fourth Estate.

BHATIA, Pratipal

1970 *The Paramāras*. New Delhi: Munshiram Manoharlal.

BLAKISTON, John Francis

1912 Nimar District. In SPOONER 1912: 41–42.

1938 *Annual Report of the Archaeological Survey of India, 1935–36.* Delhi: Manager of Publications.

BLOCH, Theodor

1900 *A List of the Photographic Negatives of Indian Antiquities in the Collection of the Indian Museum with which is incorporated the List of Similar Negatives in the Possession of the India Office.* Calcutta: Office of the Superintendent of Government Printing, India.

1908 *Annual Report of the Archaeological Survey of India, Eastern Circle for 1907-08.* Calcutta: The Bengal Secretariat Press.

BORDIA, Radhika

2007 Narmada: A River Interrupted. (Part of the documentary series *The Third Eye: India @60*, broadcast in September 2007 by New Delhi Television Limited (NDTV).[282]

CAINE, William Sproston

1891 *Picturesque India. A Handbook for European Travellers.* London: George Routledge and Sons.

CHAKRAVARTI, Niranjan Prasad

1948 A Note on the Halayudha Stotra in the Amaresvara Temple. *Epigraphia Indica* (New Delhi), XXV (1939–40): 183–185.

CHATTERTON, Eyre

1916 *The Story of Gondwana.* London: Sir Isaac Pitman & Sons.

CHOUBEY, M.C.

2006 *Tripurī. History and Culture.* Delhi: Sharada Publishing House.

COUSENS, Henry

1894 *Progress Report of the Archaeological Survey of Western India, For the months May 1893 to April 1894.* Bombay: Government of Bombay.

1897 *Lists of Antiquarian Remains in the Central Provinces and Berâr.* (Archaeological Survey of India, New Series, XIX). Calcutta: Office of the Superintendent of Government Printing, India.

282 Accessible at: http://www.ndtv.com/video/shows/the-third-eye/the-third-eye-india-60-narmada- river-interrupted-aired-september-2007-283920; [last retrieved Jan. 15, 2017].

1903 *Progress Report of the Archaeological Survey of Western India. For the year ending 30th June 1903.* Bombay: Government of Bombay.

1904 *Progress Report of the Archaeological Survey of Western India. For the year ending 30th June 1904.* Bombay: Government of Bombay.

1906 Conservations in the Central Provinces. *Archaeological Survey of India. Annual Report 1903–04.* Calcutta: Office of the Superintendent of Government Printing, India: 54–60.

CRÉMIN, Emilie

2005 *Omkareshwar, une ville sainte de la Narmada en cours de transformation.* Université Paris 8 Vincennes Saint–Denis. (Thesis submitted to the Département de Géographie).

DELAMAINE, James

1830 Account of Omkar. Sept.–Dec. 1830. *The Asiatic Journal and Monthly Register for British and Foreign India, China, and Australasia* (London), New Series, III: 207–210.

DEVA, Krishna

1975 Bhūmija Temples. In Pramod Chandra (ed.) – *Studies in Indian Temple Architecture.* [New Delhi]: American Institute of Indian Studies: 90–113.

DHAR, Parul Pandya

2010 *The Toraṇa in Indian and Southeast Asian Architecture.* New Delhi: D.K. Printworld.

FLEET, John Faithful

1910 Mahishamandala and Mahishmati. *Journal of the Royal Asiatic Society of Great Britain and Ireland* (London), April 1910: 425–447.

FORSYTH, James

1870a *Report on the Land Revenue Settlement of British Nimar; a district of the Central Provinces, 1868–69.* Nagpore: Chief Commissioner's Office Press.

1870b Mándhátá. In GRANT 1870: 257–265.

1871 *The Highlands of Central India.* London: Chapman & Hall.

GRANT, Charles (ed.)

1870 *The Gazetteer of the Central Provinces of India.* (2nd ed.) Nagpur: Education Society's Press.

HALL, Fitz–Edward

1860 Two Inscriptions pertaining to the Paramára Rulers of Málava: The Sanskrit, with Translations and Remarks. *Journal of the American Oriental Society* (New Haven), 7 (1860–63): 24–47.

HAMID, Maulvi Muhammad [MARSHALL, John Hubert]

1921 *Catalogue of the Photographic Negatives in the Office of the Director–General of Archaeology in India, Simla.* Calcutta: Superintendent Government Printing, India.

HARDY, Adam

1995 *Indian Temple Architecture: Form and Transformation.* Delhi: Indira Gandhi National Centre for the Arts.

2002 Śekharī Temples. *Artibus Asiae* (Zurich), 62.1 (2002): 81–137.

2007 Parts and Wholes: The Story of the Gavākṣa. In Adam HARDY (ed.) – *The Temple in South Asia, Vol. 2.* London: British Association for South Asian Studies: 63–82.

2012 Indian Temple Typologies. In Tiziana Lorenzetti & Fabio Scalpi (eds.) – *Glimpses of Indian History and Art: Reflections on the Past, Perspectives for the Future.* Roma: Sapienza Università: 101–125.

2014 Bhoja, Bhojpur and the Bhumija. In Michael Willis, P. Rag & O.P. Misra (eds.) – *Cities and Settlements, Temples and Tanks in the medieval Landscape of Central India.* Bhopal: Directorate of Archaeology, Archives and Museums.

2015a *Theory and Practice of Temple Architecture in Medieval India. Bhoja's Samarāṅgaṇasūtradhāra and the Bhojpur Line Drawings.* New Delhi: Indira Gandhi National Centre for the Arts.

2015b Ashapuri: resurrecting a medieval temple site. In A. Verghese & A.L. Dallapiccola (eds.) – *Art, Icon and Architecture in South Asia: Essays in Honor of Dr. Devangana Desai, Vol. II.* New Delhi: Aryan Books International: 333-348.

HAWKES, Jason D.

2014 Finding the "Early Medieval" in South Asian Archaeology. *Asian Perspectives* (Honolulu), 53.1: 53–96.

HAZRA, Rajendra Chandra

1963 *Studies in the Upapurāṇas. Vol. II (Śākta and Non–Sectarian Upapurāṇas).* Calcutta: Sanskrit College.

HELD, Patrick

*2015 *Der Siddhanātha-Tempel in Oṃkareśvar-Māndhātā*. (Unpublished M.A.–thesis submitted to the Kunsthistoprisches Institut der Freien Universität Berlin.) Berlin: unpublished.

HINGORANI, Ratan Pribhdas

1978 *Site Index to A.S.I. Circle Reports. A Cumulative Site Index to Annual Progress Reports (1881 to 1921) of Various Circles of the Archaeological Survey of India.* New Delhi: American Institute of Indian Studies.

HIRALAL

1916 *Descriptive List of Inscriptions in the Central Provinces and Berar.* Nagpur: Government Press.

1927 Śrī Magaradhvaja Yogī 700. *Indian Historical Quarterly* (Calcutta), III (1927): 408–411.

JOSHI, Nilkanth Purushottam

1992 *Devapattas*: A Less Known Chapter of Medieval Hindu Iconography. In T.S. Maxwell (ed.) – *Eastern Approaches. Essays on Asian Art and Archaeology.* Delhi: Oxford University Press: 133–140.

KIELHORN, Franz

1895 Mandhata Plates of Jayasimha of Dhara. [Vikrama–] Samvat 1112. *Epigraphia Indica* (Calcutta), III (1894–95): 46–50.

1908 Mandhata Plates of Devapala and Jayavarman II. of Malava. *Epigraphia Indica* (Calcutta), IX (1907–08): 103–123.

LONGHURST, Albert Henry

1907 *Annual Report of the Archaeological Survey of India, Eastern Circle for 1906-07.* Calcutta: The Bengal Secretariat Press.

MAJUMDAR, Susmita Basu & Vishi UPADHAYAY

2012 Did Magaradhvaja Yogī ever visit Bengal? A Case Study of three Image Inscriptions from Bangladesh. *Journal of Bengal Art* (Dhaka), 17: 177–188.

MARSHALL, John Hubert

1909 Conservation 1905–06. *Archaeological Survey of India. Annual Report 1905-06.* Calcutta: Office of the Superintendent of Government Printing, India: 1–9.

MELZER, Gudrun

*2002 *Gajasaṃhāramūrti und Andhakāsuravadhamūrti in der Ikonographie Śivas. Teil I und II.* (Revised version of a M.A.–Thesis submitted to the Institut für Indische Philologie und Kunstgeschichte der Freien Universität Berlin). Berlin: unpublished.

MITTAL, Amarcand

1979 *The Inscriptions of Imperial Paramāras.* Ahmedabad: L.D. Institute of Indology.

NEUSS, Jürgen

2012a *Narmadāparikramā – Circumambulation of the Narmadā River.* Leiden/Boston: Brill.

2012b On the Loss of Cultural Heritage in the Narmadā Valley. *Berliner Indologische Studien* (Berlin), 20: 195–248.

2013 Oṃkāreśvar–Māndhātā. Tracing the Forgotten History of a Popular Place. *Berliner Indologische Studien* (Berlin), 21(2013): 115–172.

2015 Unpublished Inscriptions from the Amareśvara Temple, Māndhātā. *Berliner Indologische Studien* (Berlin), 22: 123–150.

2016 A new type of 'Devapaṭṭa' and a few other Vaiṣṇava Icons from the Viṣṇu Temple, Māndhātā. In Parul Pandya Dhar, Gerd. J.R. Mevissen & Devangana Desai (eds.) – *Temple Architecture and Imagery of South and Southeast Asia.* (M.A. Dhaky Felicitation Volume). New Delhi: Aryan Books International: 208–220.

OTTER, Felix

2010 *Residential Architecture in Bhoja's Samarāṅgaṇasūtradhāra.* Delhi: Motilal Banarsidass.

PARGITER, Frederick Eden

1904 *The Mārkaṇḍeya Purāṇa.* Calcutta: The Asiatic Society.

1910 Mahismati, the Kaveri, and Maheswar. *Journal of the Royal Asiatic Society of Great Britain and Ireland* (London), July 1910: 867–869.

PASRICHA, Ram Nath

1972 Omkareshwar Mandhata. *Roopa Lekha* (New Delhi), XLII.1&2: 38-43.

RAG, Pankaj (ed.)

2012 *Known and Unknown. An Encyclopaedia of Historical Monuments of Madhya Pradesh, Vol. II.* Bhopal: Commissioner Archaeology, Archives & Museums.

RANGARAJAN, Haripriya

1997 *Varāha Images in Madhya Pradesh. An Iconographic Study.* Mumbai/Delhi: Somaiya Publications.

RUSSELL, Robert Vane (ed.)

1908 *Central Provinces District Gazetteers. Nimar District. Volume A. Descriptive.* Allahabad: The Pioneer Press.

SAGAR, A.P.

1979 Vajayamandira Temple of Paramāra Times at Vidishā. In R.K. Sharma (ed.) – *Art of the Paramāras of Mālwā.* Delhi: Agam Kala Prakashan.

SANKALIA, Hasmukh Dhirajlal, B. SUBBARAO & S. B. DEO

1958 *The Excavations at Maheshwar and Navdatoli 1952–53.* Poona/ Baroda: Deccan College Research Institute and M.S. University.

SEARS, Tamara I.

2014a *Worldly Gurus and Spiritual Kings. Architecture and Asceticism in Medieval India.* New Haven/London: Yale University Press.

2014b Mapping Omkareshvara's Early Medieval Past: Following Sculptural Fragments Along The *Parikrama Path.* In Michael Willis, P. Rag & O.P. Misra (eds.) – *Patrimoine Culturel de l'Eau. Cities and Settlements, Temples and Tanks in the Medieval Landscape of Central India.* Bhopal: Directorate of Archaeology, Archives and Museums: 113–131.

SHAINI, K.S.

2006 Narmada Manthan. *Outlook India* (New Delhi), October 18, 2006.[283]

SHRIVASTAV, P. N. (ed.)

1969 *East Nimar. Madhya Pradesh District Gazetteers.* Bhopal: District Gazetteers Department, Madhya Pradesh.

SIRCAR, Dinesh Chandra

1962 Mandhata Plates of Paramara Jayasimha–Jayavarman, V.S. 1331. *Epigraphia Indica* (New Delhi), XXXII (1957–58): 139–156.

SPOONER, David Brainerd

1912 *Annual Report of the Archaeological Survey of India, Eastern Circle for 1911–12.* Calcutta: The Bengal Secretariat Book Depôt.

283 Accessible at: http://www.outlookindia.com/magazine/story/narmada-manthan/235595; [last retrieved January 15, 2017].

1913 *Annual Report of the Archaeological Survey of India, Eastern Circle for 1912–13.* Calcutta: The Bengal Secretariat Book Depôt.

1924 *Annual Report of the Archaeological Survey of India, 1921–22.* Simla: Government of India Press.

THAKURIA, Tilok, T. PADHAN, R. K. MOHANTY & M. L. SMITH

2013 Google Earth as an Archaeological Tool in the Developing World. *The SAA Archaeological Record* (Washington DC), 13.1 (January 2013): 20–24.

TICHIT, Doria

*2010 *The Udayeśvara Temple, Udayapur: Architecture and Iconography of an 11th Century Temple in Central India. Volume I and II.* (Thesis submitted to Cardiff University for the degree of Doctor of Philosophy.) Cardiff: unpublished.

2012 Le programme iconographique du temple d'Udayeśvara à Udayapur, Madhya Pradesh, XIe siècle. *Arts Asiatique* (Paris), 67 (2012): 3–18.

TRIVEDI, Harihar Vitthal

1978 *Inscriptions of the Paramāras, Chandëllas, Kachchapaghātas and two minor dynasties.* (*CII* VII/II). New Delhi: Archaeological Survey of India.

1989 *Inscriptions of the Paramāras, Chandëllas, Kachchapaghātas and two minor dynasties.* (*CII* VII/III). New Delhi: Archaeological Survey of India.

WEBER, Albrecht

1853 *Verzeichniss der Sanskrit–Handschriften.* (Die Handschriften-Verzeichnisse der Königlichen Bibliothek herausgegeben von dem Königlichen Oberbibliothekar Geheimen Regierungsrath Dr. Pertz, Erster Band). Berlin: Verlag der Nicolai'schen Buchhandlung.

Illustrations

Maps

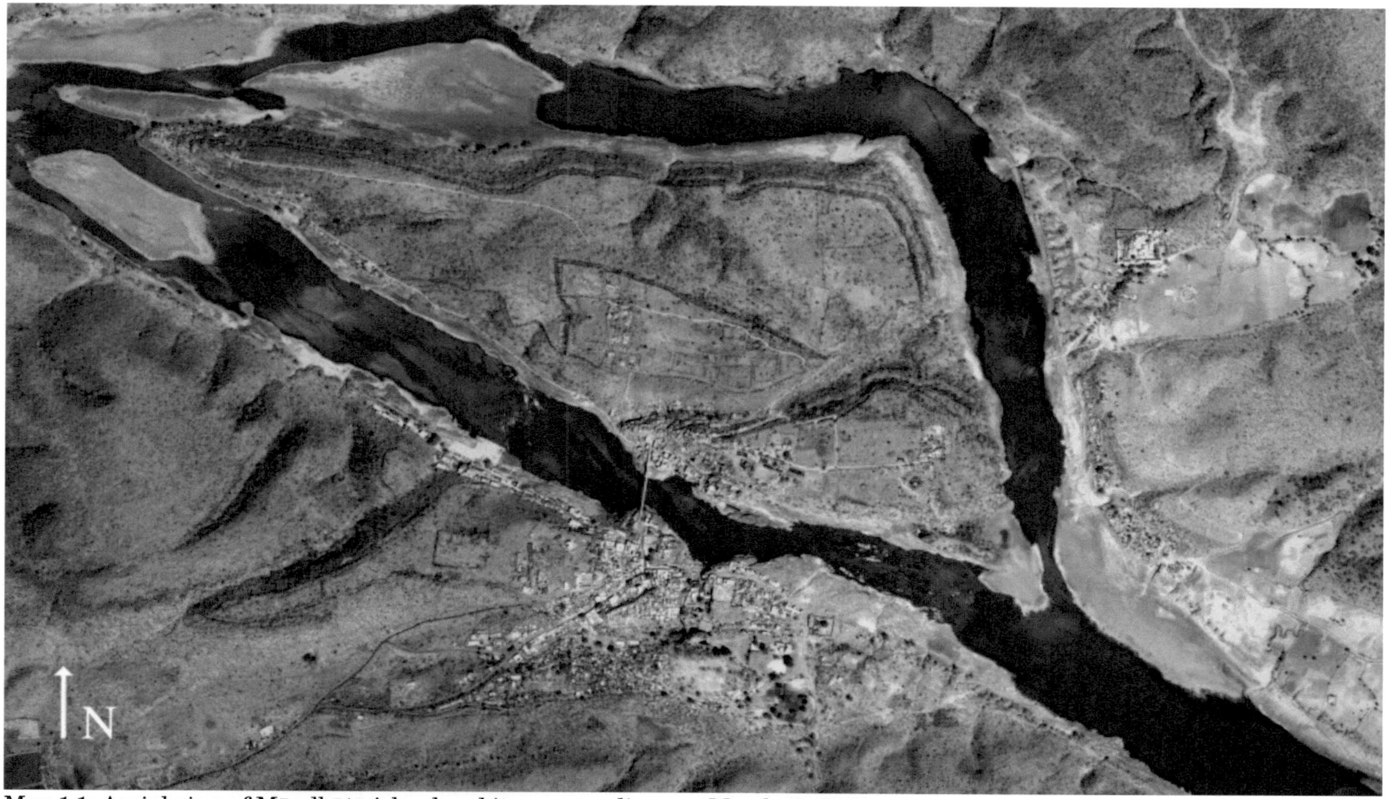

Map 1.1: Aerial view of Māndhātā island and its surroundings on March 17, 2001.

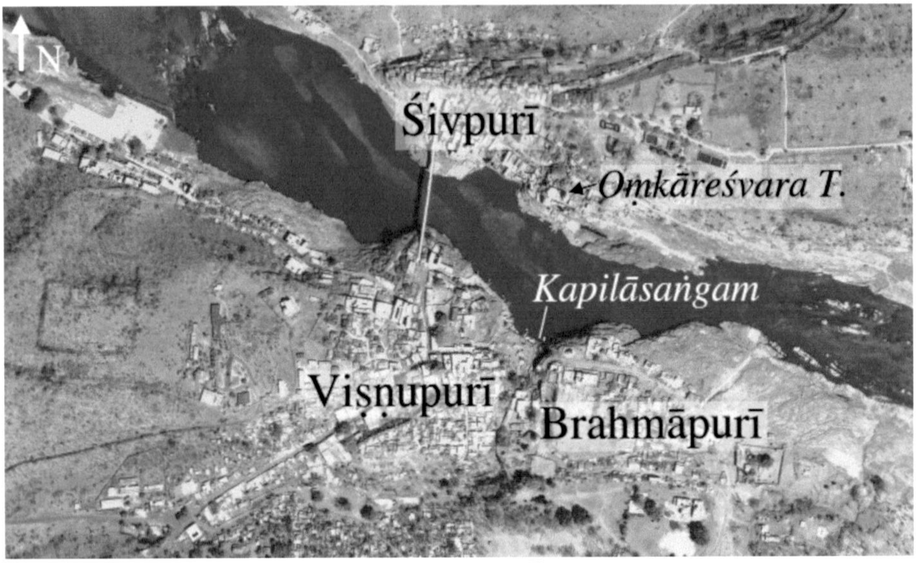

Map 1.2: Modern settlements at Oṃkāreśvar-Māndhātā.

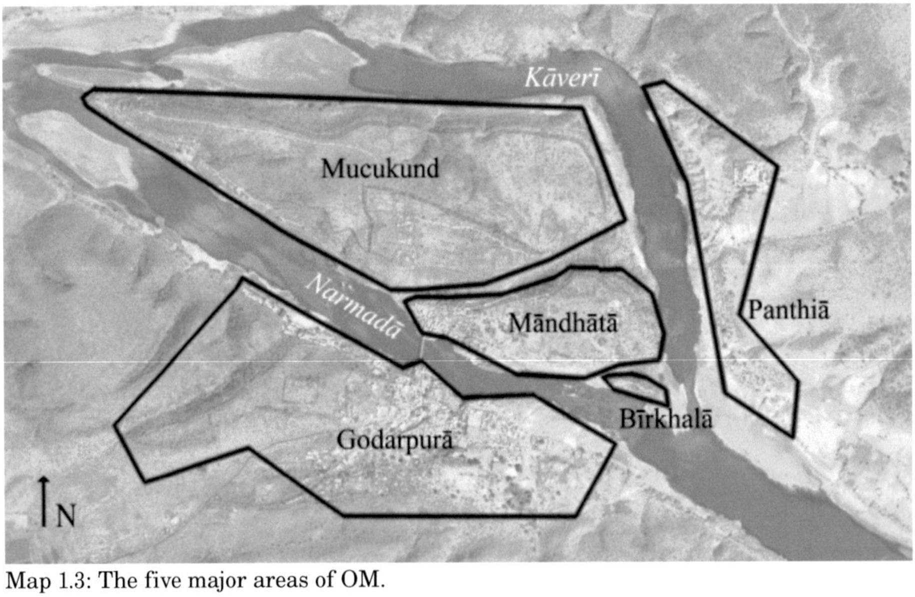

Map 1.3: The five major areas of OM.

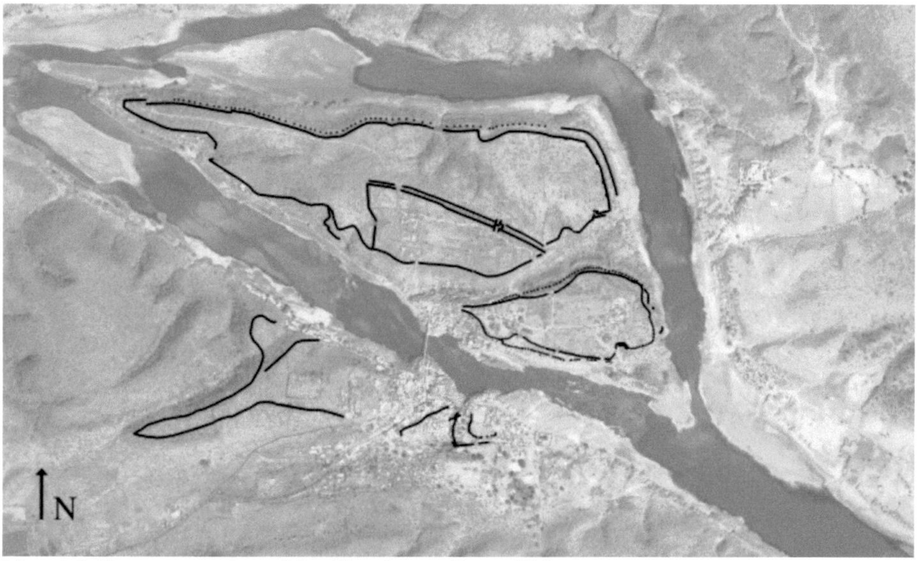

Map 1.4: Extant remains of fortification walls at OM.

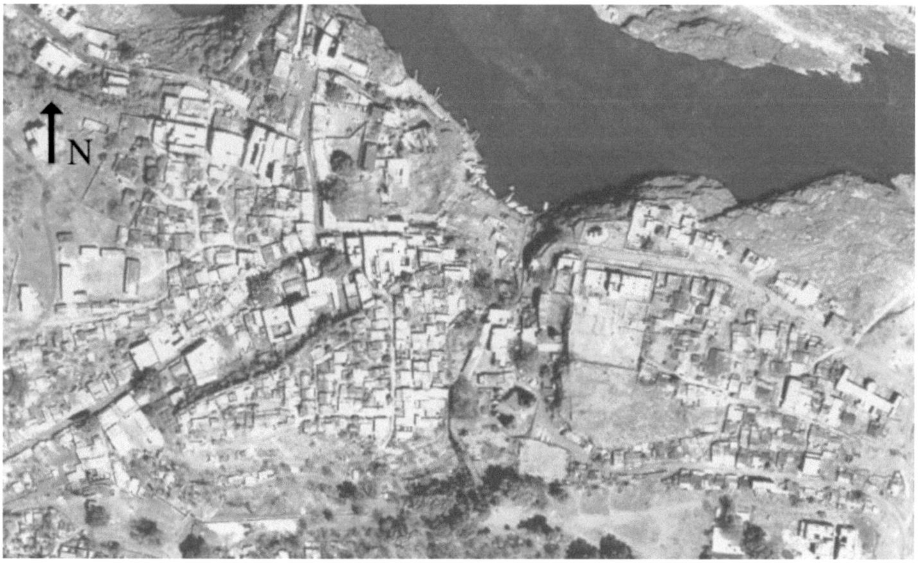

Map 2.1: Godarpurā, aerial view.

GODARPURĀ

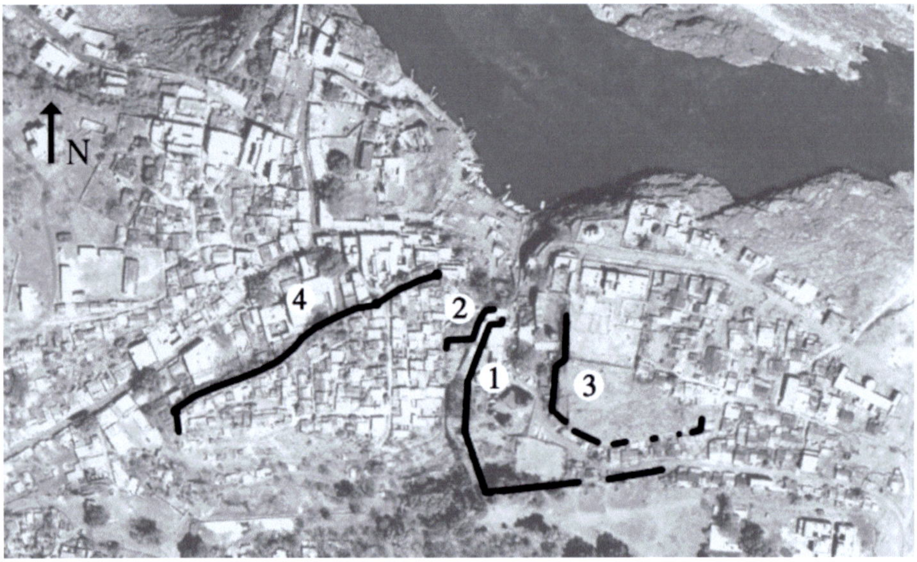

Map 2.2: Godarpurā, location of extant fortification walls.

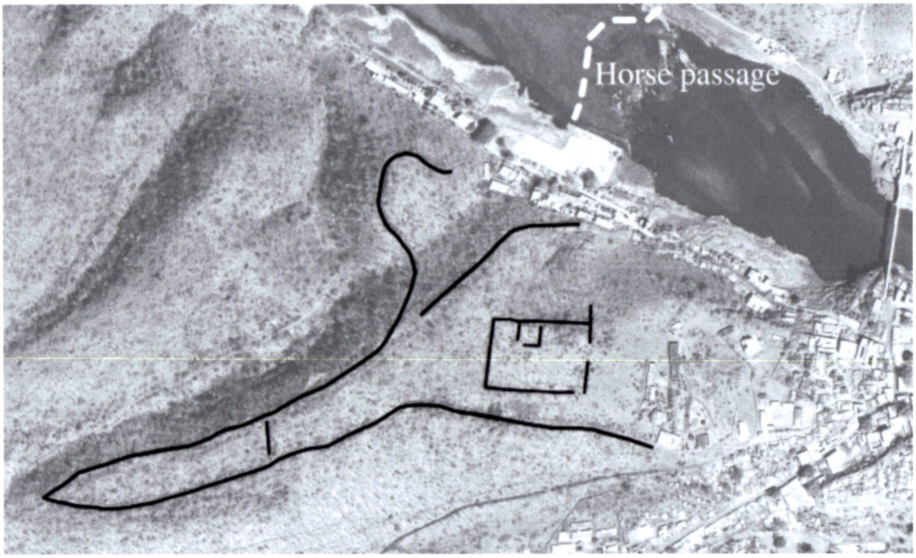

Map 2.3: Fortification walls and structures to the west of Viṣṇupurī.

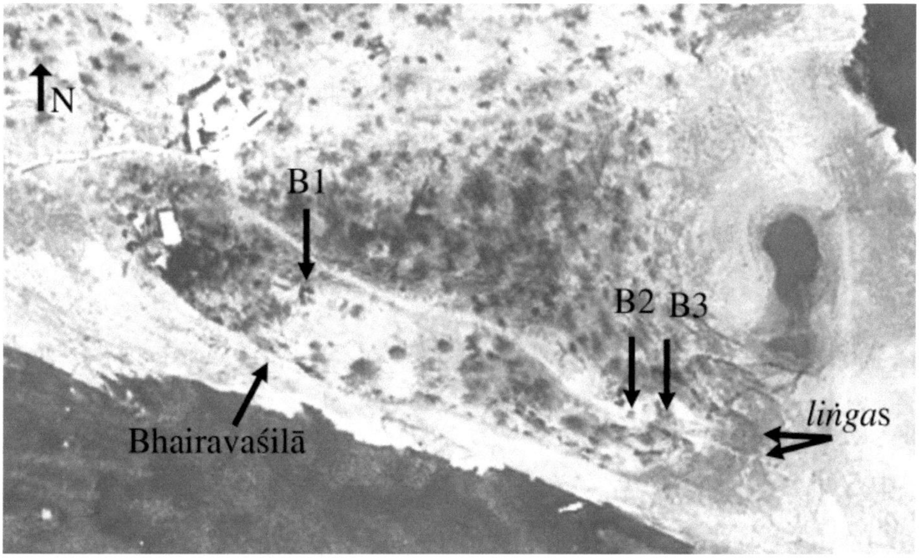

Map 3: Remains on Bīrkhalā hill.

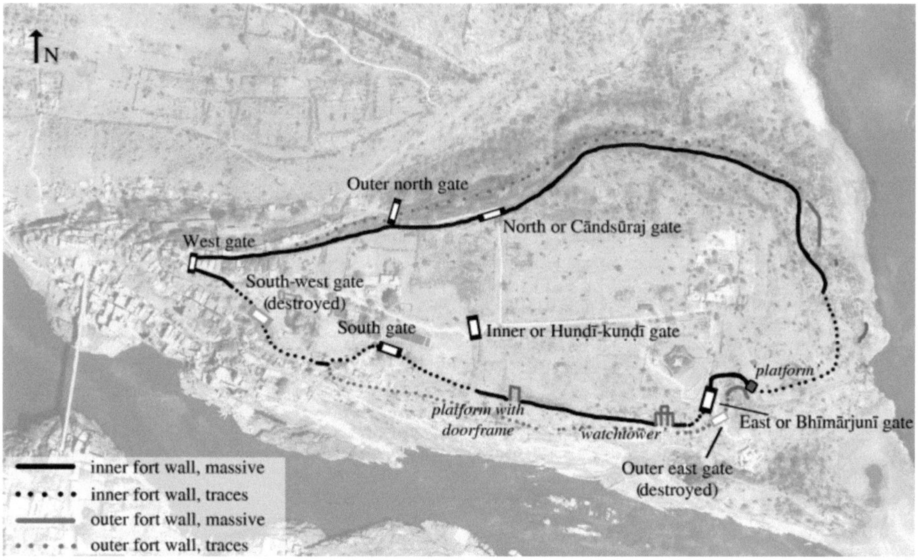

Map 4.1: Māndhātā hill, fortification walls and gateways.

MĀNDHĀTĀ HILL

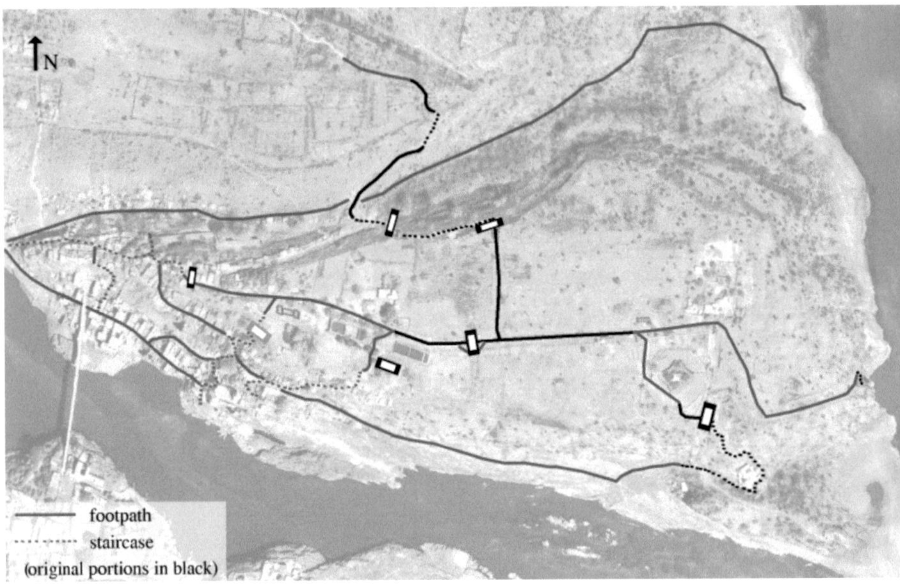

Map 4.2: Māndhātā hill, gateways, staircases and main footpaths.

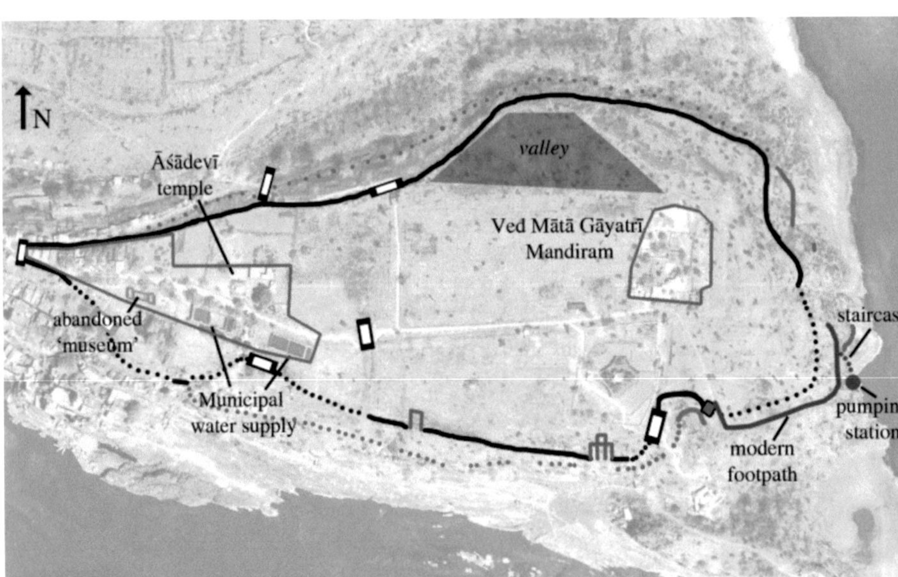

Map 4.3: Māndhātā hill, modern settlements.

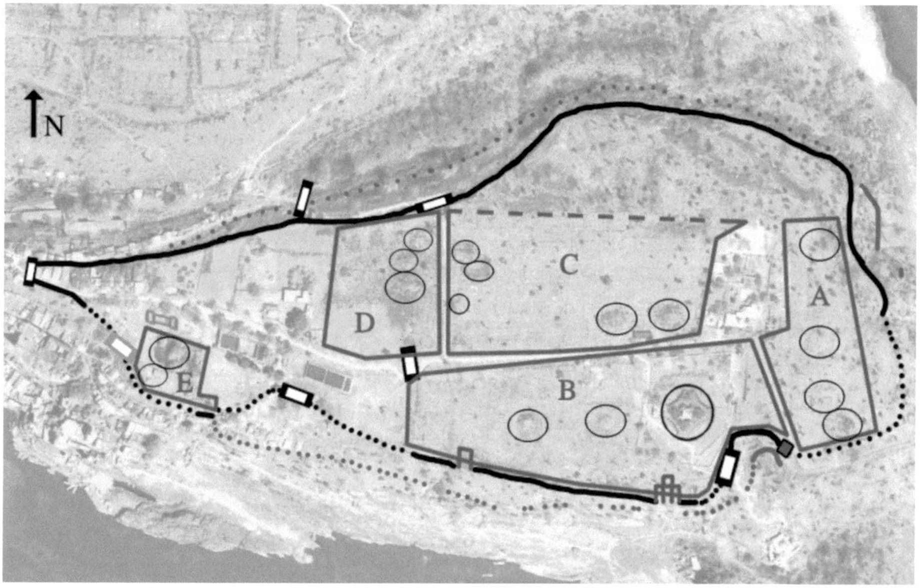

Map 4.4: Māndhātā hill, archaeological remains, settlement areas and structural mounds.

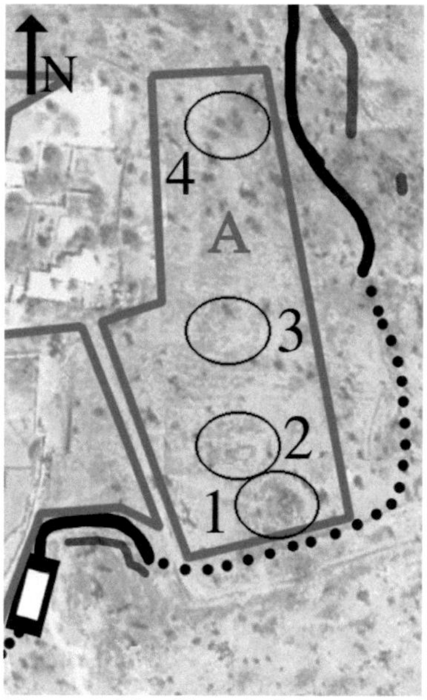

Map 4.5: Māndhātā hill, location of mounds in area A.

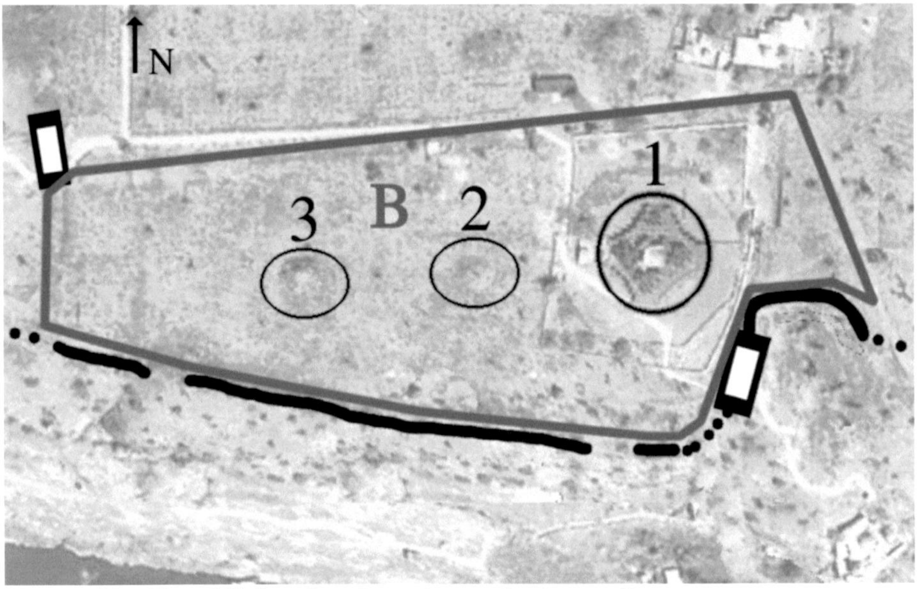

Map 4.6: Māndhātā hill, location of temple remains in area B.

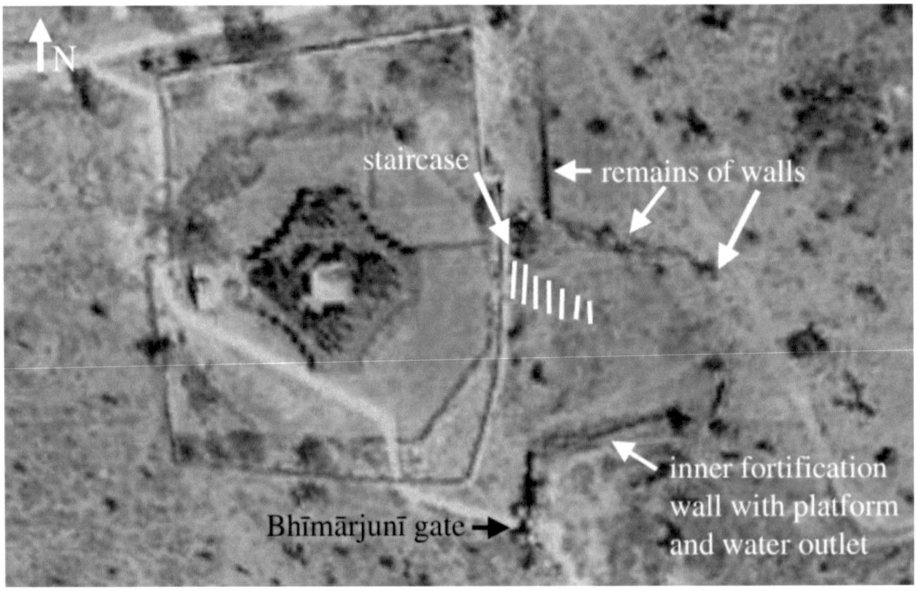

Map 4.7: Siddhanātha temple compound with surrounding area and structures.

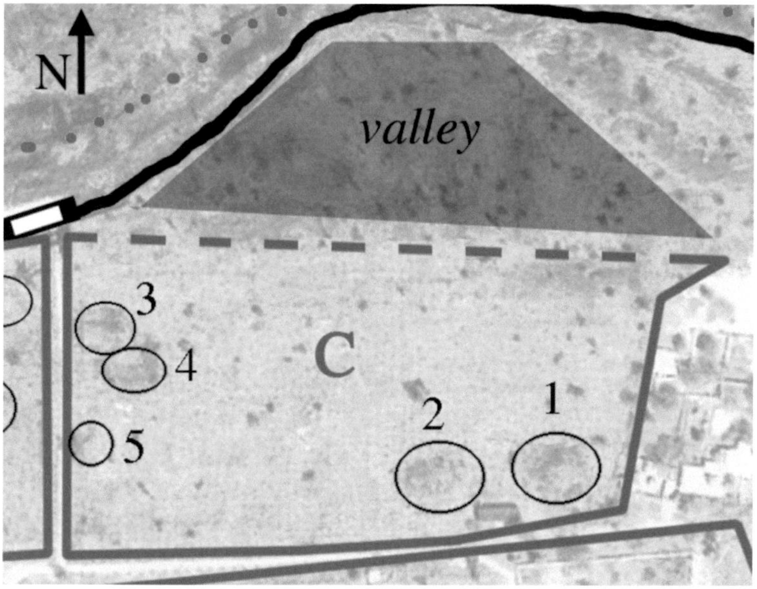

Map 4.8: Māndhātā hill, location of temple remains in area C.

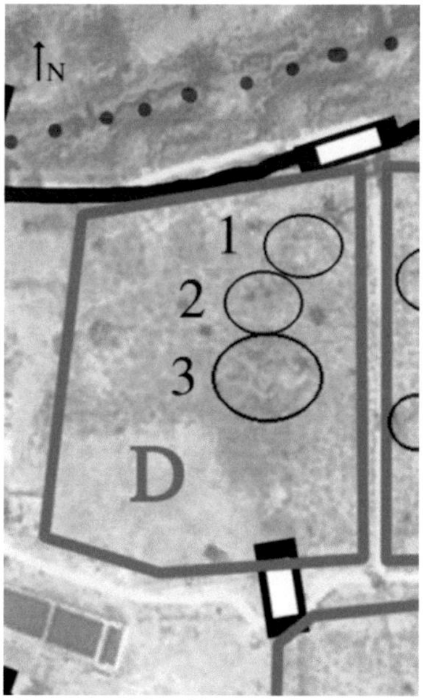

Map 4.9: Māndhātā hill, location of structures in area D.

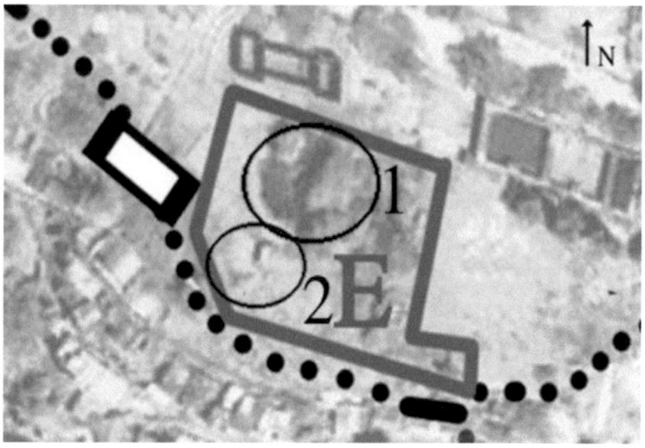

Map 4.10: Māndhātā hill, location of temples in area E.

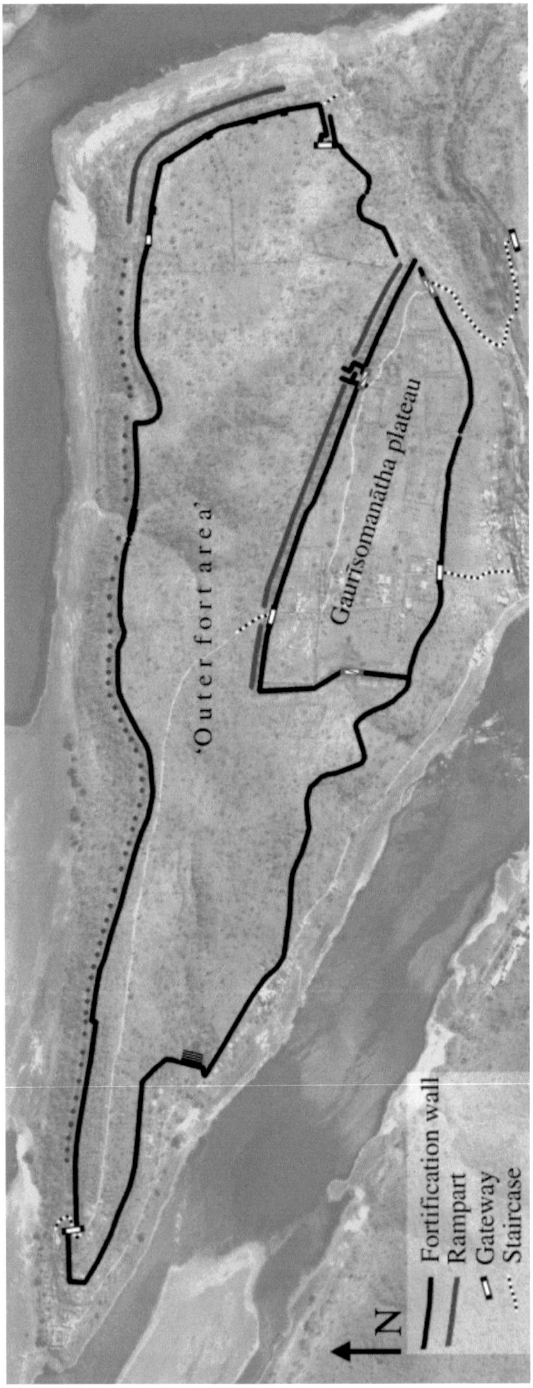

Map 5: Mucukund hill, fortification walls and gateways.

MUCUKUND HILL

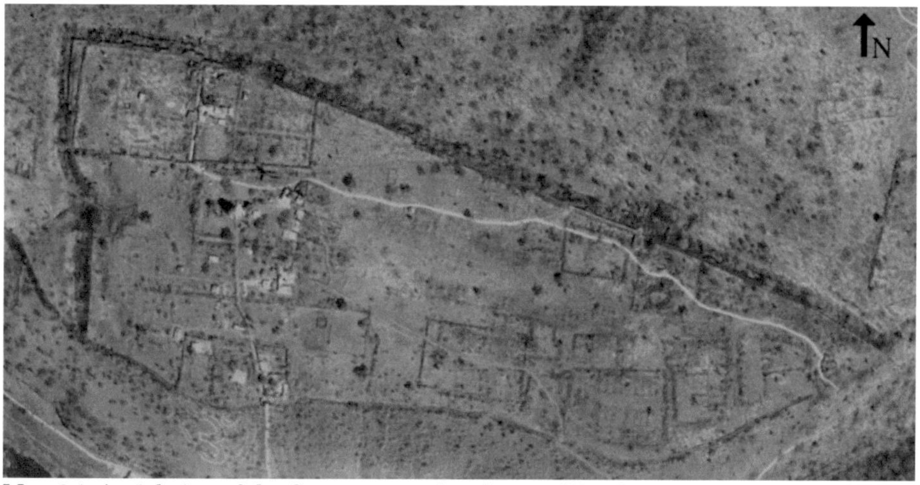

Map 6.1: Aerial view of the Gaurīsomanātha plateau (March, 2001).

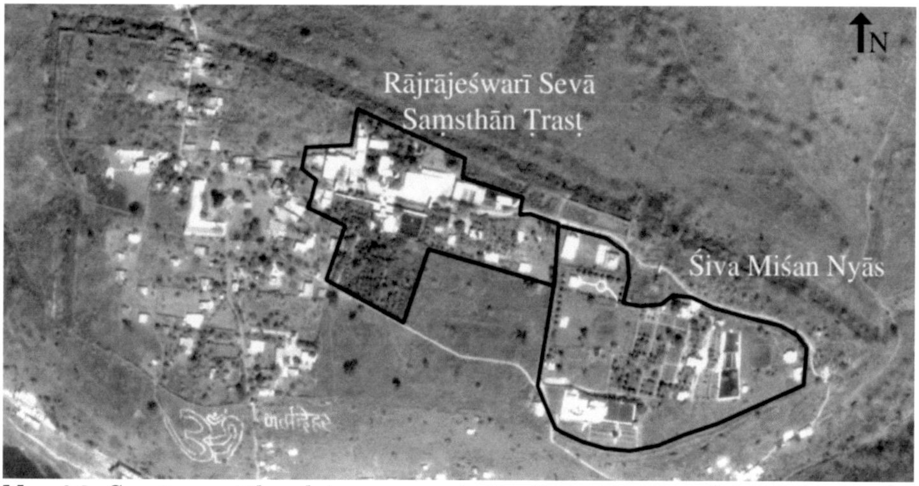

Map 6.2: Gaurīsomanātha plateau, present situation with encroachments by pseudo-religious trusts.

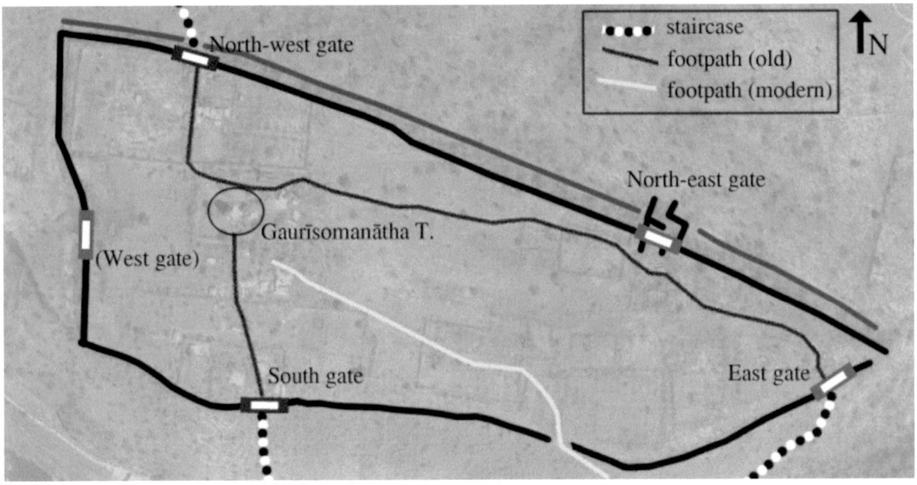

Map 6.3: Gaurīsomanātha plateau, staircases and footpaths.

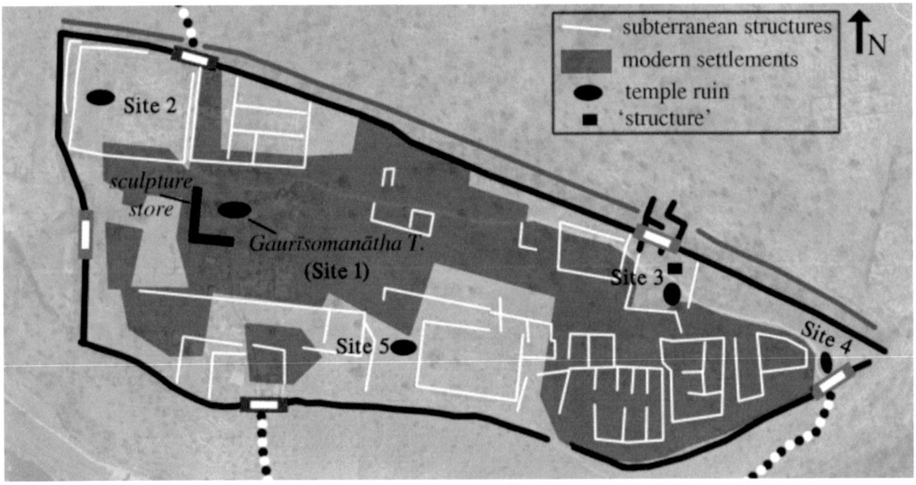

Map 6.4: Gaurīsomanātha plateau, archaeological remains.

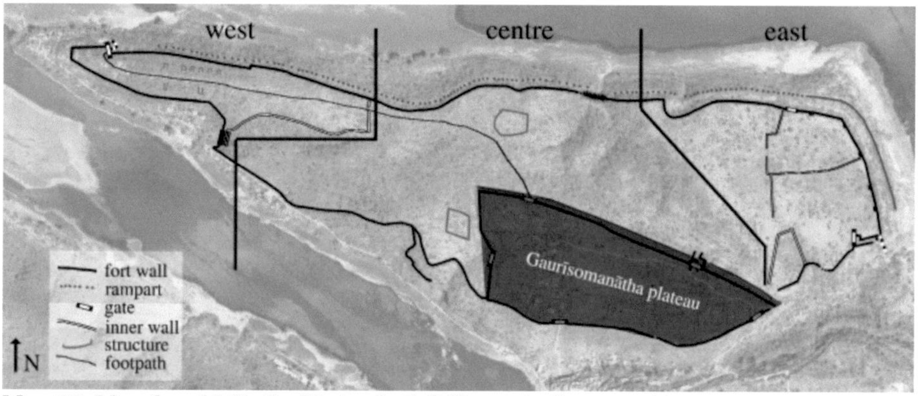

Map 7.1: Mucukund hill, the 'Outer fort', falling into three sections.

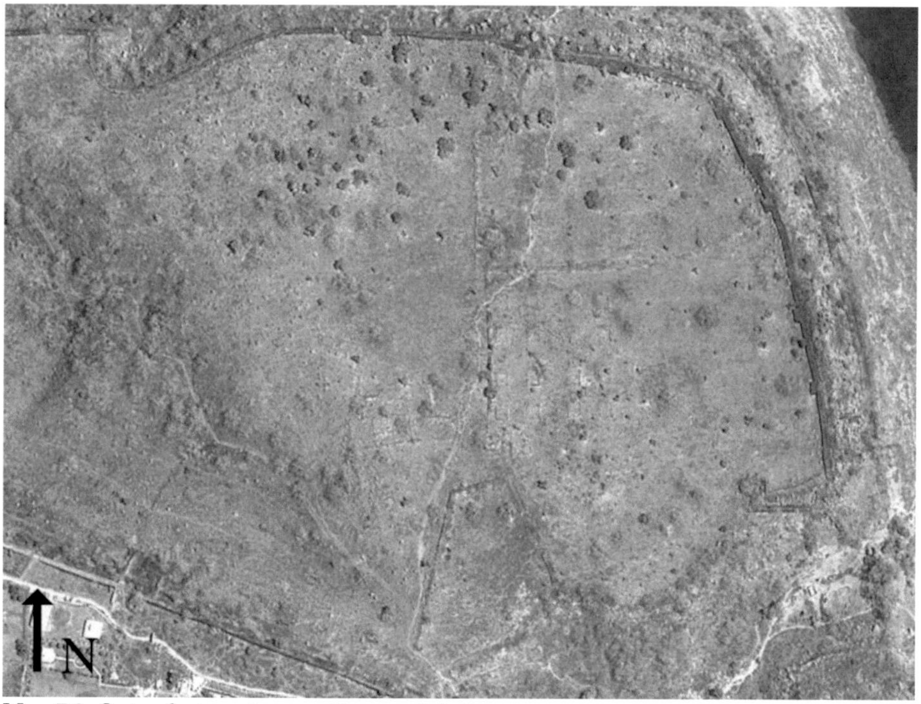

Map 7.2: Outer fort, eastern section, aerial view.

'OUTER FORT'

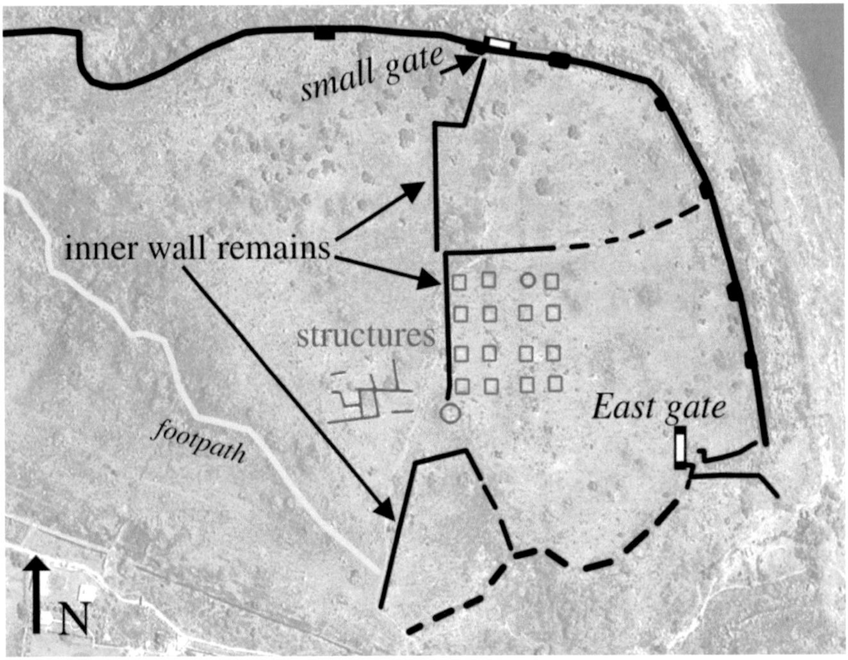

Map 7.3: Outer fort, eastern section, structural remains.

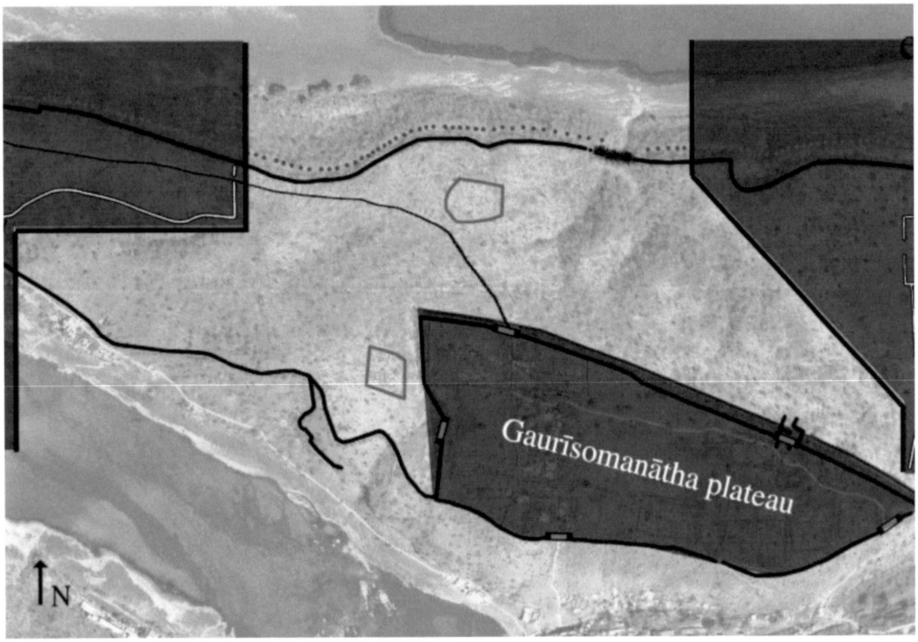

Map 7.4: Outer fort, central section, structural remains.

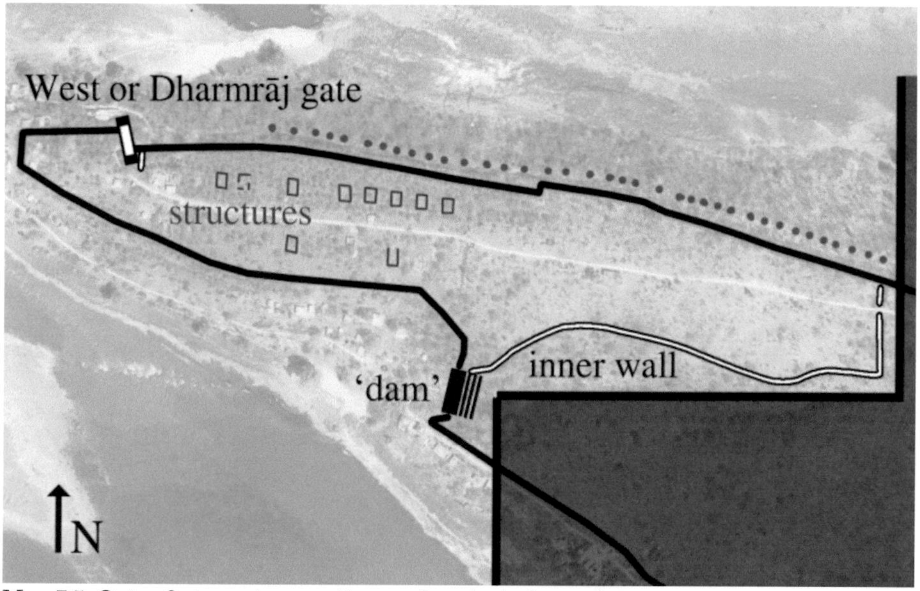

Map 7.5: Outer fort, western section, archaeological remains.

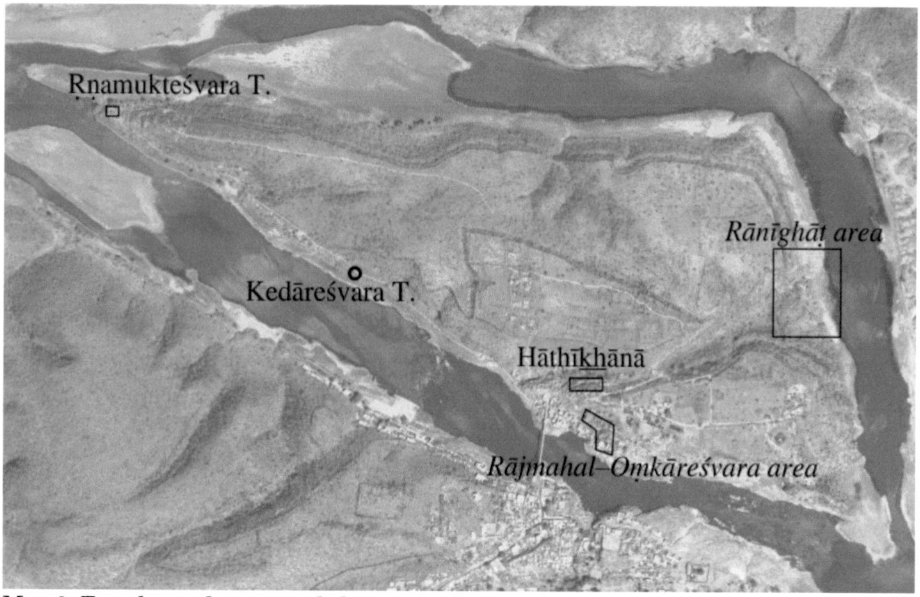

Map 8: Temples and structural clusters in the periphery, outside of fortified areas.

'OUTER FORT' / PERIPHERY

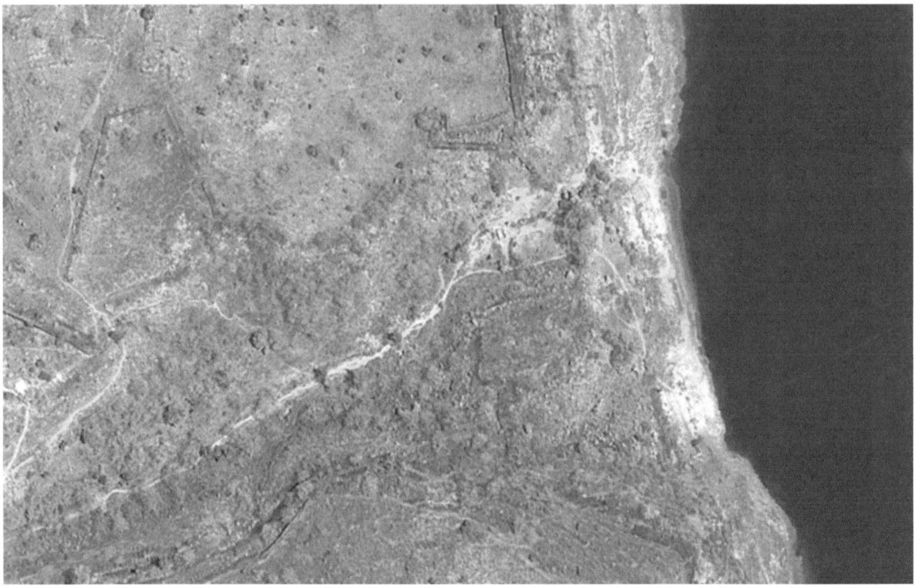

Map 9.1: The Rānīghāṭ area, aerial view.

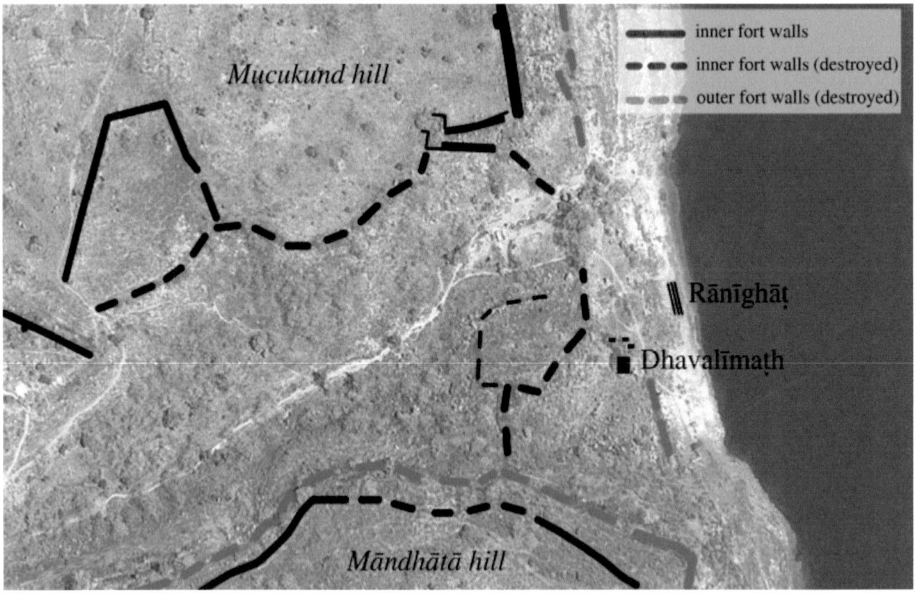

Map 9.2: Remains of fort walls and architectural structures in the Rānīghāṭ area.

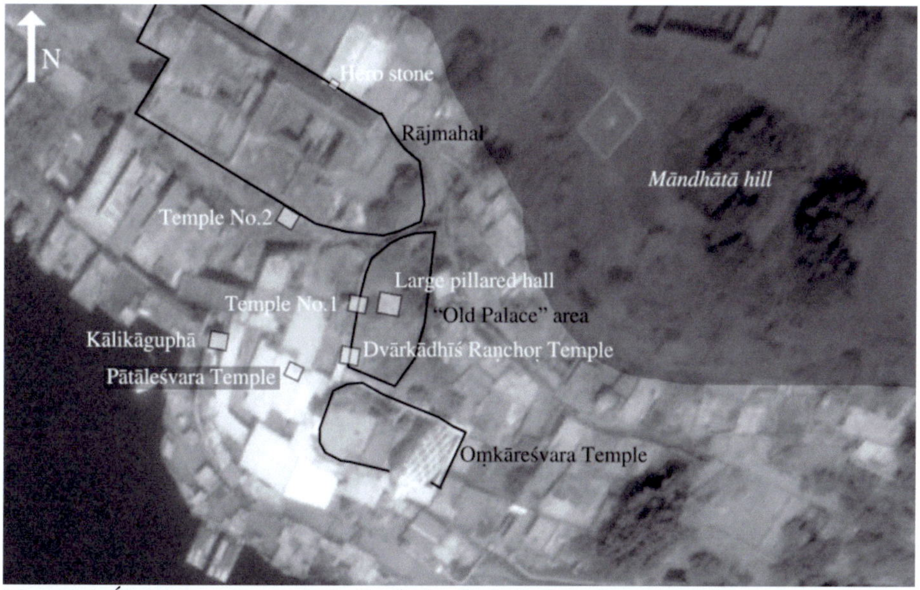

Map 10.1: Śivpurī, monuments in the Rājmahal–Oṃkāreśvara temple area.

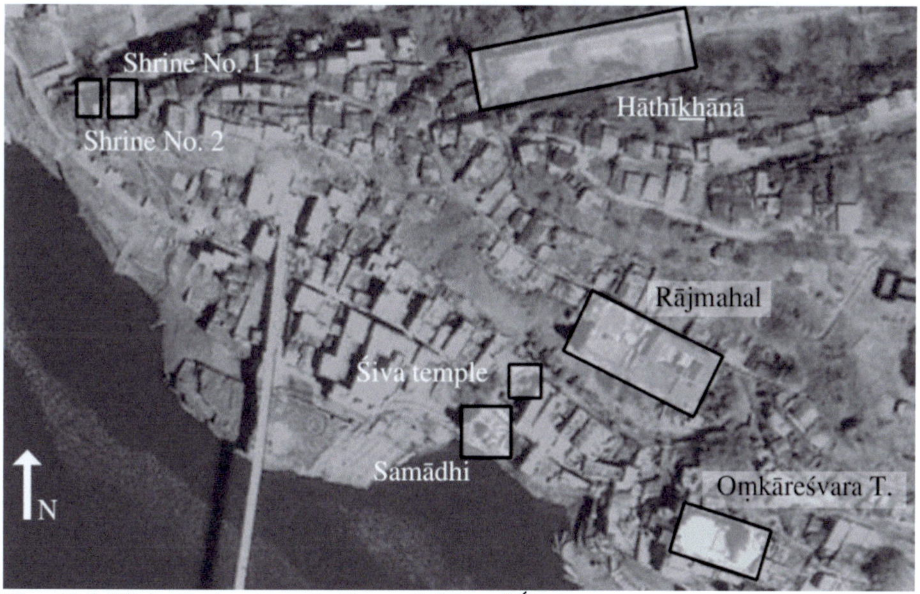

Map 10.2: Historic structures in the periphery of Śivpurī.

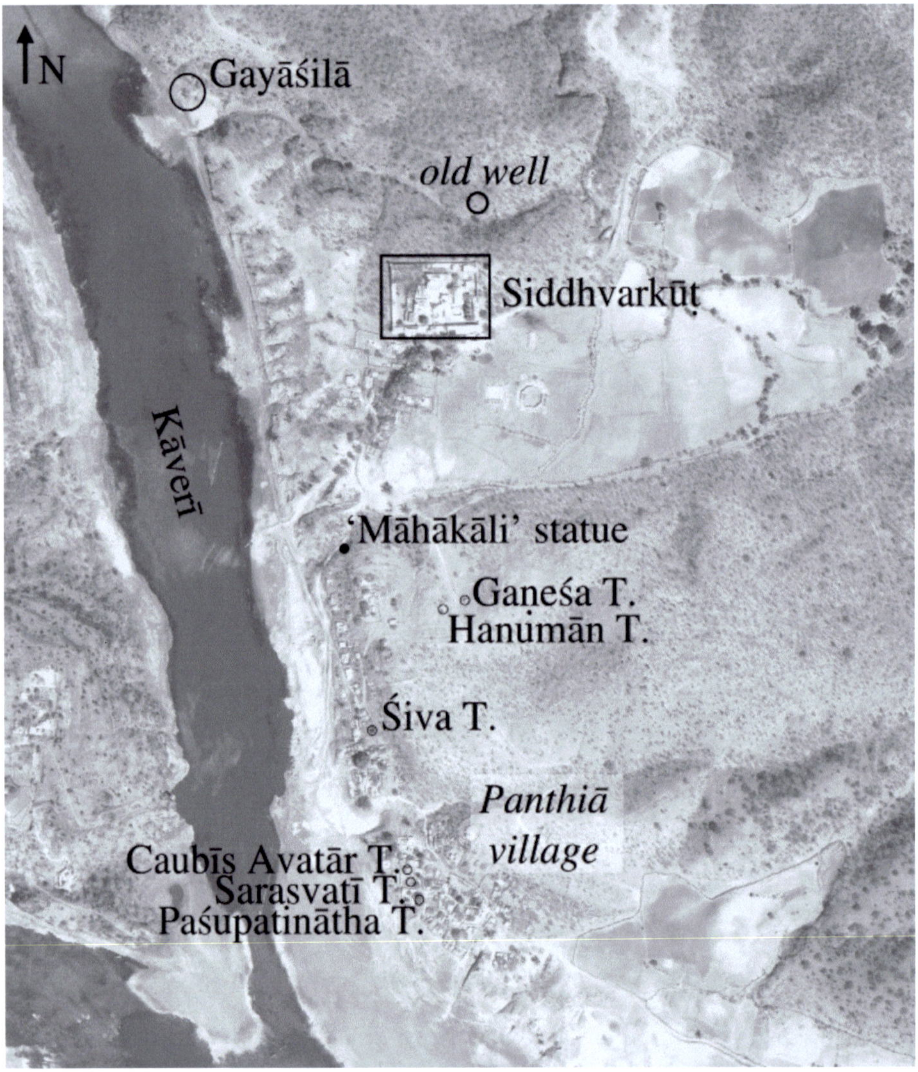

Map 11.1: Historic remains on the north bank of the Kāverī river (2001).

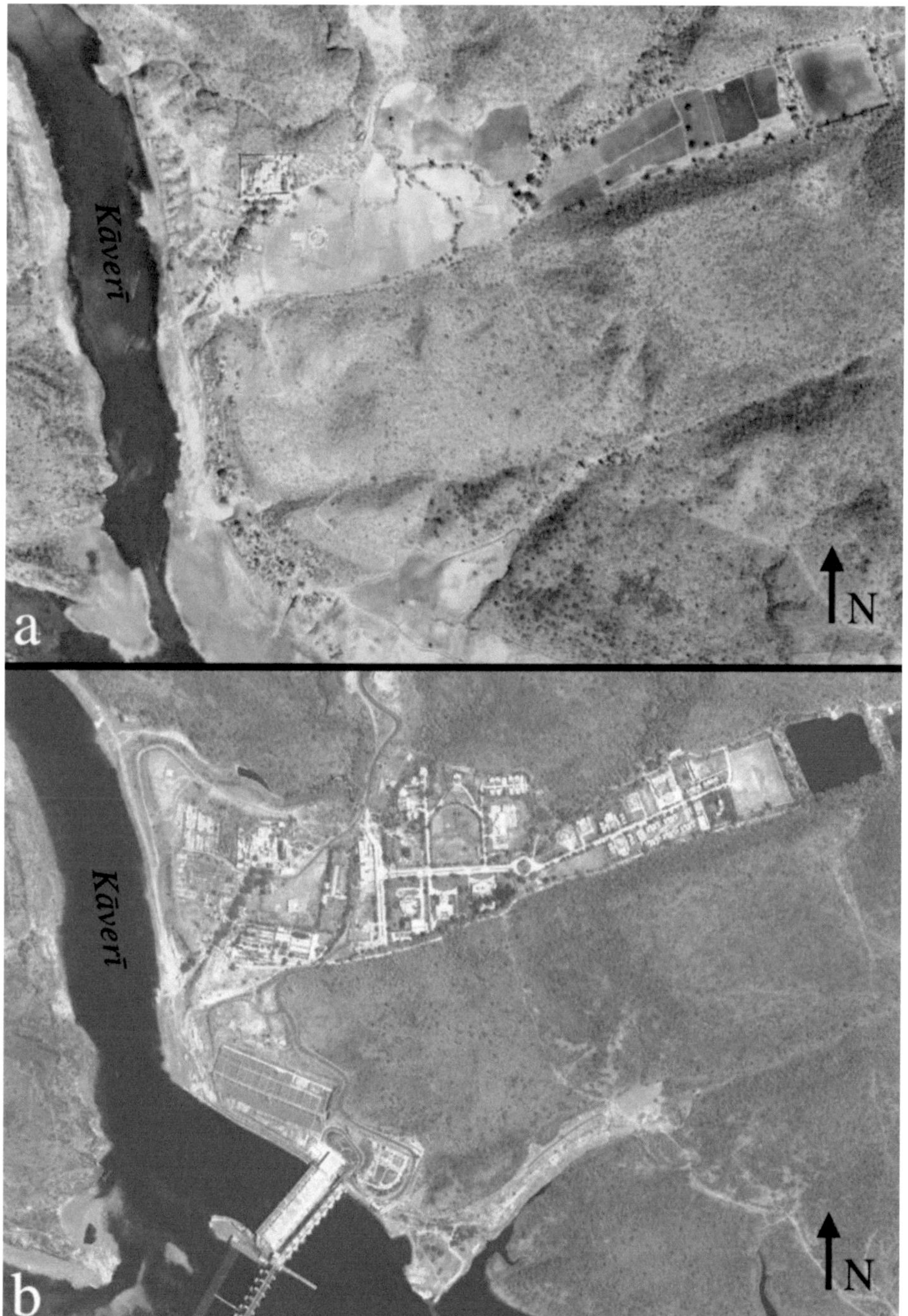

Map 11.2: Panthiā (a) before and (b) after the construction of the Oṃkāreśvar dam.

PANTHIĀ

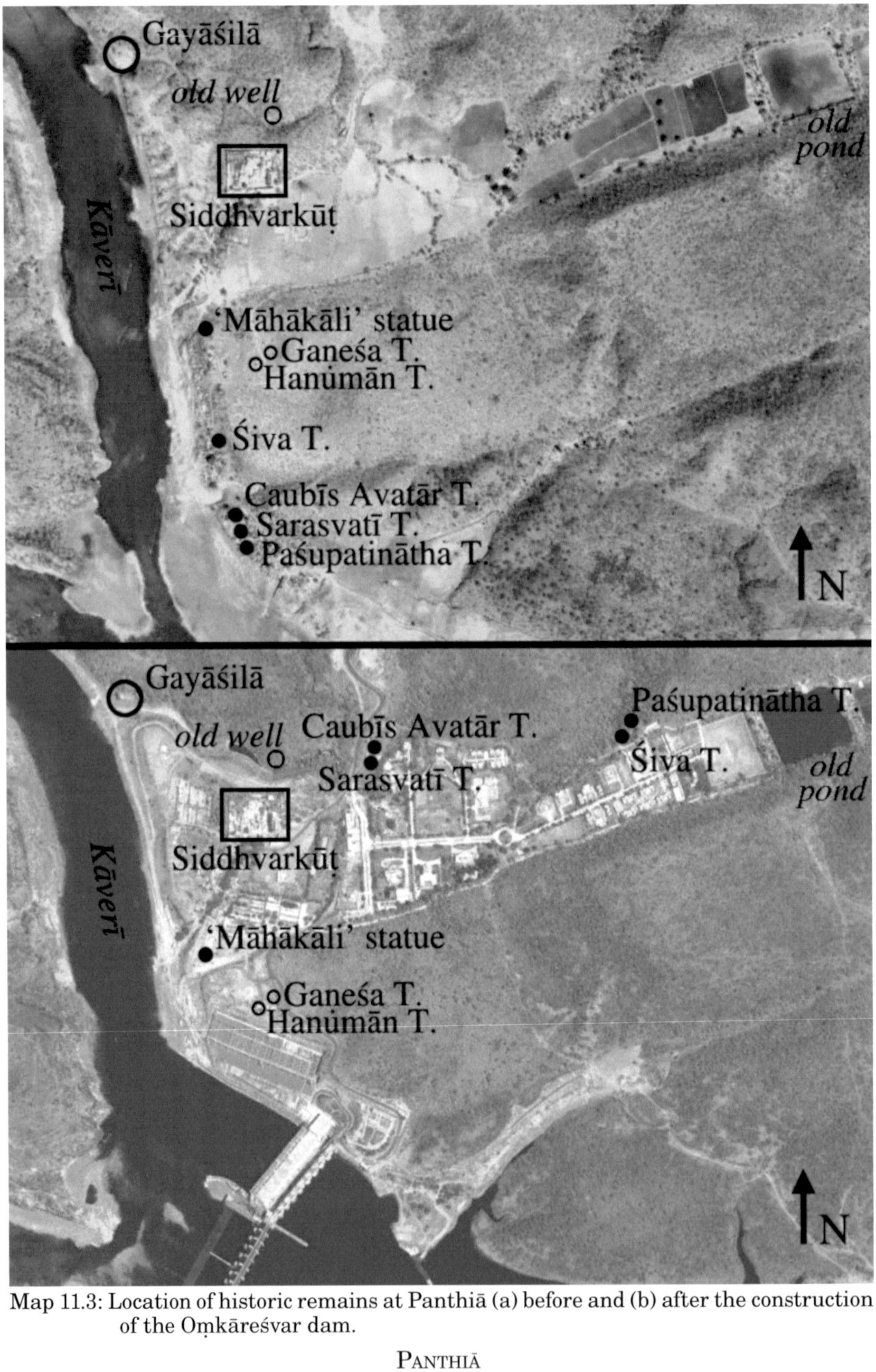

Map 11.3: Location of historic remains at Panthiā (a) before and (b) after the construction of the Oṃkāreśvar dam.

PANTHIĀ

Map 12: Location of Gayāśilā.

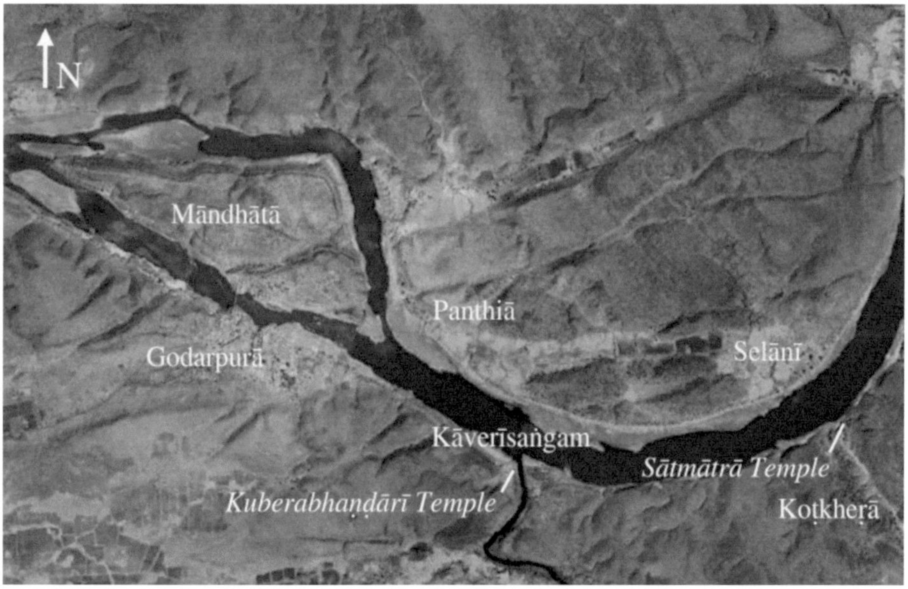

Map 13: The Oṃkāreśvar *kṣetra* (prior to the dam construction).

Illustrations

Drawings

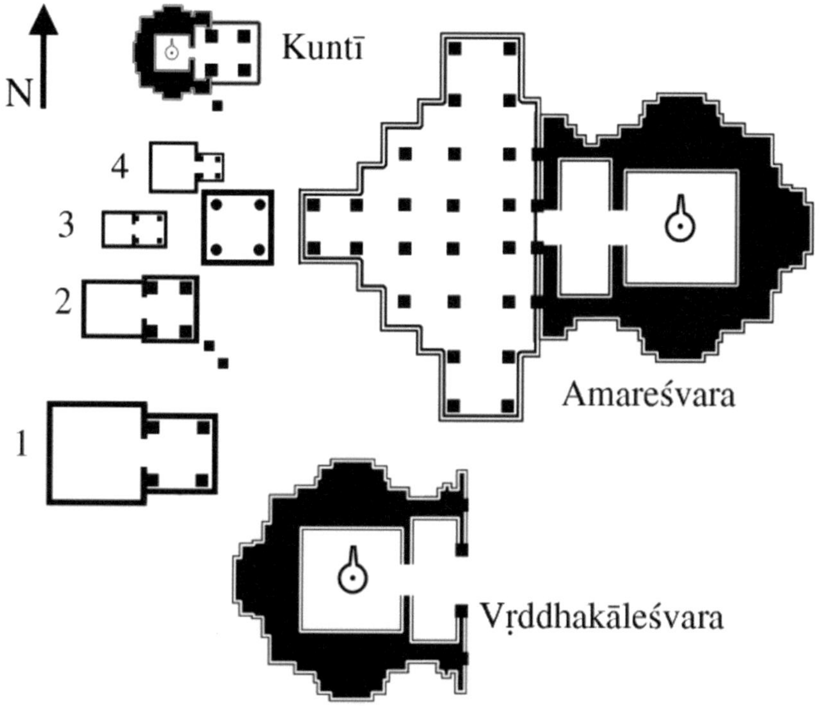

Fig. 1: Schematic ground-plan of the Amareśvara temple complex (not to scale).

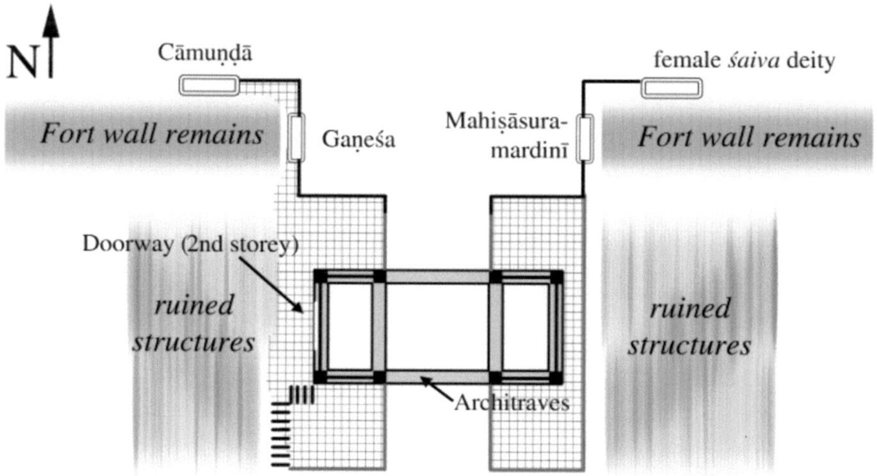

Fig. 2: Schematic ground-plan of the North or Cāndsūraj gate (not to scale).

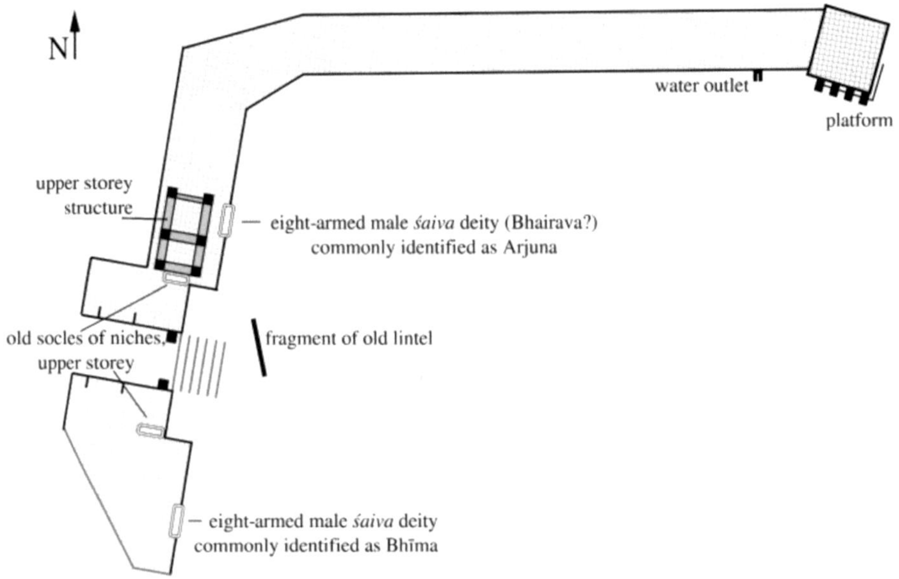

Fig. 3: Schematic ground-plan of the East or Bhīmārjunī gate and adjacent remains of the inner fort-wall (not to scale).

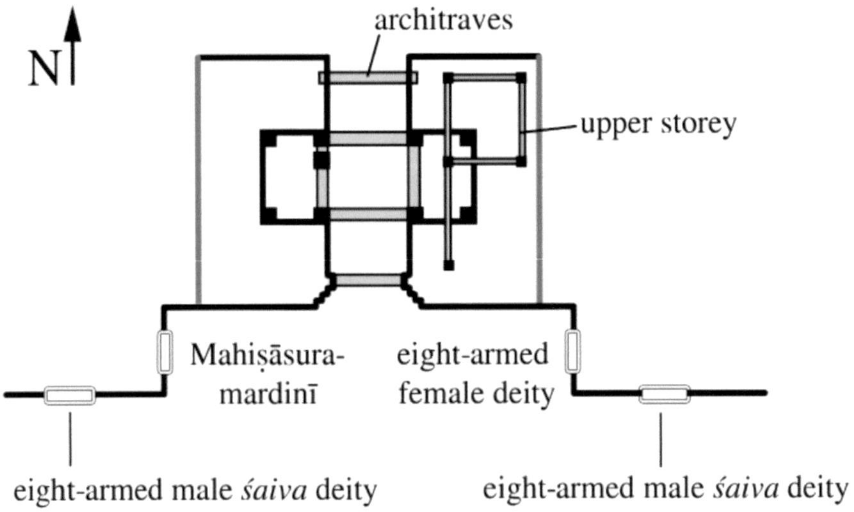

Fig. 4: Schematic ground-plan of the South gate (not to scale).

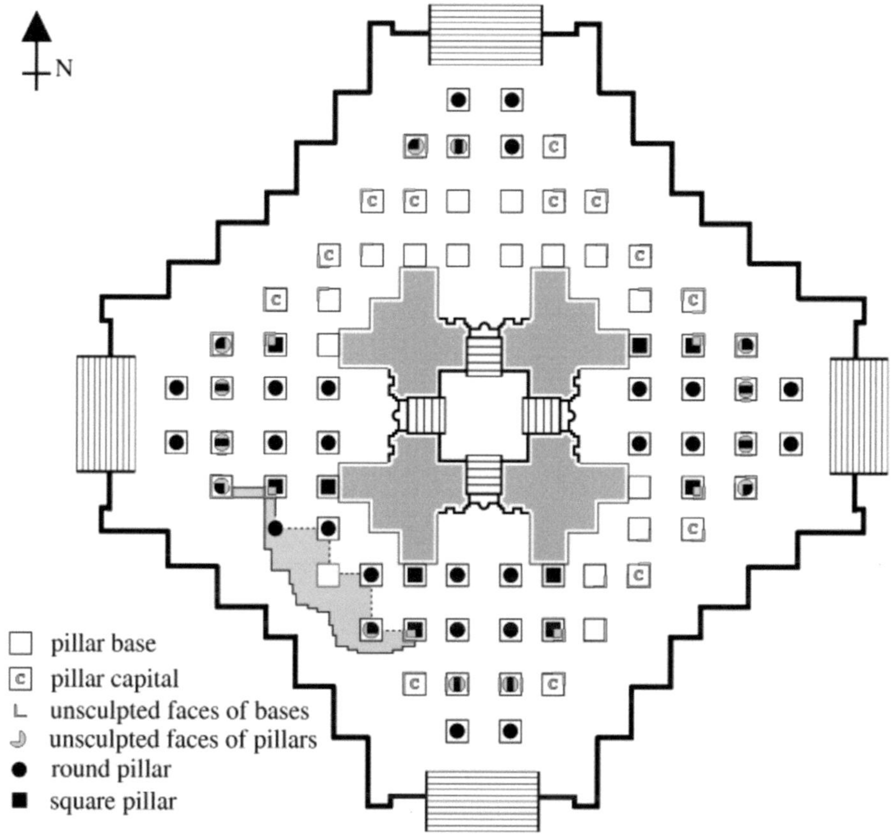

Fig. 5: Schematic ground-plan of the Siddhanātha temple.

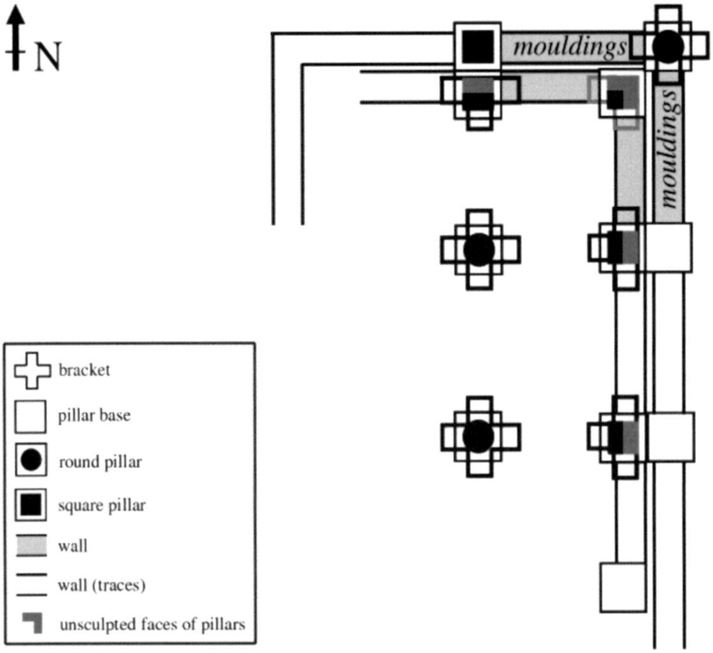

Fig. 6: Schematic ground-plan of structure E2 (not to scale).

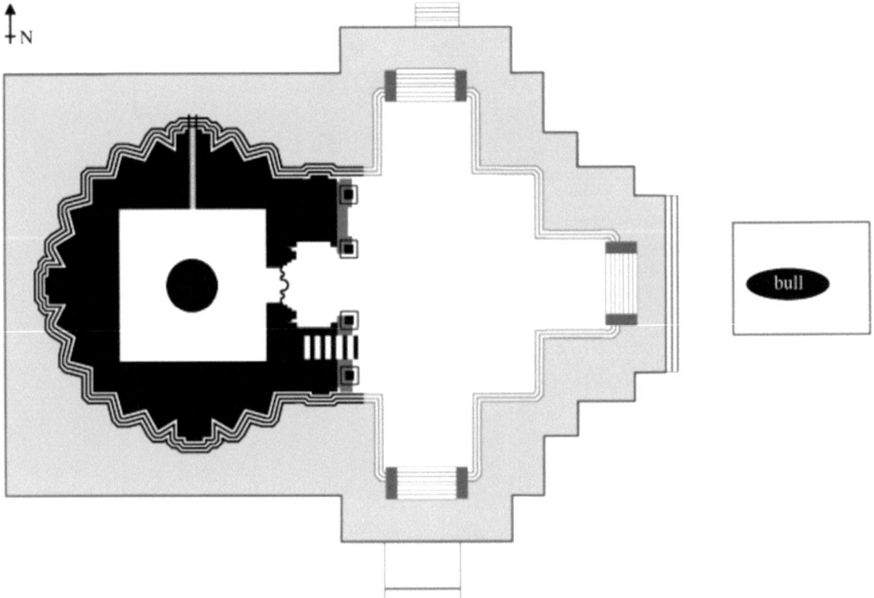

Fig. 7: Schematic ground-plan of the Gaurīsomanātha temple (not to scale).

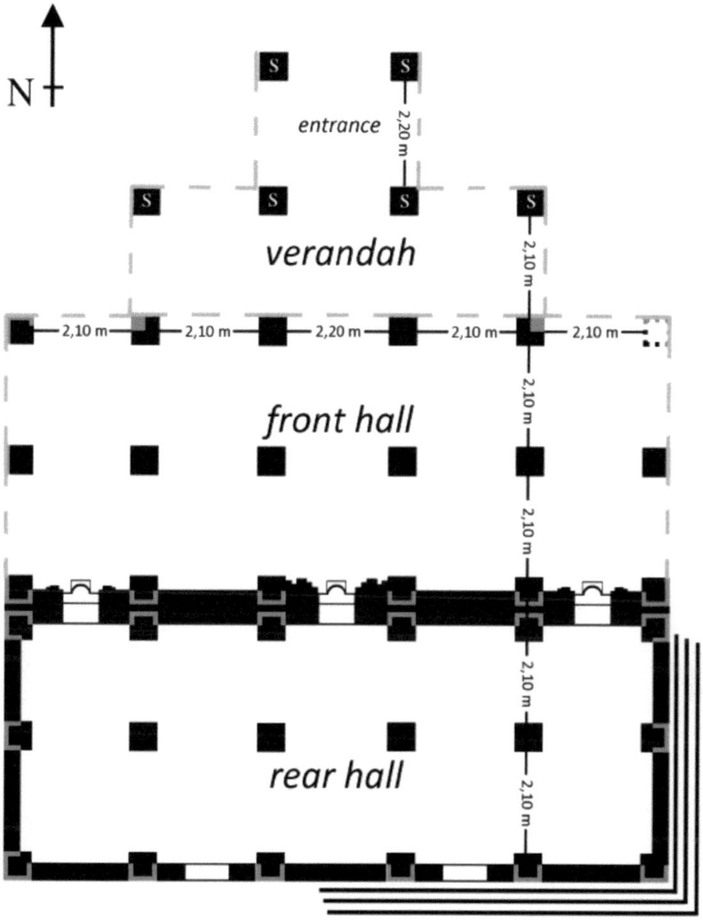

Fig. 8.1: Schematic ground-plan of the Dhavalīmaṭh (not to scale).

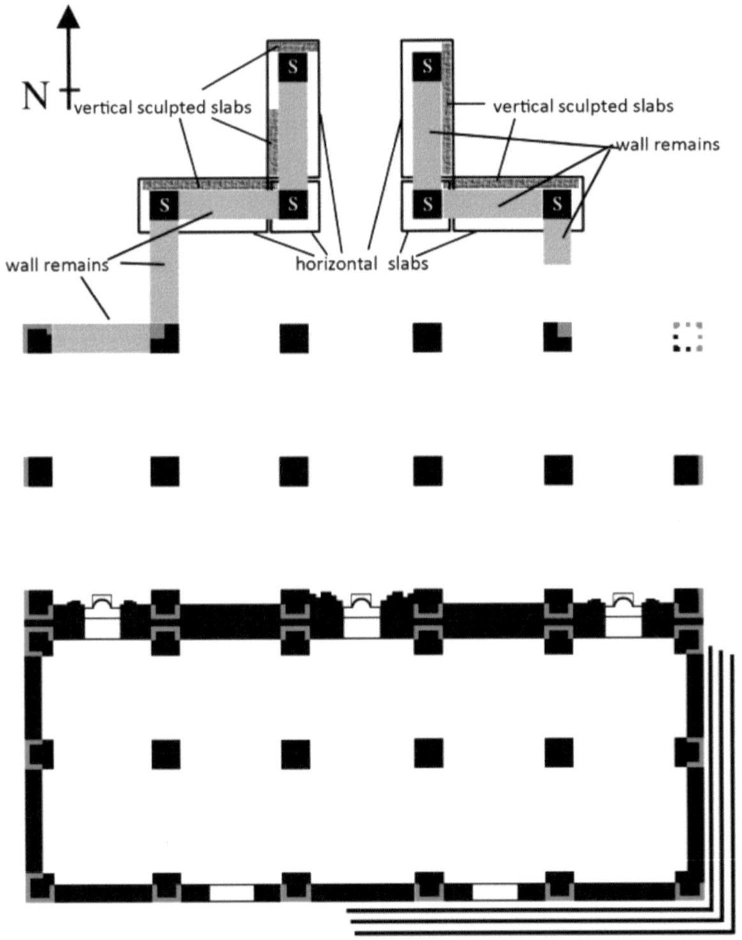

Fig. 8.2: Schematic ground-plan of the Dhavalīmaṭh, detail of the verandah (not to scale).

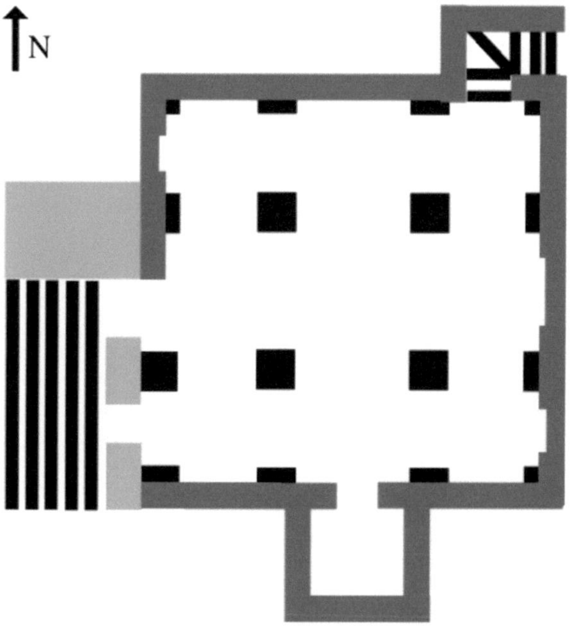

Fig. 9: Schematic ground-plan of the Kālikāguphā (not to scale).

Illustrations

Plates

Plate 1.1: Godarpurā with Brahmāpurī (foreground, left) and Viṣṇupurī (background).

Plate 1.2: Śivpurī on Māndhātā island.

Plate 2.1: Godarpurā as seen from Māndhātā island (2013).

Plate 2.2: Close-up of the Kapilā ravine (2013).

Plate 2.3: Godarpurā as seen from Māndhātā island (*ca.* 1970).

Plate 2.4: Close-up of the Kapilā ravine (ca. 1970). (Photos 2.3 and 2.4 by courtesy of Kālūrām Bhoī, Godarpurā.)

Plate 3.1: Old *praṇāla* at the Kapilāsaṅgam.

Plate 3.2: Fortification wall to the west of the Amareśvara temple complex.

Plate 3.3: Reconstructed portion of fortification wall, with incorporated head of a sculpture.

Plate 3.4: Amareśvara temple complex seen from south-west.

Plate 4.1: Amareśvara temple, south-west corner.

Plate 4.2: Amareśvara temple, north side.

Plate 4.3: Niche on the south wall with Andhakāri sculpture.

Plate 4.4: Door-frame of the *garbhagṛha*, north (left) side.

Plate 5.1: Vr̥ddhakāleśvara temple, east face.

Plate 5.2: Vr̥ddhakāleśvara temple, northwest corner.

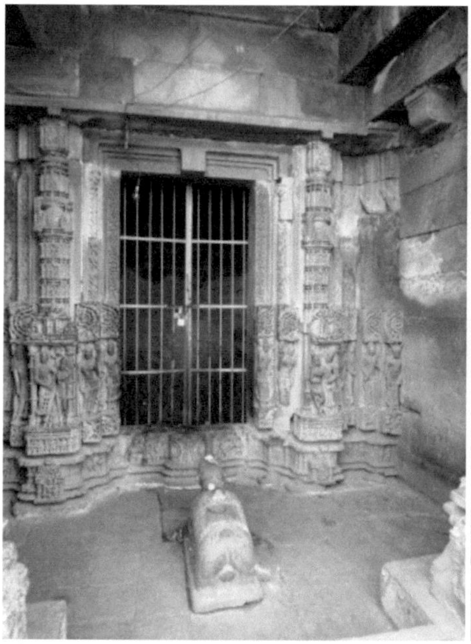

Plate 5.3: Vr̥ddhakāleśvara temple, entrance to the *garbhagr̥ha*.

Plate 5.4: Lakṣmīnārāyaṇa, *antarāla* front wall, north niche.

KAPILĀ RAVINE

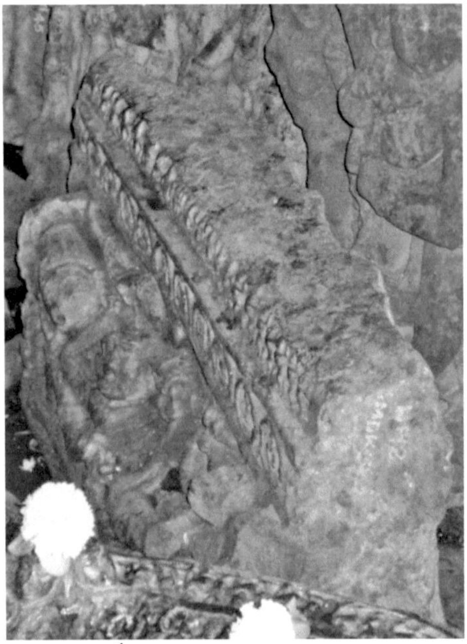

Plate 5.5: Śeṣaśāyin in the *garbhagṛha*.

Plate 5.6: Two *avatāra* slabs, behind other fragments

Plate 6.1: Kuntī temple, view from south-east.

Plate 6.2: Kuntī temple, view from south-west.

Plate 6.3: Kuntī temple, *śikhara*, east face, sculpture of a seated goddess.

Plate 6.4: Kuntī temple, door-frame.

Plate 6.5: Kuntī temple, Gaṇeśa, *antarāla* front wall, south niche.

Plate 6.6: Kuntī temple, Lakṣmīnārāyaṇa, *antarāla* front wall, north niche.

KAPILĀ RAVINE

Plate 7.1: Subsidiary shrines, view from the east (nos. 3 and 4 stand to the left, behind the *maṇḍapa* with Śiva's bull on the platform.)

Plate 7.2: Shrine No. 1, *vyāla* head at the entrance.

Plate 7.3: Shrine No. 1, Varāha (left) and Sūrya (right) reliefs in the *garbhagṛha*.

Plate 8.1: Hero stone, north face.

Plate 8.2: Hero stone, east face.

Plate 8.3: Hero stone, south face.

Plate 8.4: Hero stone, west face.

Plate 9.1: Viśvanātha temple, view from north-east.

Plate 9.2: Foundation stone with inscription.

Plate 10.1: Indreśvara temple view from north-west.

Plate 10.2: Indreśvara temple *śikhara*, south-eastern side.

Plate 10.3: Indreśvara temple, *garbhagṛha* door-frame.

Plate 10.4: Indreśvara temple, *maṇḍovara*, north side.

Plate 11.1: Candramauleśvara temple, west face.

Plate 11.2: Candramauleśvara temple, north face.

KAPILĀ RAVINE

Plate 12.1: Kapileśvara temple, general view from north-east.

Plate 12.2: Kapileśvara temple, south-western corner, remains of base.

Plate 12.3: Kapileśvara temple, *mūlaprāsāda*, north side.

Plate 12.4: Close-up of the *praṇāla*.

Plate 12.5: Door-frame, *garbhagṛha*, south side.

Plate 12.6: Close-up of the *pīṭha* and *vedībandha,* north-western corner.

Plate 12.7: Scattered fragments of the *śikhara*.

Plate 12.8: Detail of cornerstone, right portion.

Plate 12.9: Detail of cornerstone, left portion.

Plate 13.1: Brahmeśvara temple, general view, west side.

Plate 13.2: Brahmeśvara temple, *mūlaprāsāda*, north side.

Plate 13.3: Brahmeśvara temple, *garbhagṛha* doorway.

Plate 13.4: Brahmeśvara temple, *kapilī,* upper storey, south side, statue of Viṣṇu.

Plate 13.5: Brahmeśvara temple, details of *śṛṅgas* in the *śikhara*, north-west side.

Plate 14.1: Course of the southern fortification wall to the west of Viṣṇupurī.

Plate 14.2: Remains of buildings.

GODARPURĀ

Plate 15.1: Viṣṇu temple, view from south-east.

Plate 15.2: Viṣṇu temple, *mūlaprāsāda*, north side.

Plate 15.3: Inner pillars of the *maṇḍapa*.

Plate 15.4: Door-frame, *garbhagṛha*, south side.

Plate 15.5: Lintel with *saptamātr̥kās*.

Plate 15.6: Lakṣmīnārāyaṇa, *antarāla*, south niche.

Plate 15.7: Standing Viṣṇu, *antarāla*, north niche.

Plate 15.8: Mathurā *devapaṭṭa*, Viṣṇu temple, *maṇḍapa*, south wall.

Plate 15.9: Loose sculpture of Viṣṇu.

Plate 15.10: Erotic sculpture, *maṇḍapa,* south wall.

Plate 16.1: The Bīrkhalā hill, view from south-west.

Plate 16.2: The Bhairavaśilā at the south-western foot of the Bīrkhalā hill.

Plate 17.1: Temple B1 from south-west, with remains fallen down the slope of the hill.

Plate 17.2: Temple B1 and surrounding area, view from north-west.

Plate 17.3: Temple B1, south-east side.

Plate 17.4: Temple B1, west side.

Plate 17.5: Temple B1, base of the *mūlaprāsāda*, south side.

Plate 17.6: Temple B1, inscribed *akṣaras*.

Plate 17.7: Temple B1, loose statue of Viṣṇu.

Plate 17.8: Temple B1, hero stone.

Plate 18.1: Structure B2, east side.

Plate 18.2: Structure B2, old door-frame in the eastern wall.

Plate 19.1: Platform B3, view from west.

Plate 19.2: Platform B3, view from east.

Plate 19.3: Platform B3, door lintel.

Plate 20.1: The North or Cāndsūraj gate, north side.

Plate 20.2: North or Cāndsūraj gate, south side.

Plate 20.3: Cāndsūraj gate, south side. (Francis Frith 1850-70; by courtesy of the Victoria and Albert Museum, London).

Plate 20.4: Cāndsūraj gate, west side with entrance in the upper storey.

Plate 20.5: Cāndsūraj gate, *pratolī toraṇas*, view from south.

Plate 20.6: Cāndsūraj gate, south-east side, fragments of a *pratolī toraṇa*.

Plate 20.7: Cāndsūraj gate, door-frame in the upper storey, west side.

Plate 20.8: Inner niche, east side, Mahiṣāsuramardinī.

Plate 20.9: Inner niche, west side, Gaṇeśa.

Plate 20.10: Outer niche, east side.

Plate 20.11: Fragments of Bhairava statue and a pilaster, outer niche, east side.

Plate 20.12: Outer niche, west side, Cāmuṇḍā.

Plate 20.13: North gate, loose sculptures in western recess of the gatehouse.

Plate 21.1: The East or Bhīmārjunī gate, view from east.

Plate 21.2: The East or Bhīmārjunī gate, view from west.

MĀNDHĀTĀ HILL

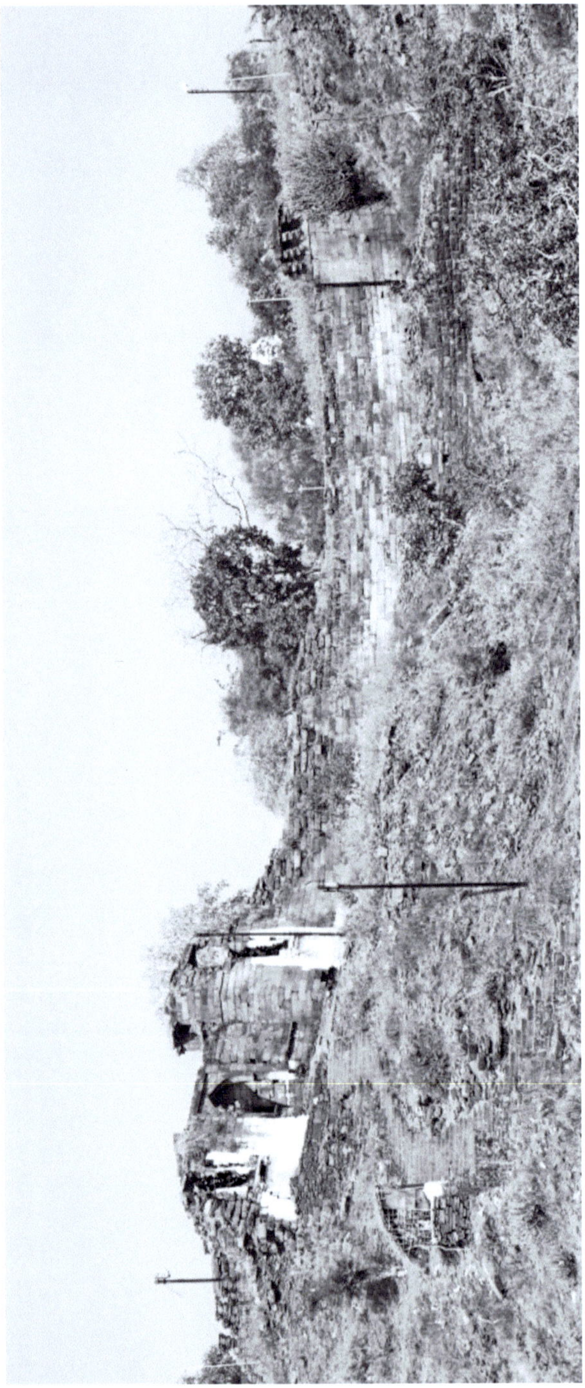

Plate 21.3: The East or Bhīmārjunī gate, view from south-east.

Plate 21.4: Loose door lintel, south of the Bhīmārjunī gate.

Plate 21.5: Old pillars and architraves in the upper storey of the Bhīmārjunī gate.

Plate 21.6: Socle of a niche, Bhīmārjunī gate, inner south side.

Plate 21.7: Bhīmārjunī gate, front wall, south niche.

Plate 21.8: Bhīmārjunī gate, front wall, north niche.

Plate 22.1: South gate, south side.

Plate 22.2: South gate, north side.

Plate 22.3: South gate, outer niche, west.

Plate 22.4: South gate, outer niche, east.

Plate 22.5: South gate, inner niche, west, Mahiṣāsuramardinī.

Plate 22.6: South gate, inner niche, east.

Plate 23: West gate, west side.

Plate 24.1: Outer north gate, view from south-east.

Plate 24.2: Outer north gate, view from north-east.

Plate 24.3: Outer north gate, detail of passage, inner east side.

Plate 24.4: Outer north gate, western row of pillars.

Plate 25.1: Inner or Huṇḍī-kuṇḍī gate, east side.

Plate 25.2: Inner or Huṇḍī-kuṇḍī gate, west side.

Plate 25.3: Area to the south-east of the Huṇḍī-kuṇḍī gate with Gaṇeśa sculpture.

Plate 25.4: Gaṇeśa sculpture south-east of the Huṇḍī-kuṇḍī gate.

Plate 25.5: Hanumān sculpture, lying north-east of the Huṇḍī-kuṇḍī gate.

Plate 26.1: Platform near Bhīmārjunī gate, view from south-west.

Plate 26.2: Platform near Bhīmārjunī gate with remains of a collapsed building, view from north-west.

Plate 26.3: Surakṣācaukī with remains of the inner fort wall, view from south.

Plate 26.4: Surakṣācaukī, view from north-east.

Plate 26.5: Surakṣācaukī, view from west.

Plate 26.6: Gate of a ruined structure.

Plate 26.7: Detail of gate, south side.

Plate 27.1: Kuntīmātā temple (A1), general view, west side.

Plate 27.2: Kuntīmātā temple (A1), loose *śṛṅga* near the south side.

Plate 27.3: Kuntīmātā temple (A1), *garbhagṛha* door-frame and statue of an eight-armed goddess.

Plate 28.1: Structure A2, general view from south-west.

Plate 28.2: Structure A2, stepped west front.

Plate 28.3: Loose sculpted architectural element near the north-west corner of structure A2.

Plate 29.1: Temple A3, general view from west.

Plate 29.2: Temple A3, eastern end of platform.

Plate 29.3: Temple A3, west side of platform, with remains of a *maṇḍapa*.

Plate 29.4: Loose architectural fragments near temple A3.

Plate 29.5: Temple A3, *śṛṅga*.

Plate 30.1: Mound of temple A4, general view from north-east.

Plate 30.2: Temple A4, exposed parts of *kumbha* and *kalaśa* portions of the *vedībandha*, north-east corner.

Plate 31: Northern limit of area B, earthwork running parallel to the footpath (right side). View from the east.

Plate 32.1: Siddhanātha temple, general view from north-west.

Plate 32.2: Siddhanātha temple, west side, with remains of a *maṇḍapa* in front.

Plate 32.3: Siddhanātha temple, western entrance to *garbhagṛha*, *udumbara* with inscription.

Plate 32.4: Siddhanātha temple, view from south-east. (Francis Frith, 1850-70; by courtesy of the Victoria and Albert Museum, London).

Plate 32.5: Siddhanātha temple, lintel with *dikpāla*s above the western entrance.

Plate 32.6: Siddhanātha temple, fragment of lintel with *mātr̥kā* figures, near the eastern compound wall.

Plate 32.7: Siddhanātha temple, remains of inner platform at the south-western corner.

Plate 32.8: Siddhanātha temple, *lalāṭabimba* with Lakulīśa above the eastern entrance.

Plate 32.9: Siddhanātha temple, graffiti on pillar reading "*magaradhvaja jogī 700*".

Plate 32.10: Bhairava on door-frame.

Plate 32.11: Old staircase to the east of the Siddhanātha temple and northern portion of a wall (right).

Plate 33.1: Māndhātā hill, temple B3, general view from north-east.

Plate 33.2: Māndhātā hill, temple B3, view from west.

Plate 33.3: Māndhātā hill, temple B3, south side, detail of exposed *vedībandha* with inscribed characters.

Plate 34.1: Māndhātā hill, platform C1, view from south-east.

Plate 34.2: Māndhātā hill, platform C1, east side with *liṅga*.

Plate 35: Māndhātā hill, platform C2 and remains of an old wall, view from south.

Plate 36.1: Māndhātā hill, temple C3, view from south-east.

Plate 36.2: Temple C3, loose door lintel.

Plate 36.3: Temple C3, fragment of door-frame.

Plate 36.4: Temple C3, fragment of *śikhara* with *śr̥ṅga*s.

Plate 37: Māndhātā hill, structure C4, view from south-west.

Plate 38.1: Māndhātā hill, temple C5, view from north-west.

Plate 38.2: Māndhātā hill, temple C5, view from south-west.

Plate 38.3: Māndhātā hill, temple C5, fragment of *śikhara* with *śṛṅga*s.

Plate 39.1: Māndhātā hill, structure D1, view from west.

Plate 39.2: Structure D1, sculptured fragments.

Plate 39.3: Māndhātā hill, structure D2, view from the north-west.

Plate 39.4: Structure D2, detail of *śṛṅga*.

Plate 39.5: Māndhātā hill, structure D3, view from the west.

Plate 40.1: Māndhātā hill, temple E1 (left) and structure E2 (right), general view from west.

Plate 40.2: Māndhātā hill, temple E1 and structure E2, general view from east.

Plate 40.3: Remains of fort wall and rectangular platform at the south-eastern edge of area E.

Plate 41.1: Temple E1, general view from west (with old sign board in front).

Plate 41.2: Temple E1, *kūṭastambhas* of *jaṅghā* at the west side.

Plate 41.3: Temple E1, cavity at the eastern side, view from north. (The white arrow serves as orientation mark for comparison with Plate 41.4).

Plate 41.4: Temple E1, cavity at the eastern end, west side, view from north.

Plate 41.5: Temple E1, east side, pillar.

Plate 41.6: Temple E1, east side, pillar.

Plate 41.7: Temple E1, eastern cavity, west side, vertically moulded stones, probably remains of a door-frame.

Plate 41.8: Temple E1, fragment of a door-frame.

Plate 41.9: Temple E1, fragment of a doorsill.

Plate 41.10: Remains of a platform to the north-west of temple E1.

Plate 42.1: Structure E2, general view, east side.

Plate 42.2: Structure E2, general view, west side.

Plate 42.3: Structure E2, south-east corner.

Plate 42.4: Structure E2, view from north-west.

Plate 42.5: Structure E2, north-west corner.

Plate 43.1: Fragment of a lintel fragment to the north of the defunct 'museum'.

Plate 43.2: Stray sculptures incorporated into a mud wall of a hut next to the Bhīmārjunī staircase.

Plate 43.3: Stray sculptures kept in another hut near the Bhīmārjunī staircase.

Plate 43.4: Remains of the inner fort wall and temple fragments to the east of the South gate.

Plate 43.5: Detail of stray architectural fragments.

Plate 44.1: The Rājrājeśvarī temple with giant Śiva statue, view from west.

Plate 44.2: Entrance to the Śiva Miśan Nyās with the demolished "Mantra Bank" building.

Plate 45.1: Gaurīsomanātha plateau, North-west gate, staircase with shops and temple (right), view from north.

Plate 45.2: Gaurīsomanātha plateau, North-west gate, staircase with temple, view from south-east.

Plate 46.1: Gaurīsomanātha plateau, North-east gate, view from north.

Plate 46.2: Gaurīsomanātha plateau, North-east gate, panoramic view from west. (Caution, view is unnaturally distorted.)

Plate 46.3: Gaurīsomanātha plateau, North-east gate, panoramic view from south-east. (Caution, view is unnaturally distorted.)

Plate 46.4: Gaurīsomanātha plateau, fortification wall near the North-east gate.

Plate 46.5: North-east gate, west side, sculpture of Mahiṣāsuramardinī.

Plate 46.6: North-east gate, east side, sculpture of Kātyāyanī.

Plate 47.1: Gaurīsomanātha plateau, East gate, view from west.

Plate 47.2: Gaurīsomanātha plateau, East gate, view from south.

Plate 47.3: Gaurīsomanātha plateau, East gate, recess at the north side.

Plate 47.4: Gaurīsomanātha plateau, East gate, remains with recess, south side.

Plate 48.1: Gaurīsomanātha plateau, South gate and staircase, general view from south-east.

Plate 48.2: Māndhātā island, general view from south-east (Deen Dayal, 1880s; by courtesy of the British Library, London.)

Plate 48.3: Gaurīsomanātha plateau, South gate, south side.

Plate 49.1: Gaurīsomanātha plateau, west side, remains of fort wall with the suspected site of a western gateway in the foreground, view from south.

Plate 49.2: Gaurīsomanātha plateau, west side, panoramic view of fort wall remains, view from east.

Plate 50.1: Gaurīsomanātha temple, south side.

Plate 50.2: Gaurīsomanātha temple, east side.

Plate 50.3: Gaurīsomanātha temple, view from north-west.

Plate 50.4: Gaurīsomanātha temple, view from south-east.

MUCUKUND HILL – GAURĪSOMANĀTHA PLATEAU

Plate 50.5: Gaurīsomanātha temple, Śiva's bull in *maṇḍapa*.

Plate 50.6: Gaurīsomanātha temple, sculptures in *kumbhaka* and *jaṅghā* at the north-eastern side.

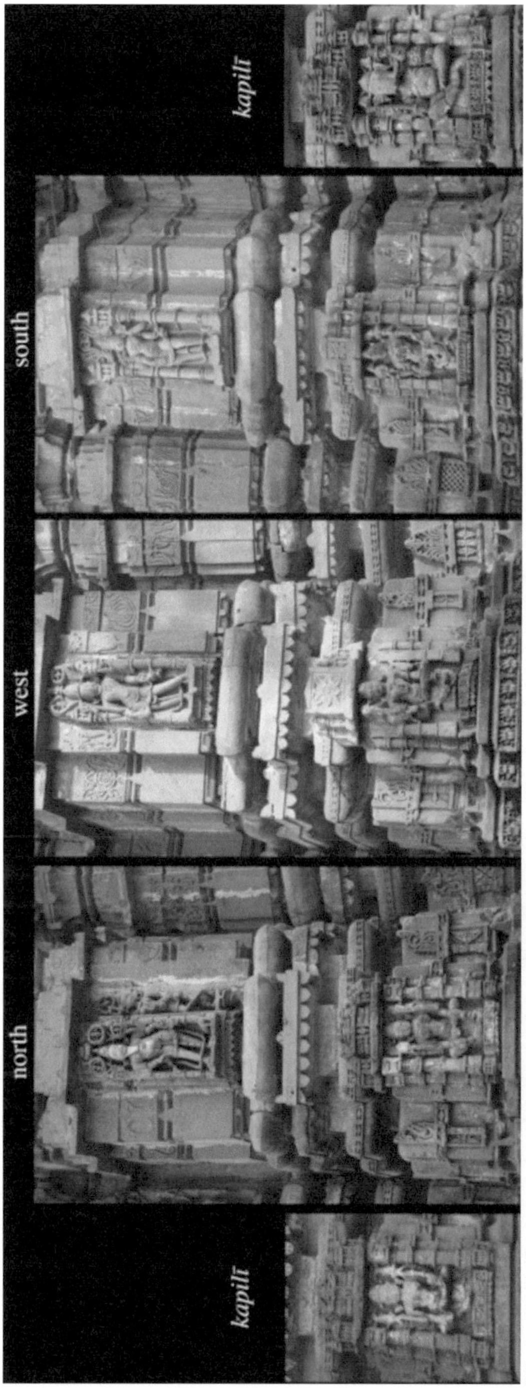

Plate 50.7: Gaurīsomanātha temple, sculptures in the *bhadra* niches of the *jaṅghā* and corresponding *kumbhakas*.

Plate 51.1: Gaurīsomanātha plateau, site No. 2, footpath with old city walls north-west of the Gaurīsomanātha temple, view from north.

Plate 51.2: Gaurīsomanātha plateau, site No. 2, fortification wall, north-west corner.

Plate 51.3: Gaurīsomanātha plateau, site No. 2, temple(?) platform.

Plate 51.4: Gaurīsomanātha plateau, site No. 2, detail of doorsill.

Plate 51.5: Gaurīsomanātha plateau, site No. 2, *liṅga* and *pratolī*.

Plate 52.1: Gaurīsomanātha plateau, site No. 3, general view from south-east.

Plate 52.2: Gaurīsomanātha plateau, site No. 3, 'structure', general view from south-east.

Plate 52.3: Gaurīsomanātha plateau, site No. 3, inside of 'structure', view from north-west.

Plate 52.4: Gaurīsomanātha plateau, site No. 3, temple platform with staircase, general view from north-west.

Plate 52.5: Gaurīsomanātha plateau, site No. 3, top of temple platform with modern cement floor, view from south-west.

Plate 52.6: Gaurīsomanātha plateau, site No. 3, temple platform, *grāsapaṭṭī* base moulding.

Plate 52.7: Gaurīsomanātha plateau, site No. 3, temple platform, loose *śṛṅgas*.

Plate 52.8: Gaurīsomanātha plateau, site No. 3, temple platform, loose sculptures.

Plate 53.1: Gaurīsomanātha plateau, site No. 4 – 'Sītāmātā temple', general view from south-west.

Plate 53.2: Gaurīsomanātha plateau, site No. 4 – 'Sītāmātā temple', rear side, view from north-west.

Plate 53.3: Gaurīsomanātha plateau, site No. 4 – 'Sītāmātā temple', south side, detail of pillar mounted on sculptured stone block.

Plate 53.4: Gaurīsomanātha plateau, site No. 4 – 'Sītāmātā temple', fragments of superstructure.

Plate 53.5: Site No. 4 – 'Sītāmātā temple', sculpture of an eight(?)-armed goddess.

Plate 53.6: Site No. 4 – 'Sītāmātā temple', sculpture of Mahiṣāsuramardinī.

Plate 54.1: Gaurīsomanātha plateau, site No. 5, wall remains.

Plate 54.2: Gaurīsomanātha plateau, site No. 5, settlement remains.

Plate 54.3: Gaurīsomanātha plateau, site No. 5, remains of a shrine.

Plate 55.1: Gaurīsomanātha plateau, sculpture store and sculptures kept in the open.

Plate 55.2: Gaurīsomanātha plateau, inside the sculpture store.

Plate 55.3: Gaurīsomanātha plateau, Naṭeśa.

Plate 55.4: Gaurīsomanātha plateau, Lakṣmīnārāyaṇa.

Plate 55.5: Gaurīsomanātha plateau, broken panel depicting Gaṇeśa and *mātr̥kās* holding children.

Plate 55.6: Gaurīsomanātha plateau, giant Gaṇeśa sculpture to the south-east of the Gaurīsomanātha temple.

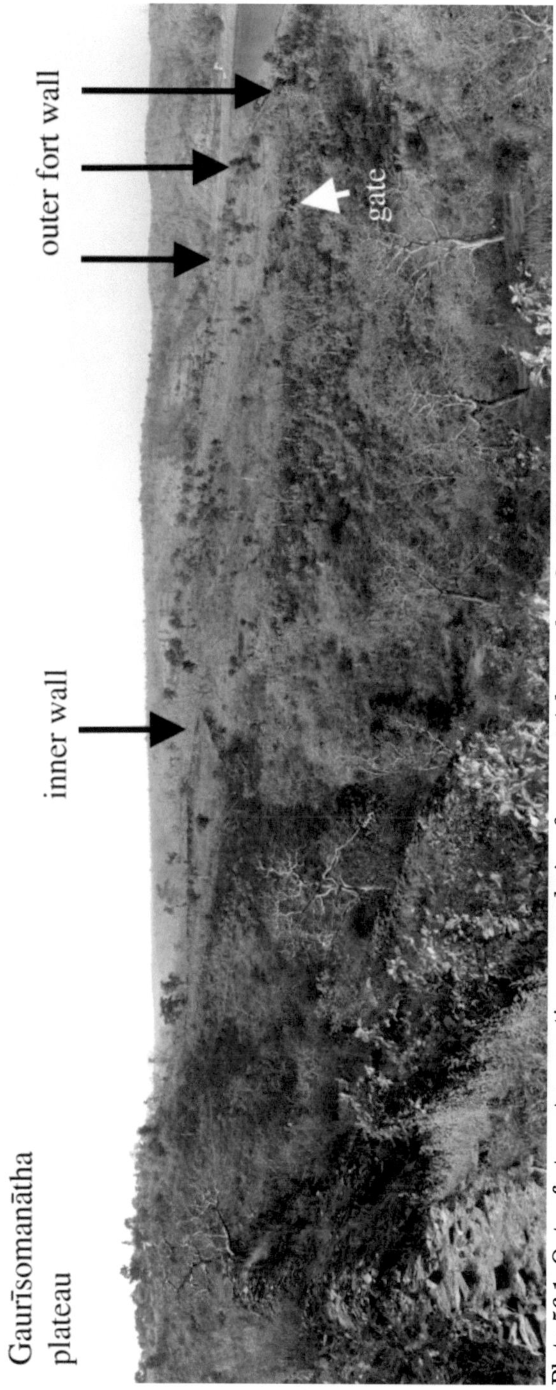

Plate 56.1: Outer fort, eastern section, general view from east (photo taken from Māndhātā hill).

MUCUKUND HILL – 'OUTER FORT'

Plate 56.2: Outer fort, eastern section, south-eastern corner with remains of massive fort wall.

Plate 56.3: Outer fort, eastern section, East gate, view from south-east.

Plate 56.4: Outer fort, eastern section, East gate, view from west.

Plate 56.5: Outer fort, eastern section, northern passage, view from east.

Plate 57: Outer fort, central section, detail of northern outer fortification wall traversing a valley.

Plate 58.1: Outer fort, western section, stretch of northern outer fort wall with merlons.

Plate 58.2: Outer fort, western section, stepped construction in the course of the outer fort wall, view from south-east.

Plate 58.3: Outer fort, western section, Western or Dharmrāj gate, view from east.

Plate 58.4: Outer fort, western section, Dharmrāj gate, view from west.

Plate 58.5: Outer fort area, western section, square structure to the north of the foot-path, view from north-east.

Plate 58.6: Outer fort area, western section, square structure to the north of the foot-path, view from west.

Plate 58.7: Outer fort, western section, sculpture of Naṭeśa, near Dharmrāj gate.

Plate 58.8: Sculpture of Mahiṣāsura-mardinī, near Dharmrāj gate.

Plate 59.1: Kedāreśvara temple, view from south-east.

Plate 59.2: Kedāreśvara temple, old door frame and pillars in front of the shrine.

Plate 60.1: Ṛṇamukteśvara temple, view from north-west.

Plate 60.2: Ṛṇamukteśvara complex, Dvārkādīśa shrine, view from south.

Plate 61.1: Rāṇīghāṭ area, general view from east, with Māndhātā hill (left) and Mucukund hill (right).

Plate 61.2: Rānīghāṭ area, architectural fragments strewn along the bank of the Kāverī river.

Plate 61.3: Remains of a fortification wall near the south-eastern corner of Mucukund hill.

Plate 61.4: The Rānīghāṭ (lower middle) and the Dhavalīmaṭh (upper left), general view from east.

Plate 61.5: The Rānīghāṭ, view from north-east.

Plate 62.1: Dhavalīmaṭh, general view from north.

Plate 62.2: Dhavalīmaṭh, general view from north-east.

Plate 62.3: Dhavalīmaṭh, wall with entrances between the front and rear halls. (Photomontage, optically distorted; the four pillars in front stand in line in reality, as do the three entrances.)

Plate 62.4: Dhavalīmaṭh, 'split' pillars at the eastern flank of the entrance, seen from inside, south-west.

Plate 62.5: Dhavalīmaṭh, vertical slabs at the outer north-eastern side of the verandah.

Plate 62.6: Dhavalīmaṭh, front hall, destroyed eastern side.

Plate 62.7: Dhavalīmaṭh, front hall, destroyed western side.

Plate 62.8: Dhavalīmaṭh, mouldings at the south-eastern corner.

Plate 62.9: Dhavalīmaṭh, outer south wall with base mouldings (arrow), view from north.

Plate 62.10: Dhavalīmaṭh, western entrance to the rear hall.

Plate 62.11: Dhavalīmaṭh, eastern entrance to the rear hall.

Plate 62.12: Dhavalīmaṭh, central entrance to the rear hall.

Plate 62.13: Dhavalīmaṭh, eastern door, *dvārapāla* figures.

Plate 62.14: Dhavalīmaṭh, western door, *dvārapāla* figures.

Plate 62.15: Dhavalīmaṭh, central door, *dvārapāla* with attendant figures and doorsill.

Plate 62.16: Inscription “कान्स” above *dvārapāla*, eastern passage, right side.

Plate 62.17: Dhavalīmaṭh, *lalāṭabimba*, central passage.

Plate 62.18: Dhavalīmaṭh, *lalāṭabimba*, eastern passage.

Plate 62.19: Dhavalīmaṭh, *lalāṭabimba*, western passage.

Plate 62.20: Eastern lintel with sitting female figures in miniature shrines.

Plate 62.21: Western lintel with sitting figures in miniature shrines.

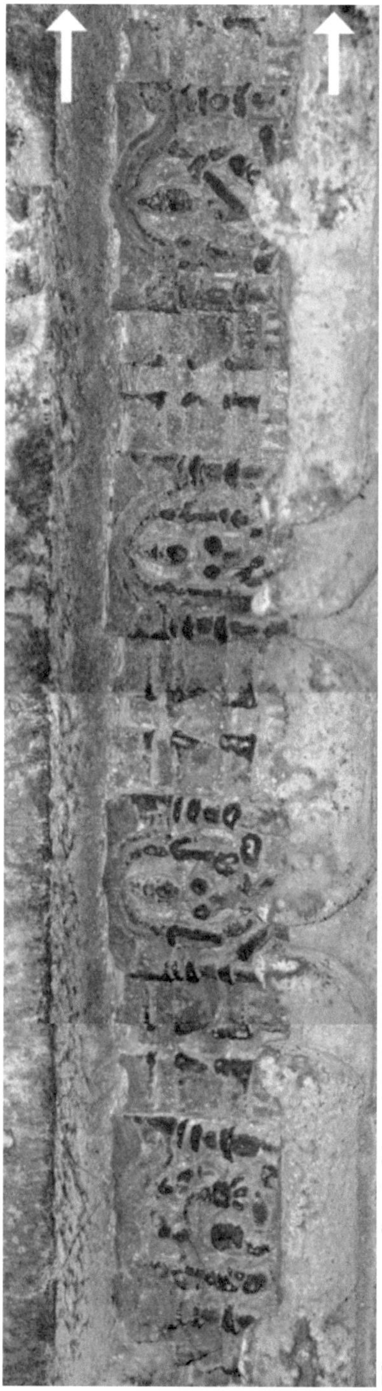

Plate 62.22a: Central lintel with sitting figures, left side.

Plate 62.22b: Central lintel with sitting figures, right side.

Plate 62.23: Dhavalīmaṭh, rear hall, eastern window in back wall.

Plate 62.24: Dhavalīmaṭh, rear hall, western window in back wall.

Plate 62.25: Dhavalīmaṭh, rear hall, west side.

Plate 62.26: Dhavalīmaṭh, rear hall, east side (eastern wall partly collapsed).

Plate 62.27: Dhavalīmaṭh, rear hall, inscriptions on a pillar and a pilaster.

Plate 63.1: Rānīghāṭ area, remains of structures to the north of the Dhavalīmaṭh.

Plate 63.2: Platform of a structure to the north-west of the Dhavalīmaṭh.

Plate 64.1: Temple fragments to the north-east of the Dhavalīmaṭh.

Plate 64.2: Remains of a temple base to the north-east of the Dhavalīmaṭh.

Plate 64.3: Loose temple sculpture, near the Dhavalīmaṭh on a footpath down to the Kāverī.

Plate 65.1: View of Śivpurī on Māndhātā island, with Rājmahal and Oṃkāreśvara temple.

Plate 65.2: Śivpurī, 'Old mahal' area with Oṃkāreśvara temple (2014, view from the Rājmahal).

Plate 66.1: Location of the Kālikāguphā (below the brick vault, right).

Plate 66.2: Entrance to the Kālikāgupha.

Plate 66.3: Kālikāguphā, central and southern aisles with entrances.

Plate 66.4: Kālikāguphā, southern aisle (view to the rear wall).

Plate 66.5: Kālikāguphā, north-eastern pillar, west face.

Plate 66.6: Kālikāguphā, south-eastern pillar, west face.

Plate 66.7: Kālikāguphā, eastern pilaster on south wall, with sculpture of a human couple.

Plate 66.8: Kālikāguphā, narrow staircase at the north-eastern corner.

Plate 66.9: Kālikāguphā, detail of rock-cut ceiling.

Plate 67.1: Statue of standing Viṣṇu, near Oṃkāreśvara temple.

Plate 67.2: Isolated *mukhamaṇḍapa* with stray fragments, view from south.

Plate 68.1: Entrance to the Pātāleśvara temple.

Plate 68.2: 'Antechamber' of the Pātāleśvara temple.

Plate 68.3: Pātāleśvara temple, entrance to *garbhagṛha*.

Plate 68.4: Pātāleśvara temple, *śivaliṅga* inside the *garbhagṛha*.

Plate 68.5: Pātāleśvara temple, doorsill and flanking *dvārapāla*s.

Plate 68.6: Pātāleśvara temple, lintel with *lalāṭabimba* showing Gaṇeśa and a seated female deity above.

Plate 69.1: Oṃkāreśvara temple (2010), general view of south side, from Godarpurā.

ŚIVPURĪ

Plate 69.2: Oṃkāreśvara temple (2006), south side.

Plate 69.3: Oṃkāreśvara temple, view from south-west during Jaypee's renovation work, September 2007.

Plate 69.4: Oṃkāreśvara temple, base and wall of the *mūlaprāsāda*, north side (view from below).

Plate 69.5: Oṃkāreśvara temple, base and wall of the *mūlaprāsāda*, north side (view from above).

ŚIVPURĪ

Plate 69.6: Oṃkāreśvara temple, *śikhara*, north-east corner.

Plate 69.7: Oṃkāreśvara temple, entrance to the sanctum.

Plate 69.8: Oṃkāreśvara temple, western *mukhamaṇḍapa*, view from north.

Plate 69.9: Oṃkāreśvara temple, northern *mukhamaṇḍapa*, view from west.

Plate 69.10: Oṃkāreśvara temple, upper storey, ca. 1893 (COUSENS No. 1389; by courtesy of the British Library, London).

Plate 69.11: Oṃkāreśvara temple, upper *maṇḍapa in* present condition.

Plate 69.12: Oṃkāreśvara temple, first floor, *maṇḍapa* with entrance to the Mahākāleśvara shrine.

ŚIVPURĪ

Plate 70.1: Dvārkādhīś, Raṇchoṛ temple, general view from west (with Oṃkāreśvara temple on the right side).

Plate 70.2: Dvārkādhīś Raṇchoṛ temple, *garbhagṛha* doorframe.

Plate 70.3: Dvārkādhīś Raṇchoṛ temple, *garbhagṛha*, sculpture of standing Viṣṇu.

Plate 71.1: The 'Old mahal' ruin, general view from north-west.

Plate 71.2: 'Old mahal', general view, west side.

Plate 71.3: 'Old mahal', general view from south-west.

Plate 71.4: 'Old mahal', staircase on the north side, with Rājmahal to the right.

Plate 71.5: "Old mahal", brick entrance inside the northern stone wall.

Plate 71.6.: Śiva statue at extreme western end of the northern wall of the 'Old mahal'.

Plate 71.7: 'Old mahal', shrine in the western wall, view from west.

Plate 71.8: 'Old mahal', shrine standing within the western wall, view from south.

Plate 71.9: 'Old mahal', shrine standing within the western wall, detail of Viṣṇu sculpture and *lalāṭabimba*.

Plate 71.10: 'Old mahal', look inside the entrance to the large pillared hall.

Plate 71.11: 'Old mahal' look into the large pillared hall with debris.

Plate 71.12: The same as Plate 71.11, but digitally overexposed to illustrate the dimension of the hall.

Plate 71.13: Detail of a pillar and a stone screen.

Plate 72.1: Rājmahal with adjacent *cūnāgaṛh* (left), general view from south.

Plate 72.2: Rājmahal, view from top showing the structure of the building, view from the north.

Plate 72.3: Rājmahal, spolia in the north wall.

Plate 72.4: Rājmahal, main entrance.

Plate 72.5: Rājmahal, north wall, hero stone, east face.

Plate 72.6: Rājmahal, north wall, hero stone, north face.

Plate 72.7: Rājmahal, north wall, hero stone, inscribed west face.

Plate 73.1: Ruined temple in front of south wall of Rājmahal, general view from south-east.

Plate 73.2: Entrance and front of the *mukhamaṇḍapa*.

Plate 73.3: Entrance and *mukhamaṇḍapa* seen from the inside of the temple.

Plate 73.4: Doorframe of the *garbhagṛha*, south side.

Plate 73.5: Doorframe of the *garbhagṛha*, north side.

Plate 73.6: Lintel with *lalāṭabimba* showing Gaṇeśa.

Plate 73.7: Mutilated sculpture of a male deity in the *garbhagṛha*.

Plate 73.8: Inscription on the inner face of the doorframe of the *garbhagṛha*.

Plate 74.1: Śiva shrine, north side of the Oṃkāreśvara *bāzār*, general view from north-east (with the superstructure of the Rāv family's *samādhi* in the background).

Plate 74.2: Śiva shrine, view from south-east.

Plate 74.3: Śiva shrine, detail of doorframe.

Plate 74.4: Śiva shrine, *garbhagṛha* with *śivaliṅga* and a niche in the back wall.

Plate 75.1: Śivpurī, south-western edge, shrine No.1 seen from a distance from north-west. (Shrine No. 2 stands immediately behind No. 1, but is concealed by the tree.)

Plate 75.2: Shrine No.1, north side.

Plate 75.3: Shrine No. 1, *garbhagṛha* with doorframe.

Plate 75.4: Shrine No. 1, emaciated goddess holding *triśūla* and *khaṭvāṅga*.

Plate 76.1: Shrine No. 2, front, view from north-east.

Plate 76.2: Shrine No. 2, front wall with entrance to *garbhagṛha* and sculpture of Gaṇeśa.

Plate 76.3: Shrine No. 2, *garbhagṛha*, sculpture on the rear wall.

Plate 77: The *samādhi* of the Rāv family, view from south-west.

Plate 78.1: The Hāthīkhānā, general view from west.

Plate 78.2: The Hāthīkhānā, entrance at the east side.

Plate 78.3: The Hāthīkhānā, view of the inside from the east.

Plate 78.4: The Hāthīkhānā (background) and remains of an adjacent structure, distant view from the east.

Plate 79.1: The Caubīs Avatār temple at its original location in 1893–94, view from east (COUSENS No. 1395, by courtesy of the British Library, London).

Plate 79.2: The Caubīs Avatār temple, at its new location, view from east.

PANTHIĀ

Plate 79.3: Caubīs Avatār temple, 'split' pillars in balustrade of verandah.

Plate 79.4: Caubīs Avatār temple, entrance to the main hall.

Plate 79.5: Caubīs Avatār temple, probably misplaced doorsill in front of the building.

Plate 79.6: Caubīs Avatār temple, entrance to the main hall, *lalāṭabimba* with figure of Gaṇeśa.

Plate 79.7: Caubīs Avatār temple, main hall.

Plate 79.8: Caubīs Avatār temple, mouldings on the south wall.

Plate 79.9: Caubīs Avatār temple, rear side, view from south-west.

PANTHIĀ

Plate 80.1: Sarasvatī temple, star-shaped base, view from north-east.

Plate 80.2: Sarasvatī temple, sanctum with entrance opening to the west.

Plate 81.1: Loose sculptures at the eastern side of the ASI compound at Panthiā.

Plate 81.2: Loose architectural fragments at the eastern side of the ASI compound at Panthiā.

Plate 82.1: Śiva and Paśupatinātha temples at their relocation site, view from north-west.

Plate 82.2: Śiva temple, north side.

Plate 82.3: Śiva temple, east side.

Plate 82.4: Śiva temple, south side.

Plate 82.5: Śiva temple, west side, entrance to *garbhagṛha* .

Plate 82.6: Śiva temple, *garbhagṛha*.

Plate 83.1: Paśupatinātha temple, east side with main entrance.

Plate 83.2: Paśupatinātha temple, south-eastern corner with side entrance.

Plate 83.3: Paśupatinātha temple, doorframe of the *garbhagṛha*.

Plate 83.4: Paśupatinātha temple, old fragments in a modern wall.

Plate 83.5: Paśupatinātha temple, *garbhagṛha*.

Plate 84.1: Statue of 'Mahākālī' at its original location in November, 1893. (COUSENS No. 1396, by courtesy of the British Library, London).

Plate 84.2: Broken statue of 'Mahākālī', view from the east.

Plate 84.3: 'Mahākālī', head and chest.

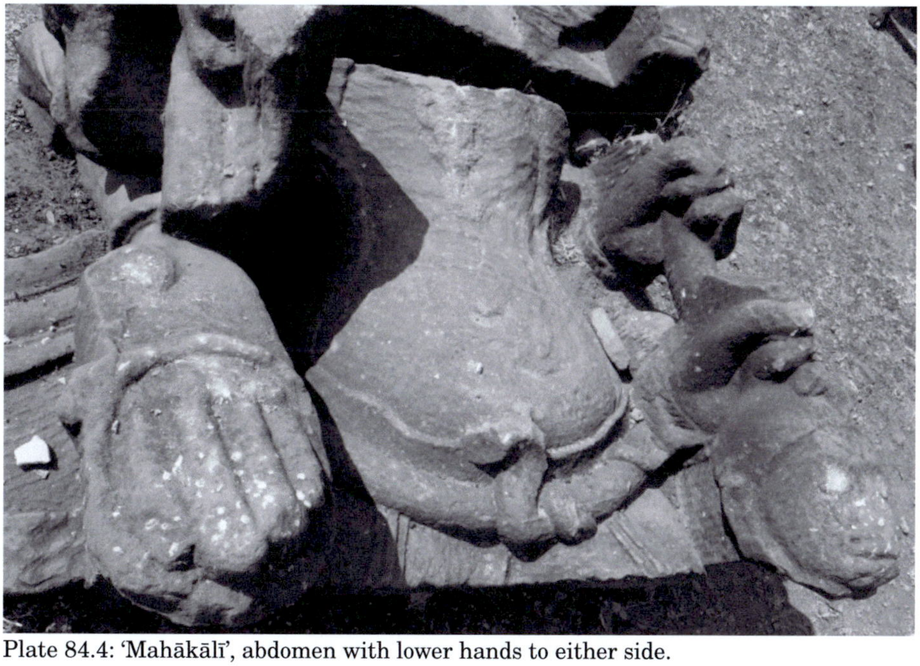

Plate 84.4: 'Mahākālī', abdomen with lower hands to either side.

Plate 84.5: 'Mahākālī', thighs.

Plate 84.6: 'Mahākālī', feet with attendant figures.

Plate 85.1: Siddhvarkūṭ Jain monastery, general view from south.

Plate 85.2: Photo No. 4426 of the Frith series, probably depicting now non-extant ruins of the former Jain monastery at Siddhvarkūṭ. (By courtesy of the Victoria and Albert Museum, London).

Plate 86.1: Architectural fragments at the south-western corner of an old pond.

Plate 86.2: Detail of an architectural fragment at the same place.

Plate 87: Remains of an old fortification wall at the northern slope of Gayāśilā.

Plate 88.1: Gayāśilāmaṭh, general view from the south.

Plate 88.2: Gayāśilāmaṭh, general view from the south-east.

Plate 88.3: Gayāśilāmaṭh, collapsed part at the eastern side of the extant hall.

Plate 88.4: Gayāśilāmaṭh, view from the south with remains of a large platform in the foreground.

Plate 88.5: Gayāśilāmaṭh, loose architectural fragments strewn all over the site.

Plate 88.6: Gayāśilāmaṭh, front wall of the extant hall, view from south-east.

Plate 88.7: Gayāśilāmaṭh, doorframe.

Plate 88.8: Gayāśilāmaṭh, lintel with figure of Gaṇeśa.

Plate 88.9: Gayāśilāmaṭh, inside of the hall, view from east.

Plate 89.1: Overgrown temple fragments, to the west of the Gayāśilāmaṭh.

Plate 89.2: Temple fragments including remains of a doorframe, to the west of the Gayāśilāmaṭh.

Plate 90.1: *Phaṃsanā* shrine, south-west of the Gayāśilāmaṭh, general view from south-west.

Plate 90.2: *Phaṃsanā* shrine, general view from north-west.

Plate 91.1: Loose sculpture of Viṣṇu with *avatāras*.

Plate 91.2: Loose sculpture of Gaṇeśa.

Plate 91.3: Loose female sculpture.

Plate 91.4: Loose *liṅgapīṭha*.

Plate 92.1: Old well near Pāṇḍukaśilā.

Plate 92.2: Staircase of the old well.

Plate 93.1: Koṭkheṛā, abandoned platform of Śiva temple on the south bank of the Narmadā.

Plate 93.2: Mātāghāṭ, relocated Cakkardevī temple, east face.

Plate 93.3: Mātāghāṭ, relocated Sātmātrā temple, west side.

Plate 93.4: Mātāghāṭ, relocated Sātmātrā temple, north side.

Plate 93.5: Mātāghāṭ, relocated Sātmātrā temple, pillars.

Plate 93.6: Mātāghāṭ, relocated remains of Śiva temple.

Plate 93.7: Statue of Bhairavanātha, Sātmātrā temple, east wall.

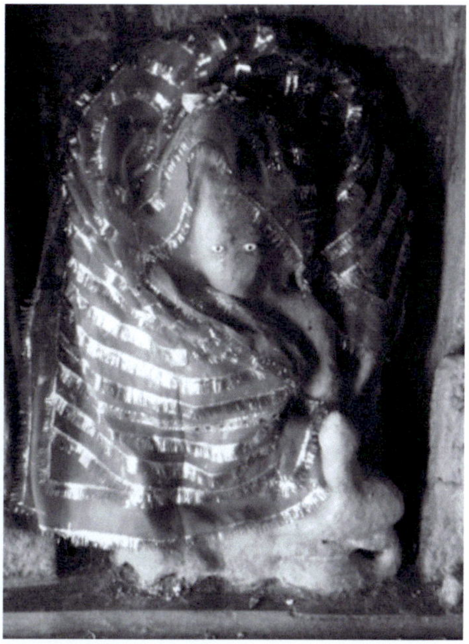

Plate 93.8: Statue of Kaumārī, Sātmātrā temple, east wall.

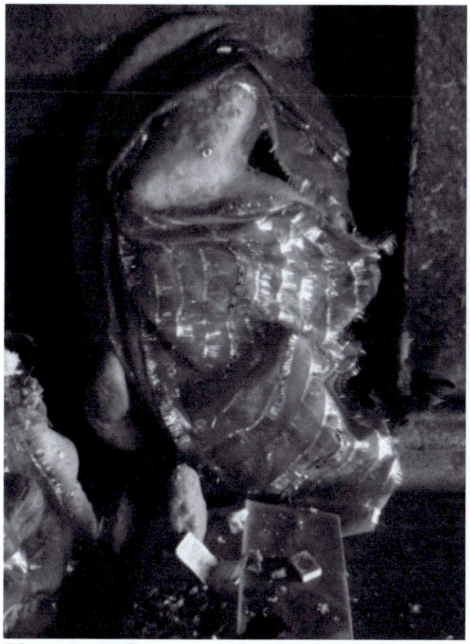

Plate 93.9: Statue of Varāhī, Sātmātrā temple, west wall.

Plate 93.10: Statue of Gaṇeśa, Sātmātrā temple, west wall.

Plate 93.11: Mātāghāṭ, statue of a male deity.

Plate 93.12: Mātāghāṭ, loose sculpture of Umāmaheśvara.

List of illustrations

Maps

DRAWINGS

PLATES

Panthiā